Vietnam, A Memoir

Vietnam, A Memoir

◆

Airborne Trooper

David S. Holland

iUniverse, Inc.
New York Lincoln Shanghai

Vietnam, A Memoir
Airborne Trooper

Copyright © 2005 by David S. Holland

All rights reserved. No part of this book may be used or reproduced by any means, graphic, electronic, or mechanical, including photocopying, recording, taping or by any information storage retrieval system without the written permission of the publisher except in the case of brief quotations embodied in critical articles and reviews.

iUniverse books may be ordered through booksellers or by contacting:

iUniverse
2021 Pine Lake Road, Suite 100
Lincoln, NE 68512
www.iuniverse.com
1-800-Authors (1-800-288-4677)

ISBN-13: 978-0-595-37414-4 (pbk)
ISBN-13: 978-0-595-81807-5 (ebk)
ISBN-10: 0-595-37414-X (pbk)
ISBN-10: 0-595-81807-2 (ebk)

Printed in the United States of America

To the Line Doggies of Vietnam,
And particularly of the 173rd Airborne Brigade

*From out of the clear blue sky,
On the wings of a snow white dove,
Comes a blood red sword,
Bringing death and destruction to the enemy below*

Ship me somewheres east of Suez where the best is like the worst,
Where there aren't no Ten Commandments, an' a man can raise a thirst;
For the temple-bells are callin', an' it's there that I would be—
By the old Moulmein Pagoda, lookin' lazy at the sea—

    On the road to Mandalay,
    Where the old Flotilla lay,
    With our sick beneath the awnings when we went to Mandalay!
    Oh, the road to Mandalay,
    Where the flyin'-fishes play,
    An' the dawn comes up like thunder outer China 'crost the Bay!

From Mandalay by Rudyard Kipling

Contents

List of Illustrations xi
Abbreviated Glossary. xiii
They Had This War Once... 1
FNG Again. 5
Really Steep Learning Curve. 26
First Blood 43
Friendly Fire 59
Second Blood 75
A Small Break, Leeches, And Snakes 91
The Delinquent Defecator 104
Buck Fever 119
Dak To, And A New Job 133
Into The Maelstrom 149
Hill 882 169
Thanksgiving 1967. 187
To Christmas 196
Kontum, And Again A New Job 214
Outta There 236

List of Illustrations

Vietnam	*xvii*
First Ambush	*46*
Second Ambush	*80*
Overview, Tuy Hoa Ambushes	*88*
Platoon AO	*112*
Dak To Overview	*156*
Hill 882	*178*

Abbreviated Glossary

EMs: Enlisted men.

DEROS: Date of estimated return from overseas tour; the date one was due to leave Vietnam.

Di-di-mau: The U.S. soldier's version of a Vietnam phrase meaning "go quickly."

ETS: For soldiers with a limited service obligation, which included just about everyone except Regular Army officers with an indefinite obligation, the date the limited service obligation was ended; in other words, the date one was due to get out of the Army.

Fire Team, or Fireteam: The smallest infantry unit, generally containing three to five soldiers. Two fire teams generally made up a squad, and two squads plus two machine gun teams generally made up a platoon.

LZ: Landing zone; in Vietnam, usually referring to a place where helicopters disembarked soldiers and supplies.

Sitrep: Situation report.

Acknowledgements

The cover and graphics are by Devon Cain.

J.B. Yowell and Rhonda Holland provided editorial comment.

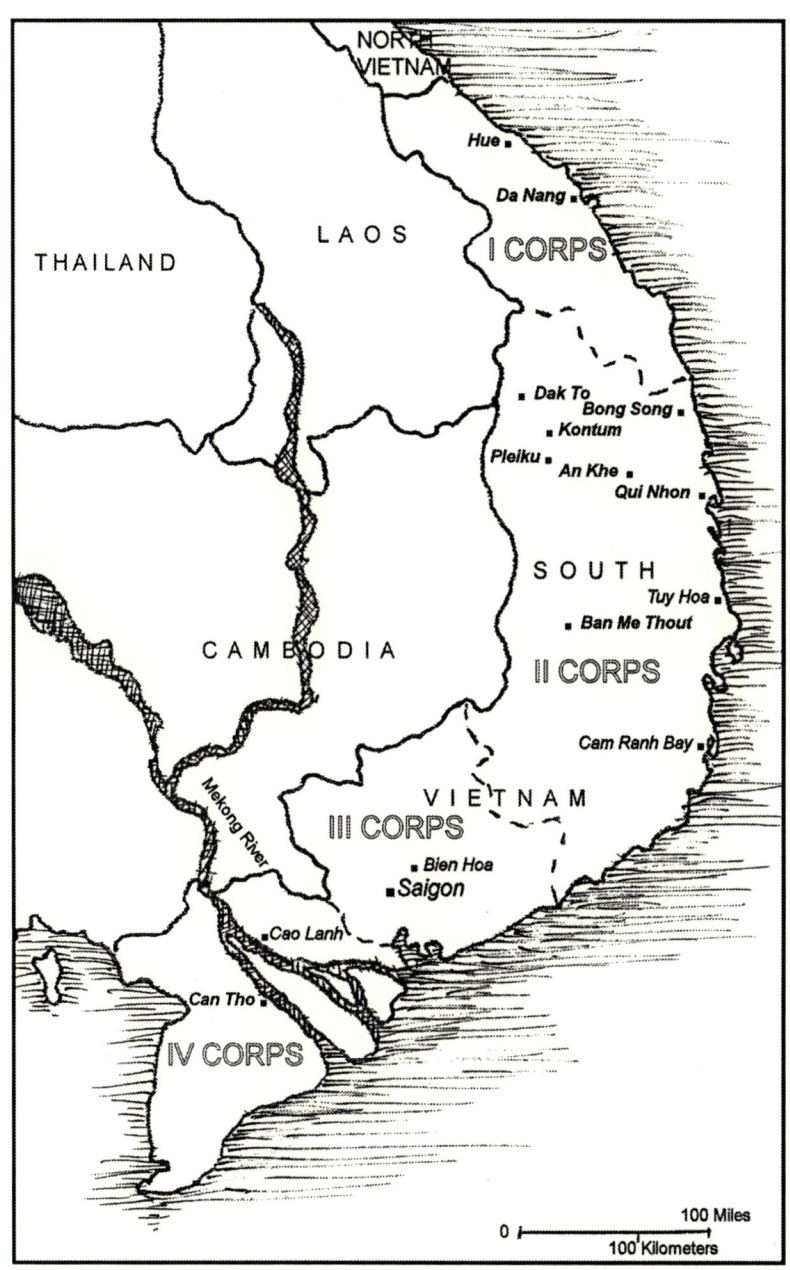

They Had This War Once...

They had this war once. It was an odd war. For one thing, it went on forever, or at least it seemed to. It imprinted a generation, some members for the better, many for the worse. The truths about this war are hard to come by. Not so the myths. They called this war, Vietnam.

This is the second volume of a trilogy on my modest participation in the war of my youth. As I described at greater length in the introduction to the first volume, *Vietnam, A Memoir: Saigon Cop*, I was no hero, and no choirboy. But few of us were heroes, and choirboys were certainly not in the majority, so in these respects I was not unusual. What may be somewhat odd about me is that I admit to a certain liking for war. In other words, I am a form of war lover. The adrenalin rush of danger, of combat is something I wanted to experience, and after experiencing it, is something I remember with a certain fondness, a nostalgia. As Douglas MacArthur said in his farewell address at West Point:

> *I listen vainly for the witching melody of faint bugles blowing reveille, of far drums beating the long roll. In my dreams I hear again the crash of guns, the rattle of musketry, the strange, mournful mutter of the battlefield.*

Being a type of war lover is not something I'm particularly proud of. But I don't think I'm as unusual as might first appear. Ultimately, we have wars because we are drawn to them. We cloak them in purpose and patriotism, but deep down inside they appeal to something visceral in our being. Not everyone feels the appeal, but enough do to have made war a central part of the human experience.

And I am certainly not completely bereft of purpose and patriotism. I think the principles upon which this nation was founded and that we strive—with occasional success—to abide by, implement, and improve upon are the human animal at its best. I think these principles are—when the stakes are high enough—worth fighting, and dying, for.

Were the stakes high enough in Vietnam? One approach to an answer is to examine the result. Fifty-eight thousand Americans died in an effort that did not result in victory. Many say we lost. But we weren't defeated on the battlefield and we didn't surrender, so to me the result was murkier. To put it succinctly, we just quit. Some historians make the argument that Vietnam was a success of sorts for the United States because the inevitability of communism as the wave of the future was called into question. North Vietnam took control of South Vietnam, but communism as a worldwide force gained little. Indeed, the long struggle likely contributed to the eventual fall of communism by allowing the internal contradictions of the system to fester and grow. But I don't think such geo-political, broad-view thinking is much solace to the loved ones of the 58,000 Americans who lost their lives.

For me in my youth, however, geo-political thinking, patriotism, and higher purpose were not how I viewed the growing conflagration in a far corner of the world. As described at greater length in the introduction to the first volume, genetically, educationally, and culturally I was programmed for a soldier, a somewhat rebellious soldier, not a peacetime by-the-numbers soldier, but still a soldier. A war appeared to be developing, lethargically at first, and I slowly realized I wanted to part of it.

And after a few fits and starts, I did become a part of it. Indeed, I had an unusual war, starting off in the military police corps and ending up in the infantry. My Vietnam years were divided into four periods: August 1966 to early September 1967, when I was a military police lieutenant in Saigon; September 1967 to late January 1968, when I was an airborne infantry platoon leader in the Central Highlands, a period that included one of the most ferocious battles of the war, the Battle of Dak To, for which the unit I was with, the 173rd Airborne Brigade, received the Presidential Unit Citation; March 1968 to the last part of August 1968, when I suffered through the agony of a demanding but excruciatingly boring staff job; and November 1968 to late March 1969, when I was an advisor to a Vietnamese infantry battalion in the Mekong Delta.

Several other periods preceded or marked the boundaries of these four periods: the pre-Vietnam year; February 1968, when I was on home leave; and September 1968, when I was debauching in Bangkok, Thailand. In addition, at times I was present in one sense but not in another. Two of these times stand out. I spent August 1967 drunker than nine skunks as I waited for an assignment to the infantry. And I spent October 1968 in the same condition as I tried to forget Bangkok and a little Thai girl and to avoid doing any work in the unit to which I had been assigned upon my return from Bangkok.

Saigon Cop, the first volume in the trilogy of my experiences, focused on the year in Saigon as a military police officer. In addition to describing the challenges, dangers, and irritations of U.S. military police work in the midst of a bustling Asian city in wartime, the volume told of my effort to join the branch of the Army that did the preponderance of the fighting, led the hardest existence, and suffered the most casualties during the Vietnam War: the infantry. That effort to transfer from the military police to the infantry was ultimately successful, and this second volume, *Airborne Trooper*, picks up the story. It is a tale that some would say exemplifies the old adage: be careful of what you wish for, you just might get it. On the cover of this volume is the infantryman's badge of honor: the Combat Infantryman's Badge, the CIB, the signature of those who have served in the infantry in combat.

A friend who read a draft of the trilogy said that it is not a very uplifting tale. He's right. It is a story of five bs: booze, babes, bureaucracy, boredom, and occasionally battle. For readers who might prefer the booze and babes portions, the majority of those—along with some commentary explaining, but not apologizing for, the less than exemplary conduct—are in the first volume, *Saigon Cop*.

The tone of the trilogy—irreverent and cynical—is the tone both of a very irreverent and cynical period in the nation's history and of my own most jaded years of young adulthood. In my lifetime, the general public's views on war, patriotism, and the military have undergone considerable change. The high respect in which the military is held in these first years of the 21st Century is certainly a contrast with, say, 1975. And how many American flags would you have encountered on a drive through a town in that year compared with the number in the post-September 11, 2001, period? If the reader finds the irreverence and cynicism a bit much, remember, the story is of a different time. But I suspect that one group might not find the irreverence and cynicism strange: this group would consist of veterans of the current endeavors in Iraq and Afghanistan, and for that matter, veterans of the other "little" wars that the United States has engaged in over the last 30 years. Irreverence and cynicism get a soldier through the day.

Also, the tone is my personal very negative reaction to the Dudley Do-Right tone of far too many war memoirs, stories, books, movies, and television portrayals. If you want your soldiers perfect, their motivations unselfish, their conduct exemplary, their religious beliefs firm, and their leaders without flaws, this trilogy might be harmful to your mental health.

Yet in spite of personal flaws and an overabundance of cynicism, sarcasm, and irreverence, I am proud, fiercely proud, of having been a soldier. I get a catch in my throat when the National Anthem, God Bless America, or a similar song is played. A fly-over by military aircraft has me yearning for a far-off battlefield. My composure is tested when a moving tribute to fallen American soldiers is read. Inconsistent you say? Welcome to the real world.

In deference to sensibilities and the privacy of individuals, most names in this narrative are fictitious. The assessments of some individuals are harsh. These assessments are subjective, the product of one whose own numerous faults and flaws have not prevented him from dwelling perhaps excessively on the perceived faults and flaws of others. Moreover, regardless of whether or not the assessments have any validity, the individuals were there, in Vietnam, in uniform, doing what their country asked of them, no matter how misguided that request may have been. Thus they are one-up on many of their contemporaries. With allowance for the usual embellishments of war stories, and subject to an occasional purposeful alteration or exaggeration, the events are as I remember them, again subjective impressions. If thirty soldiers were in a firefight, thirty different versions of what happened, of who performed admirably and who didn't, are quite possible. Finally, the dialogues are not intended to be verbatim renditions of long-ago conversations.

FNG Again

In September 1967, the 173rd Airborne Brigade (Separate) had been in-country for over two years. Bien Hoa had been its home post, and the unit had put down roots with facilities as permanent as many stateside posts. The place had two-story wooden barracks, concrete floors, asphalt roads, mowed grass, trimmed shrubs and EM, NCO, and officers clubs. And even the line doggies—the infantry—had enjoyed a little of this as they generally conducted short-term operations, returning to Bien Hoa with varying degrees of frequency, but still returning.

But things were changing. When my driver and I entered the 173rd's compound, we entered a ghost town. Since early summer, the brigade had been up north, in II Corps, in the Central Highlands. In fact, two entire platoons, almost 80 men, had been killed in June in an ambush near the spot where Laos, Cambodia, and South Vietnam joined. A small town gave its name to the area, Dak To. The ambush turned out to be just a foretaste of what that remote mountainous place held for the paratroopers of the 173rd Airborne Brigade.

Not only were the line battalions in II Corps. So were most of the support units, the brigade trains. And what was left at Bien Hoa was also preparing to go. Lock, stock, and barrel, the 173rd was moving, and was shortly to enter the most gruesome month of its existence, the month that would entitle it to membership in the ranks of the nation's most mauled military units.

My driver from the Security Guard Detachment, my last connection to the 716th MP Battalion and Saigon, dropped me at the brigade S-1 rear shop, which was an octagonal tent but with the luxury of a wooden floor. The S-1 rear was being run by an E-8 master sergeant. In fact, he was the S-1 rear. The brigade S-1, a lieutenant colonel, his assistant, a captain, and a clerk were forward, somewhere in II Corps. I was to spend the next three or four days hanging around the S-1 tent, answering the phone for the sergeant. His contact with S-1 forward, where my fate was being decided, was sporadic. The phone link was operable only infrequently, and required much yelling. There was a once-a-day mail packet, which meant about a four-day paperwork turn-around between Bien Hoa and brigade forward.

So I hung around. A one-story barracks was next door to the S-1 tent. That is where I slept. A fat E-8 who was the S-4 rear also occupied the building. My only other contact during my wait at S-1 rear was with a major, the brigade's adjutant general, who I was to encounter again in my time with the 173rd. The major had me over for a little welcome-to-the-brigade talk. Nothing special, just the usual drivel. He was an AG type, but in spite of that seemed an OK guy, a little on the heavy side.

Finally, after cooling my heels for the three or four days, I got the word. I was assigned to the brigade's 1st Battalion—the 1st Battalion of the 503rd Airborne Infantry. As with the other steps in my progression from rear echelon cop to line doggie, this one produced the usual stomach knots. I was going to an infantry battalion, hopefully—or at this point, maybe not hopefully—as an infantry platoon leader.

The sergeant drove me to the 1/503rd's area of the 173rd's Bien Hoa enclave. The area contained two-story wooden barracks and one-story admin and supply buildings. As with the other elements of the 173rd, the 1st Battalion was in the process of packing up and moving north. All that were around were a few sergeants, a captain or two, some in- and out-processing EMs, and another new lieutenant. He had been there almost a week. I checked most of my belongings into a storage area and was issued field gear.

I and the other FNG—fucking new guy—were supposed to start jungle school the next day. I was counting on the week-long course to make up for my almost complete lack of infantry training, to compensate for the ranger tab I didn't have and the paperwork way in which I had acquired the crossed rifles of an infantry officer. Most, if not all, infantry divisions and brigades in Vietnam had an in-country orientation of some sort, and the 173rd's was especially well-known. Patrolling, ambush techniques, defensive positions were all in the curriculum. I was anxiously looking forward to it as a life-saver, both mine and the men I might be commanding.

But first, I was scheduled to be the officer of the guard that night. This involved inspecting the perimeter guard before it went on duty, and then inspecting the guard bunkers once during the evening. The bunkers were on the berm, the bulldozed dirt barrier that stretched for several miles around the Bien Hoa air base and the 173rd's camp. The bunkers were constructed of sandbags and logs and were seventy-five to one hundred meters apart.

The 173rd had responsibility for only a section of the entire berm. The actual work of organizing the guard force for the 173rd's section was in the hands of NCOs. The officer of the guard's functions were, in my mind, largely ceremonial. After all, I didn't know the location of the berm, much less the 173rd's bunkers, and was totally dependent on the NCO in charge for instructions as to what to do. And like a good NCO, he got the job done. I had to make one jeep trip along the 173rd's section that night, with the NCO making the rest. During my trip, we stopped at the various bunkers. The NCO would wake everybody up, chew some ass, take some names, and we would be off. There was one suspicious incident of possible marijuana smoking, but the NCO didn't ask for my input, and I was content to let him do what he thought necessary. My main interest was to get through the night and be ready to absorb all the infantry training I could at jungle school beginning the next day.

Thus early the next morning, long before bright, the other lieutenant and I were driven to the jungle school's area. Despite little sleep, I was at peak efficiency. Adrenalin was pumping. I needed to acquire months of infantry knowledge and training in a week's time. In the whole six-year existence of the 173rd's jungle school, from 1965 to 1971 when the brigade departed Vietnam, if anyone needed the training the school provided, he was me.

So naturally, what happened? The damn school canceled its session for that week. The other lieutenant and I were the only ones who showed up, and the school wasn't going to be run for just the two of us. Besides, infantry lieutenants already had received plenty of training, so they really didn't need jungle school, right?

Thus my one chance to acquire a smidgen of formal infantry training was canceled. My companion was ecstatic. He was anxious as hell to get to his unit and considered the jungle school a waste of time. He told me he intended to have his men call him by his first name, "Jack."

"How about 'Ditmar'," I thought to myself, for no reason other than contrariness. He also said that he had been in Korea, had specifically requested a transfer to Vietnam, and saw Vietnam experience as a definite plus for the future he planned in politics. All this was far more than I needed to know.

Back at the battalion rear, the decision was made that we should go forward as soon as possible. The decision-makers saw no point in waiting a week for the next jungle school. So late in the morning, Ditmar Jack, myself, and about twenty NCOs and EMs were transported to the Bien Hoa airfield for the trip to Tuy Hoa, near where the 1/503 was operating. Tuy Hoa was on the coast. The 1/503 had very recently, within the last few days, moved there from the Dak To area on the western side of South Vietnam.

Bien Hoa airport in 1967 was a beehive of activity. Tactical jet fighter-bombers were constantly taking off and landing. Transportation aircraft—C-130s, C-

119s (I think that's what they were; planes were never my strong suit)—were coming, going, being loaded, being unloaded. Civilian 707s were bringing FNGs from the States and taking one-year veterans home. Air America, the CIA's airline, was flitting about, mostly in C-123s. Vietnamese civilian and military flights vied with the U.S. planes for runway time.

Waiting was an integral component of travel in Vietnam. I hadn't done much travel during my year, although I had certainly done my share of waiting. But airport waiting was to be a noticeable part of my existence during the next year and a half. The wait at the Bien Hoa field on that afternoon in September of 1967 was the first of many.

And it was quite a way to start. I was feeling a bit queasy, the queasiness of apprehension. Alternately pacing and sitting, I concentrated on avoiding conversation with my fellow travelers, particularly Ditmar Jack. The weather was messy. Intermittent downpours were interrupted by a hot sun that quickly steamed away the puddles of water on the concrete. The humidity was oppressive. At one point I was looking toward the runways when suddenly a jet fighter-bomber came roaring from my left, against a sky blackened by an approaching storm. The plane was about two hundred feet in the air and crossing the field diagonally. It trailed a thick cloud of dark oily-looking smoke.

Most of the group was standing and staring by the time the smoking plane reached the far end of the runway complex. At that point, it took a sharp turn skyward. Its journey was short, no more than a hundred feet. It disintegrated in a ball of fire.

Ditmar Jack was ecstatic: "I've never seen anything like that!"

Well, I hadn't either, but I wasn't going to admit it. I just grunted and sat back down, feigning nonchalance. Sirens blared as various emergency vehicles rushed to the remains. Otherwise, the incident brought nary a pause to the airfield's activity. In fact, we were soon in a C-130 flying north.

Tuy Hoa was about 200 miles north of Bien Hoa, on the South China Sea. The coastal area at Tuy Hoa was incredibly beautiful. Several miles of glimmering rice paddies abruptly gave way to towering mountains, hazy in the distance. The brightness accentuated the colors: the vivid greens of the vegetation, the deep blues of the ocean, the sparkling greenish-blues of the paddy waters. On the sides of the roads, however, and in the U.S. compounds was a dusty pallor. The steady stream of deuce-and-a-halves, five-tons, and other military traffic on the mostly dirt roads raised clouds of fine grit that settled indiscriminately on nearby objects.

We rode in a deuce-and-a-half from the Tuy Hoa air base to the 173rd's small compound, about two miles to the south. The compound was set in a sandy area, not loose sand but the hard-packed variety. The bright sun reflecting off the white sand made the compound one big glare. Tents provided the living and working accommodations in the camp: long sixteen-man tents, shorter eight-man tents, octagonal tents. Guy ropes keeping the tents erect were a constant hazard.

But Ditmar Jack and I weren't going to have to worry about guy ropes. We were told to prepare to fly out to the field that afternoon! Whoaa! This was moving a lot faster than I desired. The empty, queasy feeling in my stomach was growing. Much too abruptly, I had gone from seemingly endless waiting to the equivalent of high speed acceleration. And I couldn't find anything resembling a brake. A part of me wanted to stop this process, to shout, "Hey, I was just kidding. I'm supposed to be in the Land of the Big PX now." My situation was the result of a long stream of volunteering. Well, since I was a volunteer, couldn't I back out anytime? Wasn't there someone to whom I could say, "Look, I ain't no infantryman. I just got carried away. It was all that beer in Saigon. I don't need this as part of my life experience. You need to get me the hell outta here." I fought to control an incipient feeling of panic.

We were given three days worth of C-rations. Three days worth of C-rations in their packing boxes take up a helluva lot of room. Never having done infantry stuff before, I had no idea how to get the Cs in my already bulging rucksack. Surreptitiously, I observed Ditmar Jack, but he seemed to be struggling also.

Indeed, the rucksack itself was something of a mystery to me. The Vietnam era rucksack consisted of a large frame, stretching from the shoulders to the hips, to which a pack, or sack, was attached. The pack was about half the size of the frame and could be attached to either the top or the bottom portion of the latter. As a Saigon MP, I had received zero exposure to the rucksack. I hadn't even had any practical experience with the standard shoulder harness and pistol belt combination. Saigon Ps wore only the pistol belt.

Before leaving Bien Hoa, I had managed to get my sack attached to the top of the frame, and to figure out the harness and belt, but I wasn't yet at the stage of knowing how to pack economically. The three days worth of C-rations were a puzzle. Finally, it dawned that I had to take the individual cans out of the boxes. Moreover, the Army's idea of three days rations was too much for any level-headed grunt to attempt to carry. Most grunts had the opportunity to figure this out in stateside training, not a few short hours before going into a combat environment. I learned the lesson by looking at the pile of cans there on the sand at Tuy Hoa and realizing there weren't no way all those cans were going in that sack, which was already crammed with all sorts of equipment, useful and otherwise. Examples of what I was to learn shortly were "otherwise" included a gas mask and a mess kit.

As Ditmar Jack and I were packing, someone said that a unit was in contact. I glanced up at the distant mountains, half expecting to see evidence of an ongoing battle. The possibility of imminent fighting certainly didn't help my already rampaging feelings of inadequacy. At this point, I was just plain scared shitless and praying that I would be assigned to something innocuous, such as a supply office. The responsibility of being an infantry platoon leader without training seemed overwhelming.

Ditmar Jack and I were still struggling with straps and buckles when we were put on a chopper, a Huey, heading for the battalion forward command post, or CP. There, we were to be interviewed by the battalion commander. The chopper—it was my first ever chopper ride—bounded into the air, lurched diagonally forward at a sickening angle, straighten out, and headed for the mountains. The door was open, and there was nothing keeping me from plunging to the ground but my hand gripping a metal bar at my side. I had a fleeting thought of just letting go and getting this charade over with.

But I held on and soon we were landing on the side of a grassy hill. We first went into a tent that had several field desks and maps on easels. Three or four captains introduced themselves and questioned us on our pedigrees. They found mine—a Saigon MP—rather unusual. They were a boisterous group. One was a dark swarthy New Yorker, seemingly either Italian or Jewish, which seemed incongruous to me. I had this view that most infantry officers, which these guys were, were Southerners. A New York Jew seemed considerably out of place. Another captain was a tall redhead. They both seemed envious of Ditmar Jack and me because we were about to get combat commands, although only a platoon. They were in staff positions, probably S-2—intelligence—and S-3 air—air operations. In the brief conversation we had with them, their desire to be company commanders came through clearly.

A myth has arisen in the years since Vietnam that combat arms officers by and large served less time in the field than combat arms enlisted men, and that this was by choice. Well, the second part of that myth is bull-hockey. Yes, many platoon leaders and company commanders only put in six months in the field. But a great many were not happy with that state of affairs. The fact was that for most of the war in most units, far more infantry officers desiring line time existed than there were positions available. Thus stiff competition existed, particularly at the company commander level. Battalion commander slots—lieutenant colonels—were even more competitive, but they were much removed from my lowly status.

Some of the desire for combat commands was ticket punching. Career officers wanted that combat command experience on their resumes. Lieutenant colonels—mid-career guys at the critical junctures of their Army careers—were particularly likely to be guilty of the ticket-punching syndrome, especially since battalion commander positions were not overly hazardous. But some of the desire for combat was real. One becomes an infantry officer because one wants to KMD: "kill, maim, and destroy." One may also want to RP&P: "rape, pillage, and plunder." Throughout the Vietnam years, there were practically always more officers desiring combat commands than there were combat commands available. At least that's my impression.

Eventually, Ditmar Jack and I were ushered individually in to see the battalion commander. He was Lieutenant Colonel Shafter, and he commanded by screaming at his company commanders. I won't say they lived in fear of him, but it was not a lovey-dovey relationship. Shafter seemed to get on some of his company commanders more than others. But he didn't appear to have it in for platoon leaders. And my only contact with him—this one meeting—didn't go badly from the standpoint of friendliness. It did go badly, however, from the standpoint of my psyche.

By this time, I was one apprehensive SOB. I would have accepted any non-combat slot LTC Shafter offered. As I got closer and closer to the moment of truth, my lack of infantry knowledge and training were weighing heavier and heavier. But Shafter had a combat assignment ready and no apparent qualms about my lack of infantry training. He questioned me briefly about my background and my efforts to get to the 173rd. He then said, "So I guess you're anxious to get out to the field?"

"Well, not really," my inner self was saying. But my voice uttered, "Yes Sir," although with little enthusiasm. In any case it was a rhetorical question.

The interview had been conducted in a small five-sided tent that served as Shafter's office and sleeping quarters. After his statement about me being anxious to get out to the field, he moved toward the tent entrance, indicating that the interview was over. I unconsciously decided something more was needed, and awkwardly saluted and stuck out my hand. Shafter was caught off guard by this bumbling, and he also awkwardly saluted and stuck out his hand. Somehow, I made it out of the tent without falling on my ass.

Ditmar Jack was going to B Company. I drew A Company. Shortly after the interview, by now late in the afternoon, the colonel and I got into his chopper, a

Huey, and headed for my new home. We flew over some damn rugged terrain, steep jungle-covered hills, mountains even. There were no signs of life—no villages, no trails, nothing but many dark shades of undulating greens. We were pretty high up for most of the trip, but then we started a tight spiral downward. The door gunners, who had been boringly lounging in their seats, their M-60 machine guns in vertical rest positions, perked up. They pivoted the guns on their pipe supports. Each gunner leaned forward, looking carefully at the fast-rising green sea.

The descent took us down into a narrow valley. The tree-covered mountain sides were now even with and above the chopper. We were heading toward the head of the valley, where the mountain sides seemed to converge into an impenetrable green mass. In the other direction, to our rear, the valley broadened and curved. The door gunners, their guns at the ready, were peering intently into the sides of the encroaching valley walls. The valley floor below and ahead of us was relatively free of trees but covered with bushes and grass that appeared to be fairly high.

I began slowly to discern olive-drab figures on the ground. They were going about various tasks: digging, chopping, filling sandbags. The chopper landed inside a rough perimeter of activity, and the battalion commander and the FNG jumped out. A tall older looking soldier approached. He carried a CAR-15, a shortened version of the M-16. He turned out to be the company commander of A Company, 1st Battalion, 503rd Airborne Infantry, 173rd Airborne Brigade (Separate).

The chopper by this time had shut down, and the battalion commander introduced me to my new boss, Captain Jerome. He was about six feet two inches and stocky but gaunt. Indeed, gauntness was a characteristic of most of the troopers I saw—not an emaciated gauntness but more of a leanness. Capt. Jerome had Close-cropped dirty blond hair and about two days worth of beard. He and the colonel went off a ways, and I had the opportunity to take in my surroundings. On all sides, jungle fatigue-clad figures were preparing for the evening. Everyone had on a steel pot with a camouflage cover. M-16s, M-60s, and M-79s were casually held or within easy reach.

LTC Shafter and Capt. Jerome returned shortly. I suppose the colonel had briefed Jerome on his new platoon leader, probably, and hopefully, warning Jerome that the guy wasn't bona fide infantry. After a few more words between the two, the colonel returned to his chopper. The high whine of the starting engine began, and soon the bird was away, leaving grunts scrambling in its wake for blowing items.

FNG Again 13

Jerome was friendly enough. He introduced me to the company first sergeant, a sharp-tongued Southerner named Duckett, and to the artillery forward observer, Lieutenant Corky Blake, a hyper-active type. I was to be the platoon leader of the 1st Platoon. Jerome had the acting platoon leader report to the company CP. He was a tall lean black staff sergeant, E-6, named John Brown. The platoon apparently had been without a lieutenant for awhile. At this point I was so apprehensive and so desirous of keeping as low a profile as possible that the platoon might still think it was without a lieutenant.

Sgt. Brown took me back to the platoon. As with the other portions of the company I had seen thus far, the troops were a grimy, dirty bunch. In my relatively clean jungle fatigues and relatively shined boots, I was feeling extremely out of place.

First Platoon, whose radio call sign was Lima, had the portion of the company perimeter closest to the head of the small valley. A tree line was just beyond the perimeter, toward the head of the valley. A small stream flowed in the center of the valley. At the tree line, the valley's sides converged and became very steep. That day, the company had moved south over mountainous terrain and then down the valley. The going had apparently been extremely rough, and most of the troopers seemed exhausted. Sgt. Brown said it had been one of the toughest humps of his almost nine months in Vietnam.

Sgt. Brown introduced me to the squad leaders and a few of the men, boys really. The platoon had only two squads. The standard size for a platoon was, I believe, three rifle squads and a weapons squad, for a total of about fifty troopers. Thirty was about the most field strength I ever encountered, however. In-processing, out-processing, R&R, sickness—usually malaria—casualties, all kept field strengths from getting close to what the book said. So in one way, my lack of knowledge of the "book" was no hindrance.

The two squads each had maybe nine to twelve men armed with M-16s or M-79 grenade launchers. There was no separate weapons squad. Instead, each of the two squads had an M-60 machine gun with a two-man crew. The platoon headquarters had, with my arrival, five people: me, Sgt. Brown, two radio operators—RTOs—and a medic. My RTO was Spec. 4 Douglas Baum, a white guy from California. I was to learn that he was a conscientious, hard-working individual, almost too conscientious and hard-working. The other RTO, Sgt. Brown's, was Eugene Washington, a black guy from Washington, D.C. The medic was called, as all medics were called, Doc. One of the squad leaders was Staff Sergeant Hikaey. He was Hawaiian and proved to be fairly competent, but argumentative.

At times, he would be a real pain in the butt. The other squad leader was set to DEROS in a very short time, and I recall little about him.

Evening was fast approaching. Sgt. Brown suggested I get my "hooch" ready as the CO would shortly be having the evening meeting. My lack of infantry experience was about to become very obvious. I didn't even know the basics of grunt field living. I glanced around, surreptitiously observing other "hooches." They looked simple enough. Stretch and tie your poncho over, around, and to various trees, limbs, shrubs, and twigs.

Well, the technique turned out to require a little more precision than that. I found a downed tree trunk about ten feet long and two inches in diameter. Using it was like using steel girders to frame a beach cottage. I placed the log—that's the only way to describe it—across several bushes and laid the poncho over it, tying the corners of the poncho to other bushes. The result was, to put it mildly, a piece of shit. To return to the beach cottage analogy, my hooch was like a cottage erected by a bumbling idiot, which in a number of ways I was.

In hunting up the log, I had a chance to look at the platoon's position. Even an FNG like me could tell it was atrocious. No way that it would have passed a Ft. Benning inspection. The company had simply flopped down after getting out of the trees and into the valley. The platoon had probably six holes, each for about four people, plus a headquarters hole. The holes were small trenches, in theory designed for the occupants to stand in side-by-side. During my time with the 173rd, however, I rarely saw a hole that would have accommodated all the people it was supposed to. Time and uncooperative soil usually left the holes a little short.

Adding to the problem was a ridiculous requirement for overhead cover. All holes were supposed to have overhead cover of logs and filled sandbags. Sandbags at each end raised the logs and the sandbags on top of them enough, again supposedly, to enable the hole's occupants to observe and shoot. The overhead cover requirement meant that dirty, often wet, sandbags were part of a grunt's basic load.

The main thing overhead cover was supposed to do was to protect against artillery air bursts. The VC and NVA artillery, however, had little, if any, air burst capacity. Basic impact detonation was about the only thing on their menu. So the overhead cover requirement amounted to a hell of a lot of effort for a threat that barely existed, if at all. What the requirement did accomplish was to make many of the holes almost useless as fighting positions, and capable of sheltering only a portion of the troopers assigned to a position. The holes were useless as fighting positions because the support sandbags on the side rarely raised the roof sufficiently to allow a grunt inside enough room to aim and shoot his weapon. In actuality, most grunts planned to fight lying on the ground if the laager site—the term describing defensive overnight positions—were attacked.

Anyway, the inadequacies of the holes constructed in accordance with 173rd SOP—standard operation procedure—in 1967 and 1968 only came to me slowly over the next several weeks. What came to me that first night was that the laager site was at the bottom of a narrow valley. On three sides, the terrain rose steeply and was covered with thick jungle. Many of the defensive positions had a field of fire of only five to ten meters, and then the ground rose abruptly, disappearing into the trees. The overhead cover prevented any observation up the side of the hill, and would have prevented any firing in that direction from inside the holes. A few Charlies 30 meters or so up the slopes of the hills could have lopped grenades with impunity all night long.

It was not to be the only ridiculous defensive position I was to find myself in. And indeed, it was not long before I came to understand how such positions came about. The main culprits were time, fatigue, absurd orders from higher headquarters, and uncooperative terrain. Vietnam was not designed to provide for Ft. Benning-type defensive positions conveniently located a day's hump apart.

As I was putting the finishing touches on my hooch, Sgt. Brown came over: "Time for the evening meeting, Lieutenant. I'll go with you." He added as we trudged off: "I'll get Baum to show you how to build a hooch tomorrow night." So the thing was actually as bad as I thought it was.

At the evening meeting, Capt. Jerome introduced me to those I hadn't met yet: the platoon leader of 3rd Platoon, Lt. Jerry Kline, call sign November; the platoon leader of 2nd Platoon, Lt. Bill Roberts, call sign Mike; and the Weapons Platoon leader, Lt. Greg Monroe, call sign Oscar. All three had been in the field for close to or over six months. But it was to come out over the next few weeks that they, and most of the rest of the company, had seen little combat. The last action of any consequence had been during Operation Junction City the previous spring. Since then, the company had moved north to II Corps and spent its time humping the boonies, finding little. Actually, this was not that unusual. The widely held impression that an infantry unit was in constant combat was erroneous. Vietnam was a long war, the nation's longest. U.S. ground troops were there from 1965 through 1972. In some places and during some periods, combat was almost nonexistent. A few grunts spent a year in the field and barely heard a shot fired in anger. For others, one or two engagements were the extent of their war. Indeed, periods of continuous combat were the exception, not the rule.

The evening meeting was usually just a brief dispensing of orders for the next day. The orders given out at this, my first, meeting were not complex. The whole company would follow the valley to the south and east for no more than a couple of kilometers, or "clicks." There, we would set up a new laager site. Then each rifle platoon would undertake a short mission or patrol. Lima's mission—my mission—was to climb the valley wall to the north and check out a village that the map indicated was on top of a plateau that stretched away for several clicks.

Damn, I thought to myself. My first day on the job was going to be an attack on a village! Just my platoon! I was hoping for a little more of a breaking-in period.

After the meeting, First Sergeant Duckett and Sgt. Brown edged up to me and just started shooting the bull. It seemed to be an effort to put me at ease. I leveled about my lack of infantry experience. I asked some questions about operations, mainly about how the platoon moved in various situations. They didn't actually laugh at my questions, but they certainly seemed to find them amusing. Sgt. Brown said: "Don't worry about it, Lieutenant. It's not that complicated."

"Well tomorrow, I was, uh, thinking at the village that we could, uh, use a line formation for the sweep."

"Sounds fine, Lieutenant," Sgt. Brown said disinterestedly.

I returned to the subject of my inexperience. "Since I'm not really up on infantry stuff, I was, uh, thinking that it would be good if Sgt. Brown stayed close by me."

Sgt. Brown finally got excited about something. "Oh no, Lieutenant. The platoon sergeant belongs at the rear of the platoon. I've run this outfit for too many weeks now. You'll be okay."

He was so emphatic that I let the thought drop. It also occurred to me that he was suggesting I would be doing myself harm in the eyes of the men by having him appear to hold my hand. For better or worse, I needed to be the boss.

Capt. Jerome came over as Sgt. Brown and I were preparing to return to the platoon. "One other thing, Lieutenant Holland."

"Yes Sir?"

"We have an SOP for any contact while we're moving. It's fairly simple. The lead platoon stops and pulls back, going on line as they do. The next platoon moves up on the right flank. And the rear platoon moves up on the left flank. So what we have is a big U with the Weapons Platoon and the company headquarters inside. Then we call in artillery, air strikes, whatever is available. I believe in using our firepower as much as possible. Any questions?"

"No Sir. I think I get it."

"Good. See you in the morning."

That seemed simple enough. It didn't sound like a lot of charging or fancy Ft. Benning formations, which was a mild relief.

Sgt. Brown and I returned to the platoon. Darkness was encroaching. He called the squad leaders over, and I briefly outlined the next day's mission. I focused on the village portion of the operation, emphasizing that we would conduct an on-line sweep. The squad leaders had no questions, merely following their maps as I was giving the orders. To me, the idea of assaulting a village was a big deal, but no one else gave any indication of concern or even interest. I was anxious to get the morrow, my first day on the job, underway.

After the meeting, everyone turned in. A bona fide infantry platoon leader would probably have inspected the platoon's position. I just wanted to be as inconspicuous as possible, however. I asked Sgt. Brown about standing watch at night. He said that one person per position was awake for a two-hour shift or so, depending on the number of troops at the position. He had no official watch at the platoon headquarters. He said that the radio operators kept the radio between them and slept lightly. Only a non-infantry type like me would have bought that. A new infantry platoon leader would likely have said, "Come on Sarge, give me a break." On the other hand, that was how many platoons with months in the field came to operate. It was one thing to go to the field for an operation of a week or so. It was another thing to live there semi-permanently, as the 173rd was doing in the Central Highlands in the latter half of 1967.

Night—pitch black in the enclosed valley—soon descended. I smeared myself with insect repellant and crawled into my make-shift hooch. A few raindrops fell, but fortunately they didn't amount to much. The grass was knee-high in the platoon's area, and it was knee-high inside my hooch. I didn't even know enough to mash down the vegetation. Since the poncho was only waist-high at its peak and the grass brushed its underside at the edges, I felt cramped and confined.

Lying on my air mattress—the grunt's one bit of luxury—I felt the return of the feelings of panic and being trapped that I had experienced earlier in this long, eventful day. I had voluntarily put myself in this ridiculous situation, and the avenues of escape were nonexistent. In Saigon, I always had the feeling that if things were really disagreeable, if the Army proved too much for my tender sensibilities, a way out could be found. Tan Son Nhut and the Freedom Birds were near at hand. Furthermore, in Saigon, whatever the dangers, I was surrounded by U.S. military might.

But in this little valley in the middle of a wilderness, I felt trapped. Going back to the New Prince at night was not an option. This was a twenty-four hour a day job, a job moreover I wasn't trained for. U.S. military might was a little over a hundred gaunt, extremely fatigued GIs. My dreams of joining the infantry, of being an infantry platoon leader, of experiencing the ultimate military challenge, were being realized. And I was distinctly and almost physically feeling the truth of that old adage: be careful of what you wish for; you might get it.

Nevertheless, after a few minutes of silently bemoaning my circumstances and cursing my stupidity, I dropped into a sound sleep. It was a sleep of exhaustion. The pace of the last several days had been hectic in the extreme. So despite feeling sorry for myself, despite the tall wet grass inside my hooch, the mosquitoes, the strangeness, the newness, I dropped off quickly and slept like the proverbial rock.

Morning arrived all too soon. A brief period of "standing to" occurred in both the evening and early morning. During these periods, all troopers were supposed to be at their positions. The purpose was twofold. First, evening and early morning were allegedly the prime times for VC and NVA attack. Second, and probably more to the point, stand-to was a way to emphasize readiness and preparedness and to get the troops into a routine.

After the morning's stand-to, we packed our rucksacks and prepared to move out. Sgt. Brown and the headquarters group saw that I hadn't the foggiest idea about how to heat water for coffee. They gave me a hand, but it was obvious that I had many things to learn. In a short time, we began the day's brief hump. It was no more than two clicks, just a little more than a mile, but it beat my butt.

Lima brought up the rear. The move was relatively quick, probably no more than an hour and a half, but of a stop and go nature that I quickly learned was standard. It was stop and go because the main body waited while the point unit moved, depending on the terrain, several hundred meters and checked out the area. Only then did the main body move forward and hook up. Then the process was repeated. We only stopped a couple of times in the two-click hump. At the first stop, I was dumb enough to ask Baum what was happening. He said, "Sir, the point is securing the area."

The main thing I got from this short foray was the heaviness, the absolute dead weightiness, of the rucksack. Over the next few weeks, the ruck was to become the focus of my existence, the source of great pain, a part of my body that I only slowly became acclimatized to. Until that happened, I was to be beyond miserable. The ruck had two major problems. First, the sucker was just out-and-out heavy. Being an FNG, I was carrying far too much. Such things as a gas mask and a mess kit were totally unnecessary. But even after disposing of the unnecessary stuff, enough was left to hurt like a sonuvabitch. And the place of the unnecessary stuff was later taken by a share of the ammunition for crew-served weapons, specifically a mortar round or so. Ammunition for the crew-served weapons—the machine guns and mortars—was spread over the squads and platoons to carry.

A second problem with the ruck was the shoulder straps. Buy a backpack today in an outdoor store and you get enough padding on the shoulder straps to make a mattress. Even today's military packs are heavily padded. But the Army rucksack of 1967 had for shoulder straps only unpadded khaki webbing approximately an inch and a half wide. Despite draping a towel—a drive-on rag—around my neck and under the straps, my untrained shoulders were to be brutalized.

Since the rucksack was to be such an important part of my life for the next four plus months, a fuller description of it is appropriate. I've already noted that it consisted of a metal frame that went from the shoulders to the butt. Unlike civilian pack frames, military frames are generally not designed to extend above the shoulders. A high-riding pack frame spreads the load more but seriously hampers vision, a major concern when the purpose of being in the woods is to kill or avoid being killed rather than merely to enjoy nature. In addition, a high-riding frame only works on trails. Cross-country travel is difficult enough without equipment catching trees, branches, and vines above one's head.

The frame had one or two horizontal bars. The sack itself was about half the height of the frame and could be attached to either the frame's top half or bottom half. Most troopers attached the sack to the top half, using the bottom half for equipment and ammunition for crew-served weapons. RTOs, however, usually had the sack on the bottom of the frame and the radio on the top. Attaching—and that is the right word because it became a part of one's being—the rucksack to the body was accomplished by the aforementioned thin web shoulder straps.

In addition to the rucksack, standard equipment included web gear—the shoulder harness and belt to which ammunition pouches, canteens, and other items could be attached. I quickly noticed that many troopers were not wearing the standard web gear. A number carried their ammunition—M-16 magazines, hand grenades, and smoke grenades—in first aid or claymore satchels. These were bags that had a single shoulder strap. Others carried M-16 magazines in bandoleers across the chest, Mexican bandit-style. The bandoleers were what boxes of M-16 rounds were shipped in. Each bandoleer had about five or six pouches for the boxes of bullets. Troopers put the rounds in magazines and put the magazines in the pouches.

Among other infantry units, how extensive were deviations from the proper way of wearing gear? I don't have first-hand knowledge about other units, but I suspect the more time a unit spent in the field, the more tolerated were non-standard approaches to carrying what an infantryman needs. At this point in time, the 173rd had been in the field a long, long time.

I was very shortly to join the ranks of those who had abandoned the standard web gear. I don't know why the others started marching to a distant drummer, but I had two reasons—my right shoulder and my left shoulder. Any alternative gear arrangement that would take a little pressure off my aches was worth considering.

But these changes were several days away. For the moment, I was making my first acquaintance with agony. Fortunately, the hump was short. The two clicks took us further into the valley as it broadened and bent to the right. The valley floor was mostly treeless but covered with grass that ranged from knee to waist high. We were following a trail, which meant the going was comparatively easy. We soon arrived at the laager site. It was on the left side of the valley on a small rise in a grove of trees. First Platoon's portion of the position was on the side of our approach march and thus overlooked the valley floor.

My first day on the job was about to begin in earnest. The platoon was to cross the valley, climb the jungle-covered far side, and search the village the map showed to be there. I had ascertained from Sgt. Brown an acceptable order of march. First would be a point fire team. The squad leader would be with the fire team. I, my RTO, and the medic would follow the fire team. A machine gun would be next, followed by the rest of the lead squad, the second squad, the second machine gun, and finally Sgt. Brown and his RTO. We dropped our packs at the laager site and started across the valley. It was a relief to get the pack off my aching back, but now there were other worries. Foremost among them was navigation: where the hell were we, and where the hell were we going? MPs in Saigon did not get a lot of experience in cross-country map and compass work. Coordinates, contour lines, meandering streams, they all had little place in the life of a Saigon cop. Moreover, the intensity of map training at MP Officers Basic was, I'm sure, far below the intensity of map training at Infantry Officers Basic.

Fortunately, I had been a Boy Scout. Hey, no kidding. My Boy Scout map experience had been considerable. Indeed, the Boy Scout experience was probably crucial to my survival as an infantry platoon leader. This is not to say that map reading and cross-country navigation were not problems in those first few weeks of my infantry existence—far from it. Much of the time I had only a vague notion of where I was. But without the Scout experience, even a vague notion would have probably been absent.

Baum had given me a radio battery bag for my map. The clear plastic bag kept the map reasonably dry. The idea was to fold the map so that the portions of interest—where you were and where you were going—were visible. The radio bag was just the right size to fit into the side pocket of the jungle fatigue pants. The compass could be kept on a cord around one's neck, on a cord attached to a pocket buttonhole, or unfettered in a pocket. But that first day, mostly I kept both map and compass directly in my hands along with rifle and, before too long, canteen. We angled off across the valley, traversing a stream about five meters wide and no more than calf deep. I didn't pay much attention to it on the outward trip. Coming back it was to be a lifesaver. Due to my inexperience, we were traveling much too fast. Physically, I wasn't up to it. Security-wise, the speed was atrocious. But I wanted to get to that village for my first battle, or at least objective.

By the time we arrived at the valley's far side, however, I was a basket case. The heat, the high grass, the weight of the web gear, all were having an effect on a body dissipated by the month-long drunk in Saigon. The view at the base of the slope leading out of the valley was intimidating. The hill was covered by thick vegetation—trees, bushes, and vines—and rose at what seemed to my unpracticed eyes to be an incredibly steep angle. In a few days, I would not have any qualms about heading straight up such an incline. Panting and already semidelirious in the morning of this first day, however, I stood staring at the green wall.

According to my reading of the map, a trail up the hill existed a short distance to the east. I ordered the point to head in that direction, paralleling the base of the hill. I kept close behind, defeating the security purpose of a point unit. The point had no one to provide early warning to if the main body was on top of it. Also, my being right on its tail encouraged it to go much too fast, hastening my physical deterioration. Nothing resembling a trail appeared, and after a bit I began to feel desperate. I was supposed to be assaulting a village, but I couldn't get on top of the goddamn hill! No war movie I had ever seen or war novel I had ever read dealt with this situation. Finally, we arrived at a comparatively clear section of hillside. It wasn't ideal, just a 100-meter open area of knee-high shrubbery stretching upward before terminating in the green wall, but it was enough to attract an ascent attempt. So I headed the point upwards.

The four or five troopers on point started scrambling up the slope, followed by the Saigon cop. The troopers were moving fairly well. The cop got about fifteen meters and realized he was in deep shit. His legs were rubber, his mouth was cotton. More troubling, his vision was warning of imminent unconsciousness: objects had become lost in a bright glare relieved only by black spots. All thoughts of conquering a village were gone, driven out by two imperatives: there was no way in hell he could make it up that hill, and he couldn't embarrass himself by passing out.

I turned around and slide or fell to the bottom of the hill. Seeing their leader descending, the point stopped. The troopers who had been behind me followed me down. Per Sgt. Brown's instructions, I had been radioing back position reports every fifteen minutes or so. The last coordinates I gave had been beyond the boundary of our AO—area of operations—although where we actually were was anybody's guess. Capt. Jerome came on the horn: "Lima, this is Alpha Six." Six was the standard radio identification for a company commander. The Alpha, of course, was for A Company.

"Alpha Six, this is Lima," I managed to gasp.

"Lima, what is your location?"

Shit. I was probably going to have to put up with these location questions every fifteen minutes until I got waxed or left the boonies. I gave a six-coordinate guess, meaning—if I recall the scale of the maps we were using—that I knew where I was within 100 meters or so. That was a crock. About the only thing accurate about my location reports since the platoon had left the company was that they showed the platoon's eastward movement. Jerome realized I wasn't getting up the hill. He probably was also concerned that I was getting out of A Company's assigned area. If I was intruding on an adjacent unit, the platoon could come under friendly fire. Jerome radioed: "Lima, you'd better return to the laager site."

"Roger, wilco."

It was the best thing anyone had said to me in days. I no longer had to attempt what at the moment was clearly beyond my physical capabilities. Now the only problem was getting back. We were several kilometers from the laager site, and I was very close to collapsing. I did not want that to be the men's memory of their new leader's first day on the job.

I had two canteens on my web gear. Thus far, I hadn't drunk much, which was a mistake, but the next sip unleashed a terrific craving for water. Within a few minutes, I was through both canteens. Even though I did not know exactly where we were, the configuration of the valley made the direction back to the company readily apparent, even to me. Instead of retracing the path we had taken, which amounted to two sides of a triangle, I set a direct course toward the laager site, hypotenusing the triangle so to speak. Again, I set the point in motion and traipsed along directly behind it.

By this time, it was a little past noon. The heat was overbearing, stifling. I was soaking wet with sweat. I was beyond "numb with fatigue" because that phrase gives the impression of one being in control of a tired body. I was not in control. Rubbery, watery, without substance was how my legs felt. I staggered through the knee and waist high elephant grass and the clumps of trees. One thought alone occupied my rapidly narrowing thought processes—don't collapse.

What saved me was the "blue line," the stream we had crossed earlier. My two canteens of water had been devoured, and my body craved, needed copious quantities of fluid. The point hit the stream and moved quickly through it. I got to the middle, stopped, and started drinking. It was almost knee-deep. I first bent over and scooped up water in the palm of my free hand. Once the initial panicky thirst was momentarily quenched, I started filling the two canteens. When they were filled, I drank one with nary a pause and filled it again.

One of the troopers on point glanced back. Seeing his new platoon leader totally preoccupied with his own survival, he stopped the others. The men behind me also were halted, held up by the immobilized object in the middle of the stream. Most of them could see that object in total attention to its own very immediate needs. Sgt. Brown was near the back of the column. He made his way past the stalled troopers and joined me in mid-stream. Trying to appear as casual as possible, he asked: "Everything OK, Sir?"

"Yeah, just needed a little water, Sarge. I'll be alright now."

We resumed the move and were back at the laager site in short order. The other platoons that had missions were also back. The CO didn't seem too perturbed that Lima had failed to reach its objective. Sgt. Brown had Baum and Washington, the other RTO, show me how to construct a hooch. Instead of the elaborate log framework I had made the night before, all that was necessary was cord and a stick or so. The real trick was to use bushes and trees as tie points for lengths of cord to the corners and middle edges of the poncho. If no tie point was available, a stick jammed into the ground could serve the purpose.

After the hooch was constructed, I crept in and slept the sleep of the exhausted for a couple of hours. This was possible because A Company was enjoying a short respite of a whole afternoon. I was up later in the afternoon, more or less recovered from my near collapse of the morning. The episode scared the shit out of me. I hadn't even been humping the rucksack. This boonie stuff was going to be tough.

Two troopers from 3rd Platoon, November, came over and introduced themselves after I had dragged my butt from the air mattress. Ricky Hays and Wayne Jackson were Virginia boys. I was to get to know them much better in a few months. Also dropping by for a few minutes of shooting the shit was the Weapons Platoon leader, Greg Monroe. He was a gregarious guy, with a lot of opinions on pretty much everything.

Before too long, Jerome called a meeting to give the orders for the next day. Minus the Weapons Platoon, the company was to conduct a combat assault. It was to be just a daytime mission, and we would be returning, also by chopper, before dark. The Weapons Platoon was to stay behind at the laager site. So the good news was that we wouldn't be lugging the rucksacks. The bad news was that Lima would be in the lead, both into the LZ—landing zone—and on the subsequent move. The assault was to be observed by some media types, so Jerome said there would be beaucoup fireworks. If the LZ wasn't hot of its own accord, we would damn well make it that way. Jerome emphasized that he wanted smart-looking execution, both boarding the choppers and disembarking on the LZ.

I left the meeting with a pumping heart and a thousand questions, the exhaustion of the morning almost forgotten. The second full day on the job was to be a chopper assault into a possibly hot LZ! And Jerome had thrown out a bunch of terms—packs, chalks, lifts—and instructions that were totally incomprehensible to a Saigon MP.

Sgt. Brown enlightened me a little. Pack was an individual soldier. Chalk, or slick, was a chopper load of packs, anywhere from six to ten troopers, depending on the chopper's condition and fuel load, and the pilot's balls. Lift was all of the choppers in a group, also called a flight. Jerome had said to plan on eight packs per chalk. There were to be four chalks per lift, and three lifts. The first four choppers would pick up Lima. The second four choppers would pick up the headquarters group and a second platoon. And the third group of choppers would pick up the third platoon. The three lifts would rendezvous in the air and hit the LZ together. Jerome wanted to have the pick-up sharp, with the packs—troops—already broken down by chalks. Sgt. Brown sort of rolled his eyes at this. His experience had mainly been to line up a group of troopers, count off eight or so to the first chopper, eight or so to the second chopper, and so on. He assured me this approach would satisfy Jerome.

Well, he would turn out to be wrong. But based on his advice, I gathered the squad leaders and gave out the mission. Once the assault was completed, the company, with Lima in the lead, was to hump a few clicks to a stream, return to the LZ, and get picked up and transported back to the laager site. The point squad for the mission would be the squad that had been in the rear for today's abomination. The theory, as Sgt. Brown, had explained to me, was a continuous rotation of jobs.

Night was fast approaching. I had a lesson by Baum and the headquarters group on how to prepare C-rations, which were to be the mainstay of my diet over the next four months. C-rations were canned items: frankfurters and beans, ham and lima beans (my favorite), eggs and ham, cheese, crackers, roll, fruitcake. The trick I quickly learned was to mix and add. Melting the cheese into the ham and lima beans created, for me anyway, a quite delectable dinner. Adding condiments such as pepper and hot sauce could do wonders. A pizza could be made by slicing the rolls and putting the cheese between the slices.

C-rations were cooked with heat tablets or small pieces of C-4 plastic explosive. The tablets or C-4 were placed in a C-ration can that had air holes punched near the bottom, and lit. The stove was also used to heat water in the canteen cup for coffee. But my expertise as a C-ration cook was to take time to develop. The more immediate thing was the air assault in the morning. Even though I was dead tired, the anticipation of a possibly hot LZ kept me from sleep for a long time.

Really Steep Learning Curve

The choppers were due at 0730. The laager site was in a grove of trees, and the pick-up zone was in an open field abutting the grove. The platoon started ambling down to the pick-up zone, gathering in a sort of mob. Jerome was dumbstruck, or at least purported to be. This couldn't have been the first time Lima looked unorganized. But Jerome needed to get his new platoon leader started off right.

"What the hell you doin', Lieutenant Holland? Let's get those troops broken down."

"Right, Sir."

So Sgt. Brown had gotten me off on the wrong foot. I turned to him, "Let's get'em broken down into chalks." Sgt. Brown barked a few instructions, the squad leaders shuffled around, and the platoon broke up into four groups, about twenty-five meters apart.

"You're gonna have to get organized better next time," Jerome said. He was in a group at my chalk, to be picked up in the second lift. I made a mental note to begin taking charge. Sgt. Brown, though apparently pretty good, was obviously not going to be a completely reliable crutch.

The incoming choppers interrupt my thoughts. The distinctive whop-whop of the Hueys to this day still gets my adrenalin pumping. They landed. We boarded and were shortly airborne. The other lifts picked up the remainder of the company. The lifts rendezvoused, and we headed for the LZ. Despite the impression created by books, movies, and veterans' war stories, the number of actually hot LZs during the Vietnam War was comparatively small. That is, choppers putting down into a hail of fire was the exception, not the rule. But hot LZs did occur frequently enough to give any thinking soldier pause. And on more than a few LZs, the landing itself was uncontested but the shit hit the fan shortly thereafter.

In any case, this was my first air assault, and I was higher than a kite. What with the noise, the bouncing of the chopper, the speed of the descent, the general feeling of anticipation, air assaults would always get me going. But on this my first one, I was especially hyped. As the chopper came in over some trees to the large open area—at least a couple of football fields in size—that was the LZ, the door gunners let loose with their M-60s into the tree line. The LZ had been prepped with artillery, air strikes, and helicopter gun ships, and was smoking and smoldering. I got my first smell of freshly burned napalm, an addictive odor if there ever was one. The chopper touched down, and we quickly unassed. I noticed, however, that I was unassing quicker than most. In fact, a couple of troopers were just ambling out of the choppers toward the tree line. Apparently six or more months of no contact had reduced the enthusiasm of some of these airborne boonie rats.

I was so worked up, however, that as I ran toward the tree line, about fifty meters away, I squeezed off four or five rounds. I was into this air assault stuff! But the fun was shortly over. The company was on the ground, the choppers departed, and the quietness of the jungle returned. Jerome ended up in the tree line near me. He said, "Let's get going, Lima."

So I formed the platoon up for my first time on point for the company. The order of march was the lead fire team accompanied by the squad leader, me, Baum, Doc, an M-60 crew, the rest of the lead squad, the second squad, the second M-60, and Sgt. Brown and his RTO, Washington. Jerome and his headquarters followed. Then came the other two platoons.

The initial part of the mission was to move through a wooded area for a couple of clicks, intersect a trail, and follow it for a short distance to where it crossed a stream. Then we would move past the trail for a bit—keeping on the same side of the stream—circle around to the left, and eventually end up back at the LZ. As I did the day before, I started the platoon off at close to a gallop. Noticeable terrain features were few, so I was just following a compass heading. The woods weren't particularly thick. After a short time, Jerome came on the horn, "Lima, this is Six."

Baum handed me the headset, "Sir, it's Six."

"Six, this is Lima."

"Lima, slow down. This ain't no horse race."

"Roger," I said, charging ahead. It was going to take more than a direct order to slow me down, particularly since I had no idea of how to slow down. I knew only one speed.

Before Jerome could really come to grips with my inadequacies, the point and I were at the trail. And I proceeded to make the major mistake of my Vietnam years, one that came very close to getting two men killed. You think about the might-have-beens in life. One of my might-have-beens occurred on that September day in 1967 in Phu Yen Province, Republic of Vietnam. If men had died because of my error, my life would have been irrevocably changed. The outward manifestation would have most likely been an abrupt end to my infantry career—not a court martial or anything like that but merely being shipped from the field as incompetent. The inner manifestation would have been two dead U.S. soldiers on my conscience for the rest of my days. Others have had to cope with such a responsibility and I suppose I could have, but I shudder at the burden.

What happened was this. The point fire team, about five troopers, reached the trail. I was right behind. The rest of the company was strung out in single file to the rear, individuals being five or so meters apart. The trees and undergrowth prevented more than the first two or three troopers behind me from seeing the trail. I reported to Six: "Six, this is Lima. We have reached the trail."

"Lima, this is Six. Check it out and then follow it to the blue line.

"Wilco."

The problem was, I had two instructions: check out the trail and proceed to the blue line. Still operating in fast forward, I attempted both simultaneously. I told the fire team leader to send two troopers up the trail to the left, check it out for about fifty meters, and come back. As soon as they were off, I headed the main body down the trail to the right. Only the first couple of men behind me were aware of the two troopers checking out the trail to the left. The two were out of sight, having rounded a bend about twenty-five meters from where we hit the trail.

After about ten minutes, the point fire team and I reached the blue line. I sent the fire team, minus the two troopers who I had completely forgotten about, across the three-meter wide stream to set up security. The rest of the platoon, followed by the company, began crowding into the little stream crossing. Entirely too many people were in entirely too small a space, but I was oblivious, being content to reach the objective.

Sgt. Brown came up to me, covertly grabbed my arm, and pulled me aside. He was seething. "Sir, I almost shot those fuckers!"

"What?" I said, not grasping what he was talking about.

"Those two guys you sent up the trail. We came close to drilling them!"

"Whaaa…," I started to explain, only slowly realizing the enormity of what had almost transpired.

"Lieutenant, you can't just send men off and forget them. You gotta make sure everybody that needs to, knows what the fuck's goin' on. People get killed real goddamn easy out here."

I've never liked being corrected, but it didn't take an Einstein to conclude that I had fucked up bad and was just damn lucky two dead guys weren't the result of my second day as an infantry platoon leader.

"You're right, Sarge. I screwed up. It won't happen again."

But I could tell by the look on his face that he had no doubt I was certainly capable of other disagreeable things.

As the years have gone by, I've thought often of the incident, and of other incidents that serve to emphasize the necessity of communication on the battlefield, of keeping everyone informed. Largely because of these incidents, the importance I've come to attach to keeping people informed has rendered me an extremely uncompromising person in my professional post-Army life. I tend to view haphazard communicators in the same light as Sgt. Brown saw me that long ago day in the mountains above Tuy Hoa, Republic of Vietnam.

To digress for a moment, another Army experience—admittedly a minor one—with insufficient communication occurred in ROTC summer camp, in 1964. We were conducting a night patrol. Camp cadre members playing aggressor forces were in the area. Some shithead from Bucknell University was the patrol leader. Another cadet and I were bringing up the rear. Shortly after the patrol left the perimeter, about fifty meters away, we stopped at a small thicket. The other cadet and I were not quite at the thicket, being about fifteen meters from the front of the patrol.

The patrol started up again. When I and my fellow cadet in the rear came abreast of the thicket, we heard voices. They were only about six feet away in the darkness. We froze. The rest of the patrol moved on. Hearts pounding, adrenalin surging, barely moving, we were convinced we were close by an "aggressor" outpost. The voices continued. My companion and I were afraid to speak. I touched him, slowly raised my weapon—the bullets were blanks—and shrugged my shoulders at him in question. He shrugged back at me. We didn't know whether to fire, yell, run, shit, or go blind. Finally, we mutually and silently came to the conclusion to depart quickly and quietly. We caught up with the patrol. It had stopped, and Bucknell had started back for us, the platoon-officer-in-charge, who was an ROTC instructor, a major, in tow. I started to explain that we had heard voices. Bucknell cut me off, putting on quite a show for the instructor. "Goddammit, don't ever to that again!"

"But...."

"Shaddup. Stay closed up. We're late. Move out."

Jezz, was I pissed. This shithead fucks up by not telling the whole patrol that we were merely passing a friendly outpost, and now he was making us out to be the culprits. And the fucking instructor, he was looking on at the chewing out approvingly. Maybe they both got waxed in the 'Nam, although the major was a Signal Corps weenie and Bucknell likely didn't have the balls to be infantry.

And one more digression. To readers who say my error with the two troopers I sent off and forgot about was due to my lack of infantry training, I say, "maybe." But I saw enough official infantry officers, many with Ranger tabs, make similar stupid mistakes to be not totally persuaded. In my opinion, it was more an FNG mistake than anything else.

In any case, Army experiences made me a believer in communication, and none of my Army experiences had more impact than those two troopers who I forgot and who Sgt. Brown almost shot on my second day as an airborne infantry platoon leader.

But at the time I didn't have the luxury of dwelling on the screw-up. Just as Sgt. Brown finished his tirade, Jerome called me over. "Let's get goin', Lieutenant. We still have a lotta ground to cover. Keep goin' along the stream for about one hundred meters, then swing up toward the ridge line. We'll follow it back to the LZ. But I don't wanna be on the ridge line itself. It's open. Stay in the trees. Just parallel the open area. And, oh yeah. Slow the hell down. This isn't a race."

Sounded simple enough. But as I was rapidly discovering, fucking up simple things was pretty damn easy out here in the boonies. I extracted Lima from the congestion at the stream crossing and started through the jungle. After about 100 meters, Jerome gave the order over the radio to turn left, toward the ridge line.

The fast pace I had set in the morning now began to take its toll. All of a sudden, I was exhausted. The heat, the pulling vines, the grabbing roots, the claustrophobic jungle, were all pushing me to the basket-case stage I had been in the day before. When we broke through the tree line into the open, I felt an enormous relief. But even more, I felt repelled by the thought of going back into the trees. Consequently, I started the point paralleling the tree line, but on the uphill, open side of the line and not in the trees. As soon as Jerome broke out of the trees and saw where I was going, he called on the radio for me to get the men down into the tree line. I tried to move the point closer to the trees, but it wasn't easy. We were moving lickety-split, making a change of direction difficult. Moreover, the thought of fighting the jungle again was discouraging, to say the least.

I managed to get the point to the wood's edge, but the edge wasn't straight. It meandered in a wave-like fashion. The point fire team wanted to move straight from wave-crest to wave-crest rather than to follow the tree line down the hill and back up again. I was too tired to object. Each time we cut across an open area to the next upward push of the tree line, however, Jerome went ballistic. The company was bunched up by this time, everyone smelling the barn door and getting with the rhythm of the sprinting FNG ex-MP lieutenant from Saigon. Jerome was within loud talking distance, and noise discipline be damned, he was talking loud: "Lima, get in the trees."

"Right, Sir," I said, being incapable of even a feeble effort at getting the point off its beeline course.

Thus we proceeded in a straight-line back to the LZ, Jerome going berserk over every deviation from the wandering trees, Lieutenant Holland, in an increasingly exhausted stupor, beyond caring.

The choppers picked us up shortly after we arrived. The flight back to the laager site was uneventful, and I had recovered a bit by the time we set down, recovered enough to contemplate the fiasco that was my first two days in the field. Almost collapsing several times, coming close to getting men killed, not knowing the rudiments of sheltering and feeding myself, this was one helluva inauspicious beginning. I could have been in the Land of the Big PX. The carefree, irresponsible life in Saigon was looking pretty damn good. How much longer was this hell to last? How was I to cope? This was numbah fuckin' ten, without question.

Shortly after the return, Jerome gave the orders for the morrow. We were to climb out of the valley and move a few clicks through the surrounding mountains. Lima was to be the second platoon in line. Jerome said: "Lima, I want you to pay attention to how November moves. He's not running like a maniac through the woods but is moving slowly and carefully."

"Right, Sir," I responded. November was the 3rd Platoon.

After I had repeated the mission to the platoon hierarchy and wolfed down the evening meal, I made some preparations. Given the problems of the first two days without a pack, I was apprehensive, to say the least, about how I would function with a load on my back. I had noticed that I was the only guy lugging a mess kit, a gas mask, and an extra change of clothes. Those items had to go. The problem was that the nearest place to make an official turn-in was unreachable.

So the next morning I left Charlie a present. The standard morning procedure was to fill in the bunkers as well as could be done in five quick minutes. As the bunker of the platoon headquarters group was being filled, I dropped in the mess kit, gas mask, and clothes. Baum, the trooper doing the filling, said nothing.

Leaving presents for Charlie—food, clothing, equipment—was commonplace. And few U.S. laager sites went uninvestigated by the VC or NVA for more than a few days. Indeed, leaving a stay-behind group to stake out the previous night's laager site often produced some action. I always wondered why more stay-behinds weren't attempted.

These gifts to Charlie reduced my load somewhat. It was still a bear, but the thought of what it had been helped me mentally. I was now humping close to what my load over the next months would be: an air mattress and poncho liner for sleeping, a poncho for shelter, toilet articles, an extra pair of socks or so, a flashlight, three to five days of food (mostly C-rations), ammunition, gun-cleaning material, a small first-aid kit, and four or so quarts of water. The load doesn't sound like much, but the amount of ammunition, food, and water was substantial. All told, the load probably weighed somewhere between 40 and 55 pounds. Later I would help carry ammunition for the crew-served weapons, which could add significantly to the burden.

The climb out of the valley produced aching legs, tender shoulders, and burning lungs. Fortunately, however, the pace, as Jerome had instructed me to notice, was slow. We moved in 100-meter bounds. As the main body waited, the point went approximately 100 meters, stopped, and checked out the area briefly, often by "cloverleafing"—having a man in front and one on each side go out about ten or fifteen meters or so and return. Only then would the main body move. So the ache in the legs and the pull of the pack on the shoulders were not a never-ending thing. One just had to adjust one's self to 100-meter doses of pain followed by short periods of recoupment.

Still, for the FNG lieutenant it was one long day. As the hump neared its end, an incident occurred through which Jerome subtlety let me know that I was to solve my own problems. The lead element had closed on the night's laager site, a fairly open area bordering a small creek. One of my troopers proceeded to collapse. He was lying on the ground, pleading, "I can't go on, Sir. I just can't."

Now what the hell was this shit? I was supposed to be the weakling. This guy was supposed to be use to this stuff.

"Come on, Johnson, It can't be that bad. If a Saigon MP like me can make it, you sure as hell can."

"I just can't go any further, Sir."

I didn't believe that he was actually hurt. He didn't appear to have symptoms of heat exhaustion, and he was fairly coherent. I figured that he was testing me. But what if he really was in bad shape? His squad leader and Sgt. Brown weren't much help, just shaking their heads and moving on into the laager site. I called Jerome: "Six, this is Lima. I've got a man that says he can't go on."

"Lima, this is Six. Get him moving."

"He won't move Six."

"Well, leave him. Six out."

I turned to Johnson: "The CO is not very sympathetic, Johnson. He says to leave you."

"I just can't go on," Johnson gasped.

"I really can't see what's wrong, Johnson. Does anything hurt?"

"Just can't go on, Sir."

Johnson had a helluva limited vocabulary, I was beginning to conclude. "Well, we're just ahead," I finally said. "Get to us when you can."

I went on to the laager site. Sgt. Brown had already gotten the platoon in place, and the men were beginning their nightly digging. I asked Sgt. Brown: "What th' hell is th' story with Johnson? Is this th' first time he's pulled this stunt?"

Sgt. Brown shrugged and said, "He's just a pain in the butt."

It wasn't long before Johnson ambled in, not looking all that bad. His mouth was running a mile a minute. "I just couldn't go on, Sir. How ya doin', Sergeant Brown? I'm feeling better now."

So he appeared to have recovered. I wondered if this was going to be a regular occurrence. Being a nursemaid wasn't what I had imagined the infantry would entail, particularly the airborne infantry.

The small creek bordering the laager site was not a typical sluggish murky jungle stream. The area was rocky, and the stream was swift-flowing and clear. Sgt. Brown said, "Good opportunity ta get a bath, Lieutenant. Better take advantage of it."

After getting my hooch set up, I made my way to the water, stripped down, and waded in. A group of ten or fifteen was already there. I noticed that I was the only one with love handles and a flabby gut. I made sure to keep as submerged as possible. I also noticed that security sucked. The creek was twenty meters outside the company perimeter, which wasn't even visible. The terrain on the near side was broken, and trees and large bushes were many. The far side was a gradually rising hill covered by dense undergrowth. Yet the bathing troopers, including several senior NCOs, seem unconcerned. There must be something about this infantry stuff that I wasn't catching.

Shortly after I returned from my bath, Jerome had the evening briefing. The morrow was to be another chopper assault, to an area near the assault of the previous day. We would also return to the stream crossing where Sgt. Brown had chewed my butt. This time, however, we would continue across the stream and climb the high ground on the other side. There, we would laager for the night. I returned and briefed the squad leaders. The evening meal, stand-to, and darkness followed. It was only my third night in the field but the routine was becoming, well, routine.

The next day the chopper assault and the move went without incident. Lima not being on point, I had little opportunity to display more ignorance. That evening, choppers delivered a hot meal, something they did every three days or so as part of a regular resupply. Mail was brought in, as were replacements and returnees, troopers left for various reasons—R&R, DEROS, talking their way out of the field for some task or other—and maybe every three weeks or so, clean fatigues were delivered.

Lima had one guy leaving, a short stocky spec. 4 machine gunner. He had been humping the boonies for a full year, had seen action down south in War Zones C and D, but had enjoyed a comparatively quiet last six months. He had the cynical, laid back attitude of the veteran. I went around to say goodbye and wish him luck. He was civil, but barely, to the FNG lieutenant. Too much water had passed under the bridge, too many unpleasant images crowded his memory, for him to be kissing butt at this point.

The orders at the evening briefing were intriguing. The company was breaking up operationally into platoons for what were called bushwacker operations. Each platoon was to have an AO—area of operations—in which to do its stuff: sneak around, check out trails, find Charlies. After three or so days, we would come together for resupply and further instructions. Initially, the three platoons were to move abreast down a two-click slope toward the east. Jerome's orders were to move on line—the troops moving side-by-side down the hill. Lima was to be on the left. The company headquarters would follow the center platoon down the hill and then return to the laager site to sit around for three days. The order to move on line apparently came from battalion. The idea was to cover all possible hiding places of the elusive VCs.

It was to be my first infantry experience with "impossible" orders. The laager site was a relatively open area, with clumps of bushes broken by patches of short-cropped grass. The slope, however, turned out to be a tangled mess. It was covered by a virtually impenetrable mesh of bushes and vines about ten feet high. In truth, nothing is impenetrable, but this slope was about as close as you could get.

Cutting a path through the thicket would have been at least an all day undertaking. Several trails descended the slope, providing the only practical paths.

Early the next morning, the three platoons began the descent. As per Jerome's instructions, I put Lima on line at the top of the slope. One look, however, was enough to tell even a Saigon FNG that what was to be attempted was not to be. On the order to start, every trooper took the route of least resistance, and each route led quickly and inexorably to the one trail that descended the slope in Lima's AO. So within short order, the entire 1st Platoon was in column formation, moving down the trail.

This was apparently happening with the other two platoons as well, and Jerome was not a happy cowboy. "Lima, this is Six. Are you on line?"

"Six, this is Lima. Well…, we're trying. This stuff's pretty thick, though."

"This is Six. You're supposed to be on line."

Jerome didn't push the matter, however, which told me that his movement behind Mike wasn't going according to plan either. So we spent the rest of the morning moving the only way practical, and exploring occasional side trails. The tangled slope highlighted something that was already becoming apparent to me. The oft-expressed generalization about keeping alive in the jungle by staying off trails had its limits. There were many places and occasions where trails were the only feasible places to be. Getting off the trail might entail traversing the side of a cliff, or hacking through next to impossible vegetation.

At the bottom of the slope were a swampy area and a hut with a small garden, my first hut discovery as an infantry platoon leader. I called it in: "Six, this is Lima."

"Lima, Six."

"This is Lima. We found a hut. Some signs of recent life. Not much else."

"Well, burn it."

That was the standard procedure for this area. No humans were supposed to be around, all friendlies having long since been evacuated. It was what was called a "free fire" zone. That didn't mean you shot women and kids, but anything living was presumed to be VC.

We set fire to the thatched roof, but the thatch was too green and wet to burn much. Beyond the swamp, the terrain rose and opened up for a kilometer or so. The vegetation was high grass—elephant grass, we called it, sharp-edged stuff that cut exposed skin with alacrity. We spent the rest of the day wandering these hills, with me trying to get a handle on exactly where I was. My sitreps, short for "situation reports," were only vague approximations. As evening approached, we returned to the hut. I decided to laager there on the thought that the owners might return and we would have us some VCs.

Sgt. Brown told me that on bushwacker operations there was no digging in at night. I accepted the statement at the time but wondered about the advisability of neglecting to turn up a little helpful dirt. I was still relying on the platoon to get themselves set up in the evening. It was to be sometime before I began taking the interest in the platoon's defensive position that a platoon leader should take.

The night passed uneventfully. In the morning, we started out to explore the AO. Just on the other side of the swamp, abutting the rolling hills covered with elephant grass on which we had cavorted the previous day, was a steep jungle-covered rise. A trail invited us to climb, and so we did. The top was a small plateau, about an acre and a half. It was cultivated, with regularly-spaced mounds of something growing. The mounds reminded me of the way American Indians were supposed to have planted things.

As we were looking around, Six called: "Lima, this is Six."

"Six, Lima."

"This is Six. What's your location?"

"We're at 647825," give or take a grid coordinate or so. I was becoming adept at quickly giving wild guesses as to my whereabouts.

"Is it big enough for a two-ship LZ?"

What the hell was this? I looked around at the small field. It seemed big enough to me for two choppers, but what did I know? I called Sgt. Brown over. He had monitored Jerome's call. "This is big enough for a couple 'a choppers, isn't it?"

"I think so, Sir," he said dubiously.

With that vote of confidence, I responded to Jerome: "Six, this is Lima. I think we can get two choppers in here."

"You think or you know?"

"It can be done."

"Two choppers are on the way. They'll pick up half your men first lift, then come back for the rest. November spotted a couple Victor Charlies. You'll be inserted in at 682352 and sweep over the hill to the east. Understand?"

"This is Lima, roger."

"Six out."

I quickly briefed the squad leaders. One squad, myself, Baum, and Doc would go on the first lift. Sgt. Brown, Washington, and the other squad would be on the second lift. The choppers were already closing.

"Lima, this is Six. Pop smoke."

"This is Lima. Smoke out."

"The choppers have yellow smoke."

"That's us."

We quickly loaded and were off. The expectation of likely contact had my adrenalin pumping. The breeze in the open Huey was a welcome relief from the 90-degree heat and comparable humidity. It was only a four-click flight to the LZ, and we were shortly dropping to a small clearing at the base of a hill. The door gunners were peering intently into the fast-rising tree line. The troopers had a look of anticipation that I hadn't seen in the previous assaults. The suddenness of this one had produced a feeling that maybe this wasn't the usual bullshit.

No fire greeted us on the LZ, and we quickly made the tree line, rounds chambered, safeties off. The choppers departed for the second lift. Even before they returned, Jerome was pushing for us to get up the hill. "Lima, have you started to move?"

"This is Lima, we're waiting on the second lift. They're inbound."

"Well, get moving as soon as they get there. And go up the hill on-line to be sure not to miss anything."

This was a multi-platoon operation, but I had only the vaguest idea of the locations and missions of the other elements. Someone was blocking somewhere, and perhaps someone else was sweeping up the other side of the hill. For all I knew, Jerome and the headquarters group were occupying the hilltop. Although I was a little concerned about waxing fellow Americans—a concern that was to become more pronounced as the weeks went by and I saw how easily friendly fire casualties occurred—I was very anxious to get them VCs. As for Jerome's instruction to move on line, it was possible—the underbrush wasn't too thick—but platoon-in-column was what I was comfortable with. I wasn't ready to experiment, particularly after all the fiascos of my first few days in the boonies.

The rest of the platoon arrived, and we set off up the hill. I had briefed the squad leaders that we were looking for two Victor Charlies, but what the average trooper understood about the mission was anybody's guess. The hill was not big. And the jungle not being particularly dense, we made the top in short order, no more than twenty minutes. Mike arrived at the top about the same time, from the other side. Lt. Roberts had called me shortly before closing on the summit, so we were not totally surprised to see them. Still, a friendly fire fight was probably not missed by much.

As might be expected, neither we nor Mike had flushed any of them VCs. The men quickly lost their attitude of alert expectation, resuming the bored expressions of troops who hadn't had contact in months and were beginning to believe that none was ever going to take place. Another damn wild goose chase.

Mike and I reported the negative findings. Jerome acknowledged. When nothing more was forthcoming, I called: "Six, this is Lima. What do we do now?"

"This is Six. Continue your original mission."

I looked around at the men. It was approaching mid-day and hot and muggy as only the jungle can be. The troops had the look of having already done a full day's work. Mike was in its AO. We were four clicks from ours. I called Jerome: "Six, this is Lima. When will the choppers be back?"

"Lima, this is Six. No choppers. Get back to your AO."

"This is Lima. We have full packs, and the AO is at least four clicks away."

"This is Six. So you'd better get moving."

Christ, the troops were not going to be happy with this. I relayed the news, which was greeted with much cursing and invective. Rather than risking mutiny by starting off right away, I gave an hour's lunch-break on the hill. We might have stayed until nightfall if Jerome hadn't eventually inquired as to our whereabouts: "Lima, this is Six. Sitrep."

"This is Lima. Sitrep negative."

He asked suspiciously: "What is your location?"

"We're, uh, taking a lunch break on the hill."

"Lima, you've been there for half a day. Get yer butt back to your Alpha Oscar."

"This is Lima. Wilco, out."

So the platoon started the trudge. Bent under the packs, drowsy from the break and the heat, we moved down the hill, through a swamp, and finally arrived at the open, rolling terrain we had investigated the day before. I had in mind to cross the area diagonally, skirting the base of the plateau from which we had been lifted in the morning, and to find a combination laager and ambush site near some trails the map indicated were on the far side.

We had gone about two-thirds of the way across the two-click wide open area when we encountered fire—not bullet fire but fire fire, flames, the real stuff. Random artillery earlier in the day must have ignited the grass. The fire was small and innocuous where the grass was short, about ankle high. But where the grass was waist high, the flames were immense, leaping ten to fifteen feet in the air. We encountered the fire line just as it was meeting an area of high grass, in which we happened to be. The point fire team got through, but suddenly us in the main body were staring at a raging, charging inferno. We quickly routed to the rear, losing any semblance of a military organization and all regard for security.

The only thing that prevented us from scattering was the lack of a place to scatter to. After ten minutes or so, the fire again reached an area of smaller grass, and we began darting through the much reduced flames. Eventually, the whole platoon was assembled on the other side. I determined that no one was missing and injuries were nil, other than a few singes here and there.

As we were reorganizing for a continuation toward the far side of the open area, Johnson, the trooper who had faltered several days before, piped up: "We need Sgt. Brown to get us straightened out."

I looked at him smirking and at the generally disgruntled men within earshot, which was most of the platoon. Sgt. Brown was a little ways off. Whether he heard or not I didn't know. But I did know that this wise-ass sonuvabitch was challenging me and that the platoon was dangerously exhausted. I said quickly and angrily: "Hey goddammit! I'm the mothafucker what's in charge here and I'm th' one that gets us straightened out. Now let's get this goddamn mothafuckin' show on th' road."

The point moved out, and I and the rest of the platoon followed. Sometimes a little aggressive cursing is all that's needed to quell an incipient rebellion.

We made the far side of the open area in short order and plunged into an extremely thick stand of ten-foot high elephant grass. The visibility was the man in front of you, and the end of his machete for the guy on point. The going was extremely slow. Fortunately, after fifteen minutes the vegetation began opening up, and it wasn't long before we arrived at a trail. After conferring with Sgt. Brown, I outlined a rough perimeter to the squad leaders, with one side being within daylight sight of the path, maybe fifteen meters away. As I dropped my pack, I noticed several fine lines of blood on the backs of my hands—elephant grass cuts.

A platoon laager site such as we set up that night was not large. Generally circular like a company laager site, it was of course much smaller, maybe twenty meters in diameter. Four or five positions would be on the perimeter, and the platoon headquarters would be in the center, or sometimes also on the perimeter. Later, I would require at least minimal digging in, but in those early days, I was still following Sgt. Brown's no digging approach.

The night passed uneventfully—no VCs bobbing down our trail. I had been in the field for less than a week, but I was rapidly acquiring the attitude of much of the unit: there was little likelihood of ever seeing anything resembling an enemy. The war the American people were seeing every night on TV was not actually taking place. The action that I had envisioned happening everywhere but Saigon, wasn't.

While I wasn't learning much about the VCs, other than they were elusive little fuckers, I was learning about living as an infantryman; that is, like an animal. I was a long way from being acclimatized, however. The major problem was my shoulders. They weren't reacting nicely to humping that pack. I was in pain every moment I had it on, and the pain was definitely impacting my performance. I wasn't devoting sufficient attention to security, to map reading, to the troops' welfare, to night-time positions.

To ease the pain on the shoulders, I had discarded the web gear that I had spent much time learning how to put together during my supply room days in Saigon. It seemed only logical that two shoulder straps—those from the rucksack—would be less painful than four. This probably wasn't the case because rearranging stuff didn't reduce the overall weight, but sometimes reality gives way to appearance.

The arrangement I ended up with put most of the stuff in or attached to my ruck. On my belt, I put a gun cleaning kit, a first aid kit, and a sheath knife. Sometimes I forwent the belt altogether, putting the knife on my pants belt and sticking the web belt in the ruck. On the ruck, I attached a two-quart flexible canteen and placed two one-quart canteens in outer pockets. My M-16 ammunition was in magazines, ten to fourteen of them, which I kept in the bandoleer pouches that the cartridge boxes came in. Each bandoleer held maybe six magazines. If I was carrying the pack, the two bandoleers were in a first aid shoulder bag, along with frag and smoke grenades, and the bag was draped over the pack, or attached to the top of it. If we dropped the packs or just did a day operation, I carried the bag, adding canteens to it or putting them in the side pockets of my jungle fatigue pants.

My map, a part of a platoon leader's anatomy, went in my right pants leg pocket, in a plastic bag, generally one of the ones that PRC-25 radio batteries came in.

For the next several days, we prowled around the AO, not finding much. Trails were plentiful, and a good part of the area was short grass, indicating that people and livestock had been present in the not too distance past. One day we were sent on a wild goose chase down into a steep valley just to the west of the AO. "Intelligence" had indicated possible hostiles. When the call came to make the excursion and I saw the close-set contour lines we would be crossing, I decided to drop the packs, leaving a fire team to guard them. This would alleviate the necessity and agony of having to lug the monsters back up the hillside.

I noted earlier that the RTOs attached their radios to their pack frames. Some put the radio on top and the rucksack on the bottom, and others put the sack on the top and the radio on the bottom. In either case, attaching the radio and the sack required numerous straps and buckles. One of the disadvantages of being an RTO was moving the sack on and off the frame, depending on whether a mission required carrying all one's gear or was just a daytime out-and-back thing.

On this particular occasion, Baum decided not to disassemble his pack. Thus he humped the whole shebang—pack frame, radio, and rucksack—down and back up one incredibly steep hill. The entire move, round trip, was about four kilometers. Only Baum had the full load, everyone else traveling light. We tromped down the hill on the wild goose chase, looked around, and tromped back up, the trip taking maybe four hours. Baum wasn't slowed by carrying close to five times as much as the rest of us—seventy or so pounds versus maybe fifteen. In fact, he pretty much set the pace. It was an impressive performance, at least to me. The others in the platoon seemed to take little notice.

The nights were spent setting up ambushes. I was relying on Sgt. Brown and Sgt. Hikaey, the senior squad leader, for guidance. We weren't attempting anything sophisticated—no Ft. Benning L-shapes, X-shapes, or whatever; no claymores connected in tandem; no plastic cord explosives rigged in ingenious ways. The basic method was just to set up the circular laager site on or close to a trail, aim the M-60s along each approach, put a claymore on each approach, and wait. In theory, each four or five man position had one man awake. Sleeping on duty was more than occasional, however.

One night, we were set up on the side of a hill, in a little clump of woods. A trail ran along the side of the hill and through the clump. It was a lousy defensive position. Fields of fire up and down the hill were very restricted. The trail on one side bent upwards and disappeared out of sight very quickly, after only about 25 meters. On the other side, the trail was visible for a longer distance, following the contour of the hill.

The rationale for picking this ridiculous spot was that the clump of trees would provide cover for the ambush. The open approaches would let us see what might show up and hide exactly where we were. But if a large unit happened along and decided to make life difficult, we would be in deep shit.

Nothing in the way of enemy showed up, however, as I was coming to understand was usually the case. What did show up was a large thrashing sound very close to my sleeping position, certainly within three feet. It lasted for a good half hour. I had visions of a cobra getting irritated about all the activity in its bit of real estate and looking for something—my face—on which to vent its rage. The night was pitch black in the trees, so all I could do was listen and hope my stay in the infantry wouldn't have a premature untoward ending.

Which brings to mind a major concern of those first few weeks—my Combat Infantryman's Badge. Back in those days, the criteria for getting the CIB—the loyal order of those who have been shot at, a musket on a blue background with a laurel wreath, worn over the left breast pocket—was 30 days as an infantryman in the Republic. The individual had to have both an infantry MOS—military occupational specialty—and an infantry assignment. I suppose that someone who got whacked before 30 days might get a CIB, but 30 days was the official threshold. So I was very concerned about getting medevaced, relieved, embarrassed out of the field, or whatever before 30 days. Just give me my 30 days, my CIB, and I would be happy. Don't let this damn snake take a chomp out of me.

And it didn't. Eventually the thrashing stopped and another night passed uneventfully, which was fortunate for Lima given its decrepit location.

First Blood

The time Lima spent wandering the AO was not long—only a few days. But this being my introduction to the infantry, and to the boonies, I was on the steep portion of the learning curve, very steep.

After those few days, the company gathered for resupply. It wasn't an overnighter, just a quickie, enough to get new food and mail, and then back out to the AO. We did learn about a few problems at the headshed, however. It seems the idleness of the headquarters group and weapons platoon was not making for happy troops. You would think that not having to hump the rucks would be welcomed. But sitting around all day was evidently difficult. Apparently the headshed was incapable of running even a few light patrols.

One problem was music. There was too much of it. One of the troopers in the Weapons Platoon had a portable tape deck, and the boys were jammin'. Finally, Jerome had ordered that the thing be turned off, but a combat attitude seemed to be missing. The troops acted as if they were back at the barracks of Bien Hoa.

Also, a little friction seemed to exist between Oscar—the Weapons Platoon—and Jerome's entourage, nothing serious, but there was a clash of cultures. Oscar—actually only about fifteen guys and one 81-mm mortar—was vastly, exuberantly black, maybe four whites in the group. Jerome's headquarters group had about twelve individuals: Jerome, the first sergeant, two RTOs, a medic, the artillery forward observer, his RTO, a supply guy, two engineers, a "major domo," and a Kit Carson scout. Except for the Kit Carson scout who was Vietnamese, all were white. One of the RTOs and the "major domo" were your basic southern good ol' boys, as was the first sergeant. Although few overt racial incidents occurred in A Company, the close proximity of these two very distinct groups during an extended period of inactivity was likely to accentuate differences.

In any case, the friction and difficulties seemed to have been minor. Nevertheless, I was thankful Lima wasn't in a state of idleness.

A day after the resupply, the platoon established a combination laager-ambush at a trail junction only about a click from where the company headshed was holed up. In fact, the main trail ran to the company's location. The main trail was wide—maybe three meters, almost a small road—and well packed. A smaller trail intersected the main one at a 45-degree angle.

The platoon was set up on the side of the main trail opposite the intersection. Sgt. Hikaey selected the site. The two M-60s were aimed along the main trail, one in one direction, one in the other. This meant that one of the M-60s was aimed toward the headshed. The gunner on this gun was a lanky Indiana farm boy, Henderson, a good enough trooper but something of a complainer. The gunner on the other gun was top-notch, a Hispanic-Indian from somewhere in the West. His name was Lopez. Smart, with plenty of initiative and a steely quiet, he was an outstanding soldier. The two guns were about fifteen meters apart, each in a clump of bushes just off the trail. The rest of the platoon was in a half circle on one side of the trail. A row of bushes abutted the trail. A small clearing lay behind the bushes, and the platoon's half moon included the clearing. Two positions were just at the edge of the far side of the clearing facing into the jungle. A third position was on the straight side of the half moon, between the two machine guns, facing the intersecting trail. The platoon headshed was in the clearing.

We had arrived at the site just before dusk and gotten established in the fading light. I was about to open the first course of the evening meal, a can of apricots. The small can opener key was poised to bite into the can lid when all hell broke loose. The sound and concussion of an explosion rocked the area, followed by a ten-second burst from Lopez's M-60. Ten seconds was a damn long burst. Coming with total unexpectedness that evening in the mountains far above Tuy Hoa, it was an eternity.

A combination of terror and adrenalin surged through me, a combination I was to become familiar with in the weeks ahead. A deep, primordial fear gripped my being, but there was also great excitement. I'm sure the same two elements touch everyone who experiences combat or other life-threatening situations. What differs from individual to individual is the proportionate strength of each element. In some, the fear dominates. In others, the excitement is on top. In me, the elements seemed equal, the combination addictive. But usually in the first moments, the terror controlled. Sometimes it would only be quelled when I once again affirmatively accepted the extreme likelihood of succumbing to the infantryman's occupational hazard—death.

On this particular occasion, the initial terror was great but not paralyzing. Perhaps the reason was that I subconsciously registered the lack of incoming fire. By the time the M-60 stopped its prolonged burst, I was low-crawling through the hedge to the trail. The rest of the platoon, those not already at their positions, were also rapidly getting into place. I reached the trail a few meters behind Sgt. Hikaey, who was just behind Lopez, his gun, and his assistant gunner.

"What th' fuck is there?" I hissed.

"Something Sir," Sgt. Hikaey responded, as he craned his neck forward.

Baum whispered from back in the clearing, on the other side of the hedge, "Six wants you, Sir."

Shit, all I needed. I slithered back through the bushes. Baum gave me the handset. "This is Lima."

"What the hell is it, Lima?"

"I don't know. We're checking it out."

"You get control of your troops, Lima, got that?"

Lopez chose this moment to let go a second prolonged burst. "Lima, your men are shooting at cows! Now you get things under control, you understand?"

"This is Lima, roger."

I slithered back to the trail. Jerome's haranguing was fast subduing that exhilarating combination of fear and excitement. He had hit on one point, however. I didn't know what the fuck was happening. Sgt. Hikaey moved to solve the problem for me. "Sir, we'll go out and look around."

"Roger that." Actually, going out in the dark and looking around was a debatable endeavor. On one hand, the theory of a good ambush was that there were no survivors and that you wanted to police up the bodies and weapons before things could be moved. On the other hand, traipsing about the jungle at night was a risky proposition. You could get waxed by the enemy—perfect ambushes in which all the bad guys were killed were few and far between—or by your own men. But what the hell, no one was shooting back at us.

I called Six: "Six, this is Lima. We're gonna check things out."

"Roger. Just don't shoot yourselves while you're shooting those cows."

Shit, what the hell was this with cows? We hadn't seen cow one anywhere in the area. Sgt. Hikaey, Lopez and his gun, and a couple of troopers went poking around. They only went out about twenty meters and weren't gone long. They came back dragging two bodies.

"Looks like we got something, Lieutenant. No weapons, though."

Well, it was a free fire zone. Anything there was fair game. At least they were young males. We hadn't greased women or kids.

"Six, this if Lima. We have a body count of two."

The silence at the other end was heavy and lengthy.

"Lima, are you sure?"

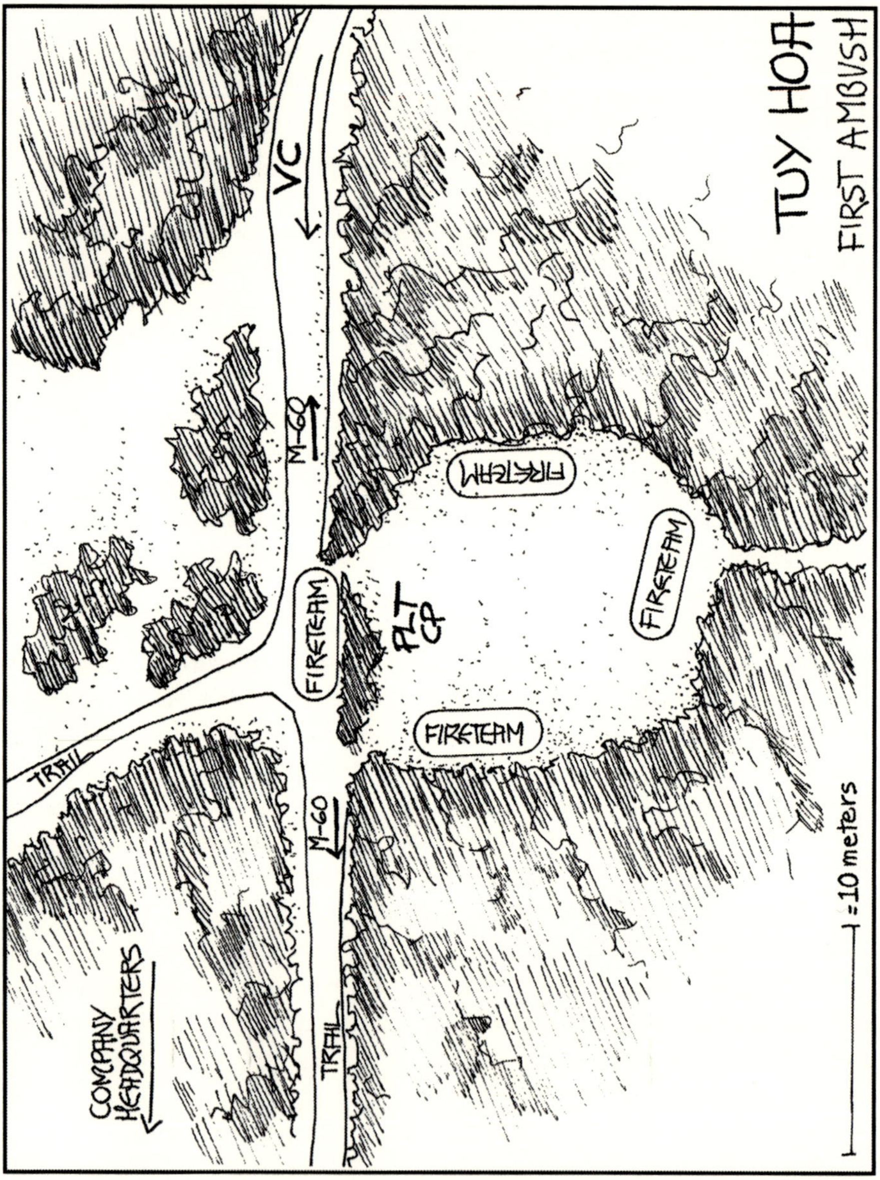
TUY HOA
FIRST AMBUSH
VC
M-60
FIRETEAM
FIRETEAM
FIRETEAM
FIRETEAM
PLT CP
M-60
TRAIL
TRAIL
COMPANY HEADQUARTERS
=10 meters

"I'm looking at 'em right now. Two young adult males. Deader than mackerels."

Jerome's tone changed considerably. He sounded apologetic, conciliatory. "Are there more?"

"I don't know. This was all that was in the open."

"Okay. We'll be firing some flares."

Shortly thereafter, the eerie subdued light of flares made its ghostly appearance. The light only added a little visibility to the open spaces. The bushes and jungle were still dark as the grave. Jerome wanted to know again if we had anything else. I told him no. He didn't ask that we search anymore, and I didn't volunteer.

So there we were with two dead guys amongst us, a long night ahead, and as yet no evening meal. After about fifteen minutes of nothing happening, I returned to the food, a little squeamishly. The dead guys had been deposited in the clearing with the platoon headquarters. They were a few feet away, but I was hungry, and I had recollections of pictures from World War II of troops eating amid the enemy dead. If the old boys could do it, so could I.

With one exception, the rest of the night passed uneventfully. The exception was when Henderson on the other machine gun smoked the company headquarters. His gun was pointed down the trail to where Jerome, his entourage, and the Weapons Platoon were holed up. Apparently feeling left out of the action, Henderson let go with a prolonged burst several hours after the first action. He claimed he saw movement. Whatever he saw or didn't see, his M-60 rounds sped unimpeded the kilometer or so to the company headquarters. The click was flat, the vegetation mostly bushes and small trees, nothing capable of halting an outburst from a high-velocity automatic weapon. The rounds snapped around the heads of the headquarters group and Weapons Platoon, sending a few stomachs into dry throats. Jerome was almost apologetic when he got on the horn to ask what the fuck was going on. He wasn't about to be too severe with the platoon that got A Company's first Victor Charlies in months.

"Lima, we're taking incoming fire from your direction."

"This is Lima. The gunner thought he saw something. Sorry 'bout that. We'll watch it."

"Well be careful. We're in your line of fire."

"This is Lima. Roger, out."

Although after the killings the night was uneventful—except for the dusting of the headshed—no one got a lot of sleep. Adrenalin levels were just too damn high. And getting people underway in the morning was not a problem. The whole platoon was up before the sun, wanting to see what was out there and wanting to get a good look at the trophies.

The platoon wasn't alone in the desire to see the dead guys. Jerome did too, as apparently did even the battalion CO. Maybe they still didn't believe us, or maybe it was just the long dry spell. In any event, Jerome said to cart the bodies back to the headquarters. I really didn't think too much of it. Hell, I was still operating on adrenalin overdrive myself. Transporting the dead dinks didn't present the platoon members with any problems. Volunteers for the macabre task were not lacking. Two troopers ended up with the job. Each threw a poncho over his shoulder to keep off the blood and gore, and placed a dead guy on top of the poncho. Thus we marched in triumph back to the company, bringing our booty.

Upon arrival, the troops seated the dead guys back to back, each propping the other up. The other two rifle platoons—Mike and November—were also arriving, and our trophies were the center of attention. Each had been killed by only one or two M-60 rounds. The entry and exit wounds were just small dark holes, so there wasn't an obvious, eye-catching reason these guys were corpses. In fact, sitting there back to back, heads down, they could have been two sleepers, although pretty pallid ones.

Just observing the corpses quickly lost its entertainment value. PFC Moste, one of Lima's finest, a hulking white teenager, took it upon himself to enliven things. He approached the two dead VC with a machete, greeted them with a graceful bow and felicitous words, and began whacking away. The blows fell with thuds, sort of hollow sounding. As the bodies were by now a number of hours old, not much in the way of blood and gore was forthcoming. All that mushy stuff inside a human being becomes stiff and less messy before the passage of very much time after death.

No one moved to stop Moste, no NCOs, no other company officers, no fellow soldiers. No one in authority was in the immediate vicinity, but many were close enough to know what was going on. Being an FNG, I felt unsure about asserting myself. Perhaps this was standard, I thought, but then remembered that the company hadn't seen bodies in a number of months. Eventually, I concluded that no one other than me, his platoon leader, was going to rein in Moste. He was beginning to look a little tired, anyway, and was probably secretly hoping that someone would put a stop to the shenanigans.

I ambled up to him and said: "Moste, knock it off. They ain't hurtin' you."

He ceased whacking. I walked back to my gear. Several members of Moste's squad were nearby. I revealed to myself the extent of my displeasure with his actions by saying to his buddies: "I hope he's that brave when we run across ones that shoot back."

They emphatically came to his defense: "Don't you worry Sir. He'll be."

It was a PFC named MacVey speaking. He, Moste, and several others in the squad were very close. They were also exuberant teenagers, the types that were trouble in high school, not evil, just trouble. Athletic, swaggering, not adverse to mixing it up, wanting to be heroes, untested but craving action, they were the backbone of the airborne. They just needed to have the reins jerked every now and then. And despite their desire to experience war, there was uncertainty, but not so much about whether they would acquit themselves well in combat. The real uncertainty, which only a few of them barely perceived, was about what combat, especially a prolonged period of combat, would do to them. They were volunteers. They wanted to see war. If they got the opportunity, all but a few of them would meet the challenge. But the aftermath, the distant future, was the real unknown.

Shortly after Moste stopped mutilating the bodies, the battalion CO flew in for a look-see. He disembarked from the Huey in his cleaned, pressed fatigues and spit-shined jungle boots. Somehow Sgt. Hikaey had become the hero of the ambush, and the battalion CO had a long confab with him and Jerome. As it was breaking up, the battalion CO asked, "Is there a sump you can throw them in?"

A sump!? Drop everything gang. Find a sump. What the hell did he think was happening out here!? A fucking sump!? What the hell was a sump, anyway!?

Unlike some other commanders I came across, Jerome was not inclined to attempt the impossible just because some higher up said to. The battalion CO departed and A Company prepared to undertake the next mission. The dead guys were left back to back, a little hacked up, a few 173rd patches stuck in their wounds.

That next mission was for the whole company to return to the ambush site, check it out for any further bodies, and move on to a piece of high ground a good distance away, eight or nine kilometers from our current location. What with moving in slow hops and stopping for the point to make its security cloverleaves, that was a long day's hump. The battalion CO had brought us a present—a tracker dog, with his handler. Tracker dogs were often used by American units in Vietnam. Most were German shepherds. Some were good. Some should have been playing with kiddies back in the Land of the Big PX. Some were trained to track. Others were trained to guard.

Prior to starting out, Jerome briefed the platoon leaders on what the company's Kit Carson scout had allegedly discerned about Lima's trophies. Kit Carson scouts were Vietnamese, usually ARVN soldiers. Generally assigned to company-size units, their main function was to serve as translators. Like tracker dogs, some were good, some were pretty close to useless.

According to our Kit Carson, the two dead guys were VC cadre-in-training. They were political types on their way to some sort of education session. It seems unrealistic that their documents would be so specific, but who was to dispute the Kit Carson? And the conclusion forestalled any embarrassing questions about the absence of weapons, although if truth be told in 1967 few questions were asked about anything that happened in a free fire zone. The bottom line was, the area was a free fire zone, and it was extremely unlikely those birds were tourists, boy scouts, or members of some other innocuous group. Most likely, they were recruits on their way to training as soldiers or political operatives. We got them before they even reached basic training. It was as if a U.S. soldier-to-be got whacked on the way to his first military haircut.

The company headed back to the ambush site. The platoons were abreast, each in column. Lima had the easy route on the trail. Mike and November were about 30 to 50 meters into the sticks, one on each side of the trail, hacking away. The headquarters section and Oscar followed Lima. Because of Mike's and November's slow progress, it was awhile before we arrived back at the ambush site.

Sgt. Hikaey once again regaled Jerome with the details of the slaughter. Meanwhile, the tracker dog was sniffing around in the bushes. And lo and behold, damned if the dog didn't find something—a young, very much alive but wounded Victor Charlie. His hand was a pretty ugly looking piece of meat. A round had shattered his wrist, and from the wound to the tips of his fingers the flesh was hugely swollen and deeply purple. A chopper shortly arrived to take the prisoner. He was sort of zombified, seemingly in shock. But he was getting out of the field. More than a few troopers watched his departure with envy.

The company returned to its journey. It was one long hot day. Lima had it comparatively easy on the trail, but we hadn't had a lot of sleep, and there was no protection from the blazing sun. The rucks bit deep. The sweat flowed liberally. Off the trail, Mike and November struggled. One trooper in Mike went down with the heat. Lt. Roberts took the trooper's ruck, balanced it on top of his own, made about 50 meters, and collapsed himself. Eventually everyone recovered, and the company broke out of the jungle onto higher ground. The area was open but interspersed with clumps of high bushes. It was to figure in my Vietnam experience on two further occasions, one in just a couple of weeks, the other approximately a year in the future. But that day, the area was just a short hump to the laager site on a small hill.

It was a beat outfit that arrived on the hill, beat and with some disgruntlement. Tired and hot troops can be that way. The most overt disgruntlement was on the part of Lt. Kline, November. He and Jerome had been together for some months and were definitely getting on one another's nerves. I don't know what set them off that day, but Kline came storming over after the company had staggered into a perimeter and was beginning to prepare positions.

"That goddamn Jerome! I haven't tied into your platoon, and I don't fuckin' intend to!"

He meant he hadn't bothered to ensure that Lima and November were lined up, or joined, properly, that there were no gaps, that fields of fire overlapped. I didn't admit that I hadn't paid the slightest attention to tying in since I had been in the field. This basic function of an infantry platoon leader hadn't even occurred to me. I just assumed that the troops were capable of choosing their own positions, tying themselves in, making sure all avenues of approach were adequately covered. Many of the troops were capable of accomplishing these functions, but platoon leaders were supposed to make certain.

Anyway, Kline was off on a tirade about Jerome. He divested himself of a good deal of anger and frustration, although I never did get what the specific problem, if any, was. After he left, I wandered over to the left side of the platoon just to see what sort of gap existed between Lima and November. There didn't seem to be much of one. Apparently the troops could do the job themselves, at least occasionally.

The orders for the following day specified a battalion-size chopper assault. Jerome said that the whole dang battalion was going to surround a large VC unit. One company was to form a blocking force. Alpha Company and the other company were to push the VCs into the block. I had been in the field not two weeks, but it was long enough to have developed the same cynical attitude about intelligence reports as I had developed back at the 716th. The troops greeted the mission with a similar level of skepticism and nonchalance.

Except for some difficulty I had sleeping, the night passed uneventfully. The difficulty was due to some developing medical problems. Scratches on my hands and right arm were not healing properly. In fact, the scratches were becoming an angry looking red, with small but growing pockets of puss. And something odd was going on with the pinky of my right hand. The joint between the finger and the hand was beginning to swell, and there was some soreness. The various pains were making sleep a little fitful.

The choppers arrived about mid-morning. The distinctive whump-whump of the Hueys, their loud roar after the quiet of the jungle, the heart-stopping speed as we raced over the nap of the earth on lift-offs and approaches, were becoming welcomed parts of my being, something looked forward to; and from the distant perspective of incipient old-age, looked back on.

As usual, the LZ was cold. It was in a valley. Alpha Company was put in on one side, at the base of a high ridge. Naturally, the next step in the mission was to climb the ridge. Once the whole company had arrived, we set about the task. The hill was one steep mutha', a real lung-burning thigh-buster. Despite the drive-on rag that I attempted to use for padding, the rucksack's thin shoulder straps bit deep. The standard drive-on rag was simply an Army-issue olive-drab towel. It had multiple uses—sweat-moper, hot canteen cup-holder, pillow, shoulder pad. On the march, it was normally draped over the shoulders, providing some cushioning for the pack straps.

Once at the top of the ridge, the company turned and followed the high ground. B Company was in the valley, paralleling our path. The high route wasn't particularly difficult, but the going was slow as battalion tried to coordinate the movement of the companies. Late in the day, the orders were given for the evening's positions. The set-up was decidedly different from what the troops were accustomed to and occasioned considerable grumbling.

A and B companies were to form one helluva long line, stretching down the side of the ridge and across the valley, to prevent the alleged VC from escaping. The only problem was, a helluva long line was a damn poor defensive position, particularly if the attack came from the back side. Lima got the far right of the company line, which meant that we had to go back down the ridge. This we did, stumbling, sweating, falling, and cursing. Our position stretched from the base of the ridge to a stream that divided the valley. It was a good 150 meters of fairly thick jungle. Seven platoon positions, including the platoon headquarters, meant about 20 meters between positions, much too far to be mutually supporting in the heavy vegetation. In essence, each position was its own little fort. Any VCs in the so-called trap could, with a little luck, infiltrate out.

Having gone down the hill, I now had to go back up for the evening briefing. At least this time I didn't have a pack, but it was still a tough hump. The orders for the next day were to keep moving down the valley. Instead of a company column, however, the company was to be on line—the three rifle platoons abreast. Fortunately, the platoons themselves didn't have to be on line; thus a platoon column formation, the easiest formation, could be adopted. Lima was to be on the right, in the valley floor. I made my way back down the ridge. Once in Lima's area, I stopped at each position and warned the troops to be damn sure before opening fire on anything—a noise, a shadow, whatever. It seemed to me our elongated line was a friendly fire fight waiting to happen. We could spend the night shooting each other up.

Fortunately, the night passed without incident. The next day was a long hump down the valley, full of stops and starts as the leadership attempted to keep six platoons—three each from A and B Companies—moving roughly abreast. The evening arrangement was to be the same as the previous evening. The two companies were to be on line. The valley had narrowed, however, so the horrendous distances between positions that had been so scary the night before were no longer necessary.

We had one additional task before settling in. Jerome gave Lima the job of retracing the route back up the valley, in part to see if anyone was following us. As I've noted, policing up U.S. laager sites was a major supply procedure for Charlie. Lima did not take kindly to the additional task. Extra missions were in theory rotated among the platoons, and the troops didn't believe it was their turn. I really didn't know, but regardless of whose turn it was, a certain logic supported having Lima perform the duty. We were the closest to the jump-off point and moreover were familiar with the route, having come down it.

In any event, the grumbling and bitching occasioned my second inspirational speech as an infantry leader, the first having been the obscenity-laden rant I had produced to get the platoon moving after the disruption of the grass fire some days previously. I halted the platoon as we were moving out, bunched them up, and said:

"Listen, you guys are bitchin' too damn much. We got this mission 'cause we're the closest to it. Maybe it wasn't our turn. But it'll even out. There's too much pissin' and moaning. Let's stop the crap and get the job done."

Elegant it certainly wasn't, but it caught the troops off guard. They probably had begun to think their platoon leader was dead in the head. At least the guy had thoughts, even if they were wrong. The patrol of course was uneventful. We found no VC following us. So we traipsed back to the laager line, hot and tired.

Lt. Waymen, the company Executive Officer, had flown in with a resupply chopper. We had a hot meal and mail. He and the first sergeant were going over some administrative stuff. I overheard the first sergeant reviewing a list of people who would soon qualify for the CIB. Christ! Had I actually been in the field a month? Well, not quite, but it wouldn't be too long. Hot damn, the CIB! But I hadn't been shot at yet. To be sure, the platoon had wasted a couple of guys. The

CIB seemed to require more than that, however. But what the hell. At least I would have proof of being a combat infantryman, although not much in the way of stories so far.

One thing I did have, though, was growing, throbbing pain from the jungle rot on my hands and right arm. And the infection in the base of my little finger was becoming particularly bothersome. Doc, the platoon medic, wasn't real swift on infections. Maybe wounds were his specialty. Doc was the dirtiest, filthiest guy in the platoon, which was really saying something because certainly one of the dirtiest, filthiest things on earth in 1967 was an infantry platoon in Vietnam that had been in the field for six months. In any case, Doc poked and prodded a little, but he didn't have much too offer. The pain was making sleep more and more fitful.

The next day was when the allegedly encircled VC were supposed to meet their fate. A and B Companies would close with the blocking C Company, with Charlie squeezed in the middle. Battalion expected a large body count.

We closed with C Company about noon. VC one was not in sight, just 300 paratroopers, three companies worth, milling around an open field. A single Charlie machine gunner on the side of the field could have bagged himself the VC equivalent of the Congressional Medal of Honor. The drill for the next hour was mill-around-mill. Troopers who had friends in other companies did some socializing, C-ration lunches were consumed, and the battalion commander chewed out his company commanders. LTC Shafter did this in full view of the three companies. Public ass-chewings were apparently his modus operandi. His company commanders—Jerome, McNevers of C Company, and the B Company CO—were no pussy cats, however. We could see them giving tit for tat.

After the festivities, the three companies parted, off on separate missions. A Company had about a four-click hump to a laager site on a hill. November was in the lead. Halfway to the objective occurred another incident that reminded me of my lack of formal infantry training. The company had broken into a large open area. It was a good two-clicks to the far side, only we weren't supposed to be going to the far side. November had gotten about a third of the way across when Jerome redirected them. They were to turn 90 degrees to the right, which would put them on a straight shot to the hilltop laager site.

The subsequent move perpendicular to the rest of the company was a work of art, infantry variety. November had been in a straight column, one man behind the other. When Kline made the turn, he called for some sort of wedge formation, a spread out array of his troops designed to give each man a wide field of fire and to avoid an enfilading attack from the front that could devastate the whole platoon in short order. This was the kind of thing you learned at Ft. Benning. Not having been through Infantry Officer's Basic, I only knew of such formations in theory. But in truth, I had not seen any evidence of exotic formations since I had been in the field. Maybe theory was where they spent most of their time. For me personally, the basic column formation was difficult enough.

As Kline and his boys paraded past, the rest of the company watched, some in awe, some in admiration, some in derision. I was close to Jerome and expected him to ask myself and Mike, "Why can't you clowns do that?" It was a damned impressive sight, and served to reinforce my feelings of inadequacy.

We made the laager site a short time later. It was a knoll that protruded from the mountains that were on its far side. The climb was fairly steep, but the top was nicely rounded and open, a rather comfortable spot. The battalion CO flew in for a talk with Jerome. He had the senior battalion medic with him. The medic's purpose was to look at one of my men, a black PFC with a severe case of jungle rot on his hands, much worse than mine. Indeed, the back of the guy's hands and his lower arms were nauseating to look at. Puss seeped from a number of inflamed open sores. He walked and stood with his arms stiffly extended about six inches from his sides.

And the dumb SOBs left him in the field! He was close to useless, obviously in pain, and the powers that be seemed to feel he was malingering. Although as the platoon leader I should have been involved in the decision, I wasn't. I was still partly in the by-stander mode, observing, and not really cognizant of my significant responsibilities regarding the welfare of my men. The poor guy would be evacuated in another day or so, but he should have gone right then, and I should have pressed the point. The lack of concern about his condition was to be in sharp contrast to how I was treated several days later. My own jungle rot was not as bad as the PFC's, but it was painful enough, and getting worse. At that point, his pain must have been excruciating.

The move for the next day was back down the knoll and along the valley to the northwest. The valley was wide, at least two kilometers in most places. The company was to move in three platoon columns. Lima was on the right, paralleling a stream that was about 20 meters wide, sluggish and deep-looking. November was a good 200 meters to our left and out of sight. Mike was on the far side of November. Shortly after we started, Mike came on the horn: "Six, this is Mike!"

"Mike, Six."

"This is Mike! We almost shot up a Mike Force! How come nobody told us about them!?"

Lt. Roberts was damned agitated. A Mike Force was a Special Forces outfit. A few officers and NCOs were U.S. Green Berets. The bulk of the unit was some type of indigenous personnel—Chinese Nungs, Cambodians, Montegnards, various other Southeast Asia mercenaries. The uniforms were generally tiger suits: fatigues with a jagged camouflage pattern of sharply defined dark green and black stripes. The reputation of the Mike Forces was impressive, although how much was due to accomplishment and how much to the Special Forces public relations machine was uncertain.

Mike—Alpha Company's Mike, that is—had run into a Mike Force operating on the company's left flank. Several of Mike's troopers all of a sudden see a couple of armed dinks grinning and waving at them. A fire fight was narrowly averted. Whether the situation was as dicey as Roberts implied is difficult to say. He had spent time with the Green Beanies at Ft. Bragg. Perhaps some of his irritation was due to familiarity.

The incident did point up the isolated world in which A Company operated, however. Most of us had no warning that a Mike Force was nearby. And only a handful of the troops had any idea what a Mike Force was. The average grunt had little knowledge of the Vietnamese and other indigenous participants in the conflict. My knowledge was due to the fact that I was an Ol' Asia Hand, with a year in Saigon hearing war stories. In the fall of 1967, the world of A Company was a world of jungle, elephant grass, rucksacks, humping, and not much else. What existed beyond the line-of-sight was largely unknown.

After a long day of paralleling the stream, Lima met up with the other two platoons for the evening laager site. Mike's encounter with the Mike Force was the only event of an otherwise uneventful day, except for what was to follow at the laager site.

The pain in the joint of my little finger was reaching heights I hadn't imagined possible. Doc was obviously stumped. By this time the joint was about the size of a golf ball, and the pinky was sticking out to the side at almost a 90-degree angle to the hand. I was convinced that the thing should be popped like a pimple, or cut, or otherwise drained. Exacerbating the pain were my shoulders. They ached. They were not yet acclimatized to the humping. Tender and sensitive were the best adjectives to describe them. The drive-on rag was not helping in spreading or padding the burden. I was spending most of my time shifting the ruck, bending over, grimacing. Physically, I was close to a basket case.

But I did have enough energy that evening to take my first serious interest in the platoon's position. A reason was the way Lima's sector of the company perimeter wandered in and out of the trees. The laager site was partly in the open, partly in jungle. This presented the problem of whether, if there was a choice, a hole should be in the woods or in a field. A position in the woods was more concealed but sacrificed visibility and fields of fire. A position in the open had better visibility and fields of fire but sacrificed concealment. In addition, the visibility and fields of fire of a position in a field stopped at the wood line.

Lima's sector was considerable, maybe a 100 meters in length. On the left side of the sector—with room for three holes—the perimeter could follow a finger of trees up a hill to the adjacent platoon, could be in an open area about 50 meters wide between the finger of trees and another wooded area, or could be in that wooded area itself. After a bit of agonizing, I chose the open area. Positions in the finger would result in the left side of the platoon's sector being considerably indented when viewed in reference to the adjacent platoon. Positions in the far woods would result in the left side being significantly extended and exposed.

That conundrum having been resolved, I took my first serious look at the platoon's weapons. I had assumed that cleaning weapons would be a top priority with grunts. I was wrong. Many of the M-16s had dirty barrels, many more than I expected. I told the squad leaders to get the damn cleaning rods in gear.

Finally, after occupying myself with these chores, I was ready for the main event. I could avoid it no longer. My finger required the attention of a professional. Doc needed to do his stuff. What he proposed to do was lance the infection, cut into the flesh with a scalpel. Three things doomed the effort. First, Doc, as I've noted, was probably the filthiest of a filthy group. Everyone had dirty hands, had fingernails encrusted with grime, but Doc's appendages were particularly grotesque. His aura of uncleanness was enhanced by a face that was home to an especially virulent crop of pimples. After all, he wasn't really a Doc, only a 19-year-old adolescent.

Second, Doc was one of the sloppier smokers around. He smoked heavily, and sucked 'em down to stubs. Even the grime on his hands couldn't completely hide the nicotine stains. As a non-smoker, I was a little nauseated by his sloppy smoking and the evidence thereof. Finally, Doc's approach to the finger was tentative. He merely pecked and jabbed. A quick slice would have done the job. The plodding probing, however, had me about to keel in short order. I felt a rush of heat to my head, sweat started flowing profusely, and the pre-faint vision of brightness interspersed with black began descending. The patient halted the operation. "Hold it, Doc. I'm about to pass. This ain't gonna work."

"Okay Sir," he said, relieved. His heart wasn't in the operation either. So I spent another agonizing night. The finger was like a really bad headache. Each beat of my heart, each acceleration of my blood, triggered a jolt of pain, only the pain was in my finger and not my head. And a handful of aspirin didn't bring it to an end.

Friendly Fire

From a purely physical standpoint, the next day was probably the worst of my almost five months as an infantry platoon leader. Moreover, it was an eventful, and tragic, day for the company. So concentrated was I on my deteriorating body, however, that I hardly noticed what transpired.

For the first few kilometers, we continued our progression along the valley, only the company was in column rather than with platoons abreast. The morning was overcast and muggy. The elephant grass was wet and waist high. The finger was aching and throbbing. The shoulder straps were viciously cutting. Moreover, the jungle rot on my hands and right arm had cut in with its own quota of pain. My right arm had two angry, inflamed places, oozing puss. One was on the upper side of my wrist. The other was also on the top side of my arm but up near the elbow. On the left hand, the nastiness was on the knuckles of my index and middle fingers. These splotches of jungle rot were extremely sensitive to the touch and had joined the finger in constant throbbing.

Shortly before noon, we began climbing out of the valley. The company went on line, with platoons abreast approximately 100 to 200 meters apart and out of sight of each other. The vegetation changed from the open elephant grass of the valley to thick jungle. Lima was on the right, which just happened to involve the steepest and longest climb. Mike and November had shorter treks to the top of the ridge. Lima's route was so steep, in fact, that hands were required to pull oneself from sapling to root to rock. This was pure agony for me. My hands were pieces of meat—living, pulsating, throbbing meat. They weren't capable of grasping and maneuvering. I was reduced to using the inside of my elbows as hand substitutes. All my thoughts and concentration went into the next few feet of climb.

As we neared the top of the ridge, shots rang out at some distance to our left. The radio began crackling. November's point had gotten a glimpse of something and let go a few rounds. For me, the activity meant a moment of inaction, a moment to ease my aching shoulders, to stop moving my throbbing hands. I promptly assumed the grunt's standard rest position—sitting on his butt, leaning back on his pack. The troopers nearby looked at me expectantly, wanting to get in on the action. I ignored them.

But the respite was brief. Six was shortly on the horn with orders. The chase was on, and a complicated chase it was to be. November was to charge straight ahead in pursuit of the alleged VC. Mike was to make a wide half-circle to the left side of November, eventually forming a blocking force to the left front in the lowlands beyond the ridge we were then climbing. Lima was to proceed straight ahead until we cleared the ridge top and then was to hang a left. This would bring us to the front, side, or rear of November, it was unclear which. And I frankly didn't care, being consumed with my physical problems.

I passed instructions to the squad leaders and those within earshot. "Okay, we're in pursuit of unfriendlies but we might be movin' into November. Be damn sure before pullin' any triggers."

We started off. I was right behind the point fire team. I glanced around and saw that the rest of the platoon was on top of me. Space discipline was nil. The troops wanted to get there and mix it up. "Hey, spread out! One machine gun burst and you're all straphangers."

There was more firing to our left front, just a few sporadic bursts. We made it over the ridge and then hung a 45-degree left. The woods weren't particularly thick, so our progress was fairly good. According to the radio traffic I was overhearing—Baum was right behind me with the radio—November had caught some women and children. There were casualties.

We caught up with the action before too long. Despite my semi-invalid state, our descent of the ridge was almost a gallop. The headquarters group and Oscar—the Weapons Platoon—were behind November in a stream bed. We plowed into them. Fortunately, no shots were exchanged. Paralleling the headquarters group and Oscar, we made our way toward November. As usual in meetings like this, too many people were concentrated in too small an area. Reminding the troops to maintain proper intervals was a never-ending chore.

Confusion reigned in November's locale. Mike was still off to the left somewhere. November's point was a hundred meters or so to the front, out of sight and hearing. Seven or eight Vietnamese women and children were milling around, fearful and moaning. Two were wounded. One of them, an adolescent girl, had a nasty looking hole in her forearm. What appeared to be a bit of bone protruded from the hole. She was lying on the ground and seemed semi-delirious, with her eyes rolled up into her head. Only a little of her pupils was visible. A medic was preparing to apply bandages to the wound. The second casualty was not as serious. The wound was a graze on a shoulder. The individual, however, a middle-aged woman, was as zonked as the young girl. Although not wounded physically, the rest of the Vietnamese appeared to be close to shock and expecting the worse.

To top off the scene, rain began falling, a slow but soaking drizzle. The whole group—the two rifle platoons, the headquarters element, Oscar, the Vietnamese—began moving slowly down the gully. A soldier carried the wounded girl in his arms. Before too long, we broke out of the woods into high elephant grass. November's point was there, having policed up a couple more Vietnamese.

A chopper was due in to pick up our booty. In the meantime, we stood around getting soaked. We had security out, but not far. Some troopers had their ponchos on. Others just put up with the water. I would have liked to be drier, but I was just too damn miserable to go through all the steps involved in dropping the pack, unhooking straps, and getting the poncho over my head and the pack too. Besides, any movement accentuated the pain in my hands and right arm, particularly in my little finger. Thus I was concentrating on keeping my arms as still as possible.

The chopper eventually arrived, as did Mike from the left flank. The Vietnamese departed for their future of who knew what, terrified and sobbing. Were they the enemy? I didn't know and didn't really care. It was a free-fire area where nobody was supposed to be. The situation was not the same as that faced by U.S. troops operating in populated locales. The magical term "free fire" was interpreted by the troops, and indeed by many company- and battalion-level officers, as a license to kill, or at least to shoot first and ask questions later. Wondering about whether the locals were friendly or at least neutral was not something you felt required to do because there weren't supposed to be any locals. As for me, if I felt anything through my own misery, it was that they were lucky they weren't dead meat.

On the other hand, I, and most of the troops, had no hatred or dislike for our just-departed captives. We weren't operating in an area with booby traps and mines, the insidious unseen evils that took casualties without giving you something to shoot back at. In some ways, I was fortunate during my two and a half years in Vietnam. One way was that I never had to command troops in a heavily mined or booby-trapped area. Later I was an advisor to a Vietnamese unit that operated in such an area. But tagging along—what most advisors really did—wasn't the same as having the responsibility of command. The point is, troops who frequently faced mines and booby traps most likely had a different view of locals than did boonie rats who were beyond the populated areas and encountered few of these nasty, maiming devices.

After the departure of our captives, the company resumed the march. Instead of platoons moving on parallel axes, however, we proceeded in a company column. The elephant grass was waist to chest high, and wet. The ground was muck. The point and lead platoon beat down a path, but they also kneaded the ground into a gluey, gripping, sucking paste. By the time Lima arrived at a spot, each step was a struggle. We crossed several streams, at least one of which had high banks. Sliding down the embankment and crawling up the other side insured that the muck was distributed over our whole beings. After a couple of hours of this, we arrived at the evening laager site in the middle of a wide valley. Several small groves of trees were within the company position, but mostly the vegetation was elephant grass.

Shortly after arrival, Six gave out the evening responsibilities. Generally every night, two of the three rifle platoons put out a fire team-size ambush or outpost—OP. An ambush was designed to catch some varmints. The purpose of an OP was to give early warning of an attack on the company position. In reality, there was little difference in how the troops set up and operated an ambush and an OP. When your main goal was merely to rest, to sleep, to do as little as possible, the grandiose techniques taught at Ft. Benning and other training centers got short shrift.

The troops generally didn't mind the ambushes and OPs. The troops were beyond the apparent safety of the company's position, but they didn't have to mess with digging holes. Just head out to a quiet spot, spread out ponchos, poncho liners, and air mattresses, and get sack time. In theory, at least one guy was always awake. The platoon CP kept in touch by radio. The standard procedure was for the OP or ambush not to talk when the platoon asked for a sitrep—situation report—but merely to acknowledge alertness and health. "Lima Two, this is Lima. If you are pingpong, break squelch twice over."

If someone at the OP or ambush were awake, two pushes of the talk button would produce two short bursts of static. On occasion, however, the OP or ambush was slow in responding: "Lima Two, this is Lima. Wake the hell up out there."

Eventually, a sleeper would awaken and break squelch. Even when silence lasted for awhile, there was little fear that the OP or ambush was in trouble. Real, bona fide trouble would have been signaled with explosions and small arms fire. Silence just meant some bozo was again sleeping on guard duty.

Jerome's instructions were for ambushes for Mike and Lima. He gave out the grid coordinates, and Lt. Roberts and I departed to get the troops out before night fell. I gave the fire team their instructions and sent them on their way. I then turned to my hooch. We were in elephant grass, away from all but a few trees. I was attempting to hammer several sticks into the ground to tie out the poncho. The hammers were an entrenching tool, the side of a machete, and my helmet. Whatever I tried, each blow sent a sharp, almost unbearable throb of pain up my arm. The level of pain was well beyond any I had yet experienced. I was in such obvious distress that Sgt. Brown came over: "You okay, Sir?"

"This damn finger is killing me."

We both looked at my misshapen, swollen, inflamed pinky. It was not a pretty sight. "Let me help you with your hooch."

"I ain't gonna refuse."

As Sgt. Brown was pounding in the stakes and I was suffering, Lt. Roberts came up. "Hey Lima, I gave my ambush the wrong coordinates, your coordinates, could we trade?"

Jesus Christ. This was all I needed. I couldn't think as it was, and here was Roberts with some weird problem. Because he gave the wrong order, I was supposed to try to relocate my men by radio? It was hard enough to position them when you could give the instructions face to face. Roberts saw my indecision. "Both ambushes are now in the same place. One needs to move."

"Well, how come you can't move yours?"

"Look, I'm asking for a favor. How about letting me owe you one?"

What was this? Pick on the FNG? All I wanted was for the pain in my hand to stop. I didn't want to get involved in this nightmare. "Hey, I'm sorry, but my guys are in place, the right place. This is your screw-up. You can straighten it out as well as me."

Roberts stomped off. I probably should have been a little more accommodating, but I was in too much agony. After a few minutes, I called Lima's ambush. "Lima Two, this is Lima. Are you alone yet?"

"Negative. Mike is just moving off now."

"Make sure you know where they go. We don't want to fire each other up."

"Roger."

"Lima out."

The specter of friendly fire casualties was a growing concern to me. Part of this was the legacy of my year with the 716th, whose troopers had not been adverse to shooting first and asking questions later. Blowing hell out of any friendlies who happened to be in the wrong place at the wrong time had not been standard procedure in the 716th, but it had certainly seemed so on occasion. Another source of my concern about friendly fire was that anyone who was at all familiar with war stories—including Vietnam war stories—knew that friendly fire casualties were pervasive. So I was worried about shooting, or getting shot by, my own troops, and the more I contemplated how easily such events could occur, the more worried I became. As for the here and now, I was sure that Mike's ambush wouldn't be far from Lima, so I reiterated my fears.

"Lima Two, this is Lima."

"Lima Two."

"Contact Mike Two directly when you think they are settled in. Be sure you know which direction they are and how far."

"Roger."

"This is Lima, out."

Darkness was rapidly descending. An intermittent drizzle kept the knee-high elephant grass soaked. Any movement resulted in more water on already drenched pants and boots. Wet, miserable, and in much discomfort, I crawled into my hooch. The damn finger was driving me nuts. I could tell there would be little sleep, what with the constant throbbing. Each beat of my heart sent a jolt of pain to the finger and back up my arm.

I lay there listening to the drizzle on the poncho, feeling extremely sorry for myself. With excruciating slowness, the minutes turned to hours. Sleep wasn't close. Other than the rain, the only thing breaking the silence of the night was Oscar's H and I fires.

H and I stood for harassment and interdiction. Artillery of all sizes, from Oscar's 81-millimeter mortar, to the battalion's four-deuce mortars, to the 105-millimeter, 8-inch, and 155-millimeter guns of the artillery batteries, engaged in H and I fires. The targets were simply grid coordinates of locations where someone thought a VC or NVA soldier might hang out, maybe a stream crossing or a mountain pass. Avenues of approach into the company position were also frequent targets. H and I fires were fired both day and night. For a company on the move during the day, however, H and I fires from its Weapons Platoon were only possible at night.

Firing a mortar was a relatively simple affair. A mortar consisted of a base plate, a firing tube, and a bipod. The rear of the tube rested in the base plate. The bipod supported the front of the tube at a fairly steep angle. A sight on the bipod enabled direction and distance fine-tuning. The sight focused on aiming stakes set ten to fifteen meters away from the gun on a known azimuth. Estimates of directions and distances to targets, which were rarely visible from the gun, were translated by a chartman, who carried a chartboard two to three feet in diameter, into settings for the sight. The settings were set with reference to the aiming stakes. At night, flashlights with red lenses were attached to the aiming stakes.

A mortar lobbed shells on a high trajectory. Accuracy wasn't the weapon's strong point. What it did was deliver a high rate of fire over an area. The distance a mortar shell went depended on the angle of the tube and the number of powder charges on the fins at its base. A shell came with five or so powder charges in little packets, and the gunner removed an appropriate number to enable the shell to go less than the maximum distance for a given tube angle. The number of powder charges was one of the calculations provided by the chartman.

A rifle company normally had several 81-mm mortars. In Vietnam, however, with the chronic under-strength condition of rifle companies, several mortars in the field were often impossible. Alpha Company had one mortar in its 15-man Weapons Platoon. The company carried about 45 mortar shells, which were big heavy muthas, about ten pounds each and about two feet long. Oscar carried about thirty shells, and the remainder were apportioned out to the two rifle platoons not on point.

The platoon didn't fire H and I fires every night. Whether it did so depended on the situation, the length of time to the next resupply, the company commander's desires on a particular evening, and the like. A typical night's firing would be nine rounds—three about 2100, three around midnight, and three at 0300. The procedure up until this particular night was that a gunner would get up, do the firing, and return to his air mattress.

My misery was pretty close to complete on this drizzly evening. The finger, hands, and arm throbbed. The shoulders ached. I couldn't sleep. I wondered about the ambush and whether it would get through the night without firing up Mike. I wondered about the platoon's position that I hadn't checked, as usual. Maybe I even wondered about what the hell I was doing there when I could have been back in the Land of the Big PX. I didn't often think that, but the idea did cross my mind during the really low points.

I was still wide awake at midnight, tossing and throbbing on my air mattress, when from the direction of the company CP—command post—came a brief whine followed by an explosion. Immediately, there was much shouting and activity from the CP area, which was about 40 meters away. The radio, which was with Baum and his hoochmate about ten meters from me, began crackling. I whispered loudly, "What the hell's goin' on?"

"Don't know yet, Sir."

No other explosions occurred, and there was no small arms fire. My first thought was incoming mortars. But if it was hostile fire, there would likely have been more than one round. The next thing that I thought of was a friendly grenade. The troops carried grenades in abundance and carelessly, strapped on ammo pouches, stuffed in pockets and bags, squirreled away in corners of the rucks. It was a wonder a grenade pin didn't work loose every day.

By this time, Baum and most of the others in the platoon CP were up and at the platoon bunker. Sgt. Brown was still in his jungle hammock—a mesh thing he had acquired from some deceased VC. When he could, Sgt. Brown strung the hammock between trees and tied his poncho overhead. I felt I should be investigating but was just too damn exhausted and hurt to do so. I lay on my air mattress, the only bit of luxury in a grunt's life, in absolute misery. Eventually, one of the members of the platoon CP went over to the company CP and reported back. "The mortar misfired. Wentworth's dead. Two others are wounded."

"Shit," someone said. "Fuckin' mortar's not worth a rat's ass."

The ambush patrol broke radio silence, wanting to know what was going on. I told Baum to tell the patrol everything was under control, to hold their position. The activity at the company CP continued. Noise and light discipline had been pretty much abandoned. Any VC mortars would have had a hard-to-miss target.

So the night passed. I finally fell into about an hour of troubled sleep. The drizzle continued intermittently. At daybreak, the company went to stand-to, with each position fully manned and all personnel supposedly wide-eyed and bushy-tailed. At the end of stand-to, a chopper came in to take out the one dead and two wounded. The battalion commander also came in. He stayed only briefly. Jerome seemed in no danger of being relieved. Company commanders were relieved for a lot less in Vietnam, but Jerome was the battalion CO's main man. Clashing personalities often led to relief from command for minor errors or mishaps. Meshing personalities often saved commands when even egregious errors were involved. Although a soldier was dead, this particular incident probably qualified as no more than a minor mishap. Blame? The war was to blame. Putting a bunch of men with lethal implements in close contact was to blame. Only an arm-chair soldier or a media crusader out to make a name could find blame in this situation.

Shortly after the choppers departed, Jerome called for the platoon leaders. It was a somber gathering. Jerome told the story. A mortar round during the midnight H and I firing had not dropped fast enough down the tube but had merely slid slowly. The powder bags had apparently not all ignited properly, and the round just plopped out of the tube, going maybe fifteen meters. It landed close to where Wentworth, a supply guy in the company CP, was sleeping in a jungle hammock strung between two trees. The ground-level explosion sent shrapnel outward and upward, riddling Wentworth suspended three to four feet off the ground. The two wounded were on air mattresses on the ground.

Jerome didn't cast any blame. He said that the wet weather was probably the major cause of the accident. Water could have gotten on either the inside of the gun tube or the powder bags, or both. Jerome did tell Monroe, the Weapons Platoon leader, that henceforth either the platoon leader or platoon sergeant was to be awake for, and was to supervise, any H and I firing. Jerome then specifically thanked November, Lt. Kline, for coming to the company CP and helping out. I took this as an unstated criticism of myself and Lt. Roberts for not coming to the CP at the time of the incident.

Criticism at this point, however, was immaterial to me. I was just too miserable to give a shit. Fortunately, this turned out to be my mental and physical lowpoint.

Jerome issued another order—no more sleeping in hammocks. This was going to hit Sgt. Brown hard. He loved his hammock. Finally, Jerome laid out the mission for the day. We were to continue up the valley, laagering in a saddle about five clicks away.

The move went quickly. The route offered little in the way of thick forests, just a lot of knee-high elephant grass. The drizzle had let up but the sun stayed hidden behind clouds. The temperature was a comparatively cool low 80s. We made the saddle a little after mid-day. Mike and November were given afternoon patrols. Lima was to spread out and occupy the perimeter. Doc apparently felt badly about his inability to cure my infections and jungle rot. He came up to me as I was pitching my hooch: "Sir, I talked to Calvert, the company medic. He wants to take a look at your hand."

"Alriiightt. I'm goin' to a specialist, huh?" I was feeling better already.

"Yes Sir. He's good."

Calvert was a tall white guy, maybe twenty or twenty-one, from California. He had a feather in his helmet and several strings of beads around his neck. He was a paratrooper hippie, but I didn't know it at the time. I had been in Vietnam for 14 months, since August 1966, and was only vaguely aware of the explosion of the counterculture back home. Calvert's beads were merely an interesting oddity to me, of no larger significance.

But Calvert was a damn good medic. He took one look at my finger, whistled, and went for his scalpels. I immediately felt the onslaught of severe squeamishness, but Calvert was having none of it: "Relax Sir. This is a piece of cake."

"Yeah, well, I don't take to knives very well."

Calvert grabbed my hand, arched the palm side up, and made a quick deep slice into the puffy inflamed flesh at the base of my little finger. None of the poking and picking that Doc had attempted. Half a shot glass or more of bloody puss dripped to the ground. The edges of the cut pulled back. The sides of the cut were red pulpy material. Calvert then kneaded the ends of the cut between his thumb and forefinger, peering into the abyss. I could swear that I could see the bone, but that's probably an elaboration of the years.

In hindsight, Calvert's next step was obvious, and if it had been done a week or so earlier, might have saved me a week of torment and anguish. He gave me a shot of penicillin. Simply as that. Have an infection? Attack it with antibiotics. Why the hell couldn't Doc have thought of that? He must have been hung over that day in medic school. After receiving the shot—which was in my butt as I stood with my pants around my ankles in the middle of the open saddle—I went back to my hootch and slept for the rest of the afternoon. It was my first extended bit of rest in days.

The other platoons returned before nightfall. The orders for the morrow were to remain in place, sending out day patrols. In other words, no humping the ruck. My shoulders were ecstatic. It rained during the night, steadily for several hours. The next morning, the platoon leaders gathered with Jerome early to get the specific assignments. November was sopping wet and grinning like a shit-eating cat. He volunteered that he had been up since 0300 checking out his positions. Where the hell was the guy getting the energy and enthusiasm? I wasn't even participating regularly in the platoon CP's radio watch, was in a permanent state of exhaustion, and here this sonuvabitch was spending half the night harassing his men. If that was being a good platoon leader, I had a long damn way to go.

Lima's mission for the day was to cross the mountain to the immediate north and take up a blocking position on the next mountain over. A VC platoon had allegedly been flushed a few clicks to the east and was headed our way. I had heard enough false "they're on the way" warnings not to be particularly expectant about the approaching hoard, but still it was an explicit bit of intelligence. You never knew.

The destination was only a couple clicks away, and we were shortly there. The mountain was a jungle-covered jagged little peak. I set up the platoon CP on the top, which had about a ten meter by ten meter flat spot. The rest of the platoon was spread around below the CP. I promptly went to sleep. I didn't realize it at the time, but within the last twenty-four hours I had begun a rapid recovery. The penicillin, the sleep, and a day without the ruck were having an effect. In fact, the whole platoon took advantage of the respite for a couple of hours rest. I suppose a few troopers were awake, but the prospect of a platoon of VCs coming Lima's way wasn't rousing much interest. Sleep was a precious commodity to a grunt, and he took it when and where he could. Rumors of impending enemy appearances weren't enough to prevent the ZZZs.

A little after midday, we got the call to return. Apparently the VC platoon had other business. Still, I was a little uneasy crossing the saddle between the mountain we were on and the mountain before the laager site. The saddle had no vegetation other than the knee-high elephant grass. It was subject to fire from the mountain we were headed for and from the side of the saddle to the east. The side of the saddle was not much lower than the saddle itself. An automatic weapon in the tree line about 75 meters away could have swept the saddle with devastating effect. But we made it across with no problem. The proper ways to have done it were to send the point across, to send elements to each side, or to walk around. Proper ways, however, did not always get followed in the day-to-day mind-numbing grind of humping the boonies.

Back at the laager site, we received welcomed news, of sorts. The following day, A Company was to be extracted by chopper and was to be the guard for a new fire support base for a few days. This was standard procedure, although A Company hadn't caught the duty for some time. The way the 173rd operated during this period, which was a common way of operating, was that a battalion went into an area, established a fire support base consisting of an artillery battery of four or so 105mm howitzers, the battalion's Four-Deuce Mortar Platoon, assorted communication facilities, and the battalion TOC, or tactical operations center. The line companies were generally assigned areas of operation within artillery range of the fire support base. Often one company would be held back to guard the base, manning some of the perimeter defensive positions. Usually, palace guard duty, as it was called, lasted only a few days. It meant a respite from humping the ruck, but also scrutiny from the battalion hierarchy.

The evening passed without incident, and the next morning we were picked up bright and early. Alpha Company led the assault on the site of the fire support base. There were no hostiles. Lima's section of the perimeter was open and rolling. A ravine angled across the right half of the section, joining the perimeter on the platoon's far right. Jerome gave instructions that each position was to have a range card, a standard Ft. Benning defensive position item. A range card, which was hand drawn, showed fields of fire, terrain features, and estimated distances. Accompanying a range card were field-of-fire stakes. The fire of each position, of each individual, in fact, was in theory controlled by stakes to the left and right. If an individual tried to swing his weapon too far to the left, he would hit a stake; similarly if he tried to swing too far to the right.

Of course, I was basically ignorant, and therefore contemptuous, of the details of the range card and stakes business. But in truth, range cards and stakes weren't much in evidence in my parts of Vietnam. My impression was, and is, that they were products of a previous era. Their applicability to a mobile environment with just about every infantry gun an automatic weapon seems questionable. But what do I know? I never received the benefit of Ft. Benning training. Anyway, I put out the order. Shortly after, the company medic came around and told me that the battalion surgeon would be at the fire base later in the day and would look at my finger. It seemed much better to me but was still not pretty.

Before the doctor arrived, however, Jerome decided to inspect the perimeter, giving his platoon leaders some instruction in the process. Since by this time I was getting a bit cocky about my infantry abilities, I approached the session with not the best of attitudes. Jerome walked from position to position, asking about fields of fire, final protective fires, and other defensive esoterica. All went well until we got to the M-60 machine gun position on Lima's right flank. Jerome turned to me and asked where the final protective fire line was, the line on which the gun would be fired if an enemy assault was in its final stages.

I drew a blank. Somewhere deep inside me the concept of final protective fires lingered from a long-ago ROTC class. Automatic weapons such as M-60s were supposed to fire across a unit's front. But the concept was too far buried. I blurted out a straight ahead direction, at a right angle to the platoon's portion of the perimeter, smacked dab into a hillside about a click and a half away. In fact, I envisioned grazing the top of the hill, which would have had the rounds travelling many meters in the air between the position and the hill. Thus the only thing any VCs in the space between the position and the hill would suffer would be loud noise.

Jerome looked at me with a touch of disgust. "Now Lieutenant. You want to fire the M-60 across your front. Do you really think anyone is going to be standing on the top of that hill?"

Well, now that you mention it, no. It did seem unlikely that any attacker would be perched complacently on the hill. The ravine that came in diagonally to the perimeter entered just about at the M-60's position. Firing down the ravine would be firing across the front of the platoon's position and would also negate the attractiveness of a major avenue of approach into the perimeter. So that was where we agreed the main fire of the gun should be.

The ordeal of examining the perimeter ended soon thereafter, much to my relief. And the doctor was on the scene. He was a youngish guy, in hindsight maybe a little too caring. He took my hand, squeezed and manipulated a bit, peered into the meat, and exclaimed, "I'm sending you to the rear."

I should have objected. The finger looked a mess, but it was much improved from a day or so earlier. The throbbing pain that had dominated my existence for more than a week was gone. I knew I was on the way to recovery. But, somewhat guiltily, and without thinking it through, I leapt at the opportunity to get to the rear for a few days. What the hell, who was I to argue with the Doc? Besides, all the company was going to be doing for the period was play palace guard.

So I grabbed my gear and was shortly on a chopper bound for Tuy Hoa. Sgt. Brown didn't appear particularly happy to see me go. The monkey was now back on him. The chopper rose out of the mountains and set a path for the coast to the east. Soon, the rice paddies of the coastal plain were below us, simmering in the tropical heat. About a quarter of a mile from the ocean, the chopper descended to a landing pad close to the 173rd's compound. Invalid Holland hopped out. No one was issuing instructions as to where to go or what to do, so I found my way to A Company's tiny portion of the rear area. This was half a large tent containing about sixteen cots.

The tent was largely deserted. A couple of shirtless troops were lounging around. I asked the way to the aid tent. They warily gave directions, not sure who I was. I didn't have any rank on, just a set of unmarked jungle fatigues with several weeks of dirt. At the aid tent I approached a shirtless black trooper who looked like he had some authority. "Whadda you want?" he growled.

"I'm Lieutenant Holland, A Company. I've got a diseased finger." I grinned and waved my bandaged hand at him.

He didn't seemed amused. "Let's look at it, Sir." A deep tint of insolence surrounded his "Sir." I was beginning to get an uneasy feeling. The trooper looked at the hand. As he was doing so, a doctor came over. He was dressed in pressed jungle fatigues with full insignia—rank, doctor branch, name, jump wings, 173rd patch, what all. He took a quick look, said "soak it for a few days," and was off.

Insolent trooper said "C'mere." I followed him to a rear chair and table. He prepared a solution in a pan and growled, "Put your hand in."

As I did so, he continued: "An enlisted man wouldn't have been able to get out of the field with that. I've been out there, and I've seen troopers with a helluva lot worse have to keep on humping."

To say I was taken back would be putting it mildly. I was caught completely off guard by this direct charge of shirking. I should have locked the insolent bastard's heels, but instead all I could manage was a lame, "The doctor out there told me to leave."

The trooper grunted and grandly tromped off. I felt like an asshole and was pissed at the trooper, and myself. Of course, what he said was largely true. Just a couple of days earlier one of my own men, the trooper with rotting arms, had left the field, but only after the powers that be had kept him there much longer than proper. And I had certainly jumped with considerable alacrity at the chance to visit Tuy Hoa.

But in hindsight, something was going on that was much larger than the insolent black trooper and my own malingering self, and was to develop into a real problem for the Army. The matter of race relations in that second decade of the civil rights revolution was running up against a war in the incipient stages of going sour. Among some black soldiers, a rebellious attitude was developing, an attitude that reached its peak in the early and mid '70s. My run-in with the black medic was to be the first of several race-related incidents I experienced in the 173rd. Fortunately, I was to see only the early stages of the full rebellion.

In any case, I soaked my finger quickly and got the hell out of the aid tent, determined to make my stay in the rear as short as possible. I returned to A Company's tent. A few more troopers were there than when I first arrived. The company XO, Lt. Wayman, was at Bien Hoa, assisting in the 173rd's departure from its home of over two years. An E-6 was the man in charge in Wayman's absence. I told him who I was and tried to ascertain the procedure for temporary life in the rear. There didn't seem to be much in the way of such procedure. The sergeant just said to grab a bunk and implied that I was on my own. I was supposed to go back to the aid station that afternoon for another soaking. So what to do in the meantime? The PX, of course.

At that time, the 173rd's corner of Tuy Hoa was just a temporary dust-bin. The main air base where I had flown in just a few weeks before—it seemed like another eon—was fairly permanent, however, with wooden buildings for the Air Force and other personnel who were assigned there. The base had a sizeable hospital and the ubiquitous PX. A shuttle bus ran periodically about the area. I hopped one and eventually dismounted close to that facility. It had a large selection. Most of the patrons were well-scrubbed Air Force and rear-echelon Army troops. Only a few grubby field grunts like myself were wandering about, wide-eyed from the cultural shock. I shuffled up and down the aisles, not really looking to buy anything but just soaking up the consumerism after the days in the boonies. The desire to observe the trappings of civilization was eventually satiated, and I returned to the 173rd's camp.

After another soaking of the hand, I had a shower and a meal. By then it was dark. Maybe twelve troopers were in A Company's tent. There wasn't much conversation. The presence of an officer probably stifled some talk, but the transient nature of the clientele and the general level of exhaustion among grunts were the main curtailers of normal adolescent exuberance. Someone gave me a couple of beers, my first in awhile, and I put myself to sleep.

The next day started with another soaking of my now obviously healing finger. Then it was another trip to the PX. I picked up a bottle of bourbon. Although we hadn't discussed my bringing back some liquor, I was sure Sgt. Brown wouldn't refuse a little snort. I missed a shuttle back to the 173rd, and rather than wait for the next one, started walking and hitch-hiking. I got a ride to a helicopter unit about halfway back. While walking through the area, I stumbled upon a face from the past, a warrant officer who had been my next door neighbor at Ft. Rucker. He had almost talked me into buying a motorcycle as a way of soothing my growing unhappiness with being the BOQ Billeting Officer. Instead, I had volunteered for the 'Nam. How long ago that was.

He was with a captain. In my grubbiness, bandaged hand, and unmarked uniform, I could tell I was making an unsettling impression. The last time he had seen me, I was a wet-behind-the-ears second lieutenant hotel keep and he was a swaggering chopper instructor motorcycle jockey. Now I was a grubby airborne line doggie, with a bandaged hand to boot. He and the captain were on the way to some commitment, but he invited me to his quarters that evening for a beer and to catch up on our lives. To his evident chagrin, I accepted. I got the impression that he found my reappearance in his life somewhat troubling.

So that evening I showed up at his doorstep. I quickly came to a conclusion as to why my presence was unsettling. Despite being a pilot, he had latched onto a rear area desk job and was quite content. The swaggering, daring motorcyclist of Ft. Rucker days was nowhere in evidence. I sat on the door stoop of his room drinking beer and fiddling with my bandaged finger. He sat at his desk, making a model airplane. It was as if he hadn't left Alabama. The conversation was rather stilted. I tried to talk about the boonies, about my time in Saigon, about Vietnam in general. His contributions, such as they were, were mostly inane. He seemed disconnected from Vietnam, existing in a comfortable, air-conditioned cocoon.

After a few beers, we said our farewells. I trudged the mile or so back to the 173rd's area. I felt both irritated and superior: irritated because he hadn't acknowledged the substantial move I had made from Ft. Rucker BOQ Billeting

Officer to airborne infantry platoon leader in a combat zone; superior because the macho rider of mean-ass motorcycles seemed a little too happy with piloting a desk.

Second Blood

I woke the next morning anxious to get back to the field. I felt dangerously close to being a bona fide malingerer. After a perfunctory soaking of my obviously improving finger, I headed for the chopper pad to catch a ride. A Company was due for a resupply that day. Contrary to the usual practice, it had spent only one night as palace guard for the fire support base, and was back in an AO, the acronym for area of operations. In fact, I learned that the afternoon before Mike had been in a fire fight. I was missing the damn action!

No one had checked me in when I had left the field, so I figured there was no one with whom to discuss my departure from the rear. The informality of it struck me as a bit odd, but undoubtedly folks unknown to me were keeping track to prevent a mass congregation to the rear. In any event, I shortly caught a chopper to the battalion fire support base. I was to wait there for several hours until the A Company resupply chopper made its run. While waiting at the fire support base, I encountered my ol' buddy from my first days in the battalion: Ditmar Jack. He was a platoon leader in B company, which had assumed the fire support base guard assignment from A Company. I was lying in the grass beside the LZ when he strode up: "I heard you had some contact."

"Yeah, we got a few."

"What was it like?"

Now how do you respond to that? Hadn't he been in the field long enough to know something about "what was it like?" Besides, nobody shot back to speak of. I wanted to ask him if he actually had gone through with his plan to have his men call him by his first name, "Jack," but thought better of it. Instead, I gave a noncommittal response: "It wasn't that big a fire fight."

"Yeah, but what was it like to kill someone?"

So that was it. Ditmar Jack still hadn't experienced the grim reaper first hand. He was wondering what he would do around his first dead body. Give me a break, I thought to myself. Some stuff you just don't talk about. Besides, I had seen bodies, blood, and gore in Saigon. The handiwork of our ambush had not been that shocking.

"Well, the dead are dead. I seen enough of 'em in Saigon."

The way I grunted must have convinced Ditmar Jack that further conversation would be unrewarding, so he departed.

Not long after, the A Company resupply chopper appeared. I clamored aboard and was soon descending to the company's laager side. It was on the long, gradual slope of the hill we had moved to the night after the ambush. In fact, it was just off the trail we had followed from the ambush site. After traversing a little less than ten clicks of wooded, rolling terrain from the ambush site, the trail broke out onto the slope of the hill, which stretched another click or so to the hill's summit. The vegetation on the slope was in clumps—patches of high bushes and small trees ten to fifty meters on a side. The open areas had only short, ankle-high grass. The current company laager site was mostly in the bushes, near the point where the trail left the woods.

The chopper was on the ground only a moment. I and the resupply—mail and food—were quickly off. Jerome was close by and briefed me on the situation. The company had been inserted into the area the previous morning and had undertaken several platoon-size patrols. Mike's patrol was in the vicinity where we were presently located. The other two platoons had been on the far side of the hill.

Mike had sent a squad down the slope to the point where the trail entered the woods and rugged terrain. The squad had set up an ambush on the trail, just a simple thing with an M-60 and a claymore aimed down the trail, which at that point climbed steeply out of a gully. Several Victor Charlies had entered the ambush kill zone. They had apparently suspected the presence of trouble because they had been crawling up the trail. The claymore hadn't been properly set. It was behind a small mound in the trail and aimed out horizontally into space rather than down the trail. When the first Victor Charlie stuck his head over the mound, the triggerman set the claymore off. The VC's last mortal view was a claymore a foot from his face. Decapitated was too neat a word for what befell him. His head literally disintegrated.

This made for a nice gruesome story for any Mikes who survived the war to tell their grandchildren, but it didn't make for a successful ambush. Only the first VC died. The ones behind him quickly disappeared into the bushes that hemmed in the trail. Soon the ambush squad was receiving a goodly amount of fire. It began pulling back up the slope. Near the top of the hill, Mike saw the retreating squad, and even caught sight of the advancing VC. He headed down the hill with the remainder of the platoon. From the other side of the hill, Lima, November, and the company headquarters soon followed.

The Victor Charlies were driven back with neither side suffering casualties, and the company laagered for the night. We were now in the next day, and the company was still located in the spot. Two platoons had patrolled earlier in the day but had come up empty-handed. After the fill-in by Jerome, I found Sgt. Brown. He appreciated the booze. Lima seemed to have functioned adequately without me. The platoon had not been much involved in the previous day's fight.

Just before dark, the platoon leaders assembled for the evening briefing. A light rain was falling, so we squeezed under Corky Blake's hooch, which he had set up in lean-to fashion. Blake was the artillery forward observer. I sat on his air mattress and promptly put a hole in it with my trusty sheath knife, the tip of which had cut through the bottom of the sheath. A line doggie's air mattress was his only piece of luxury, the one bit of comfort in an otherwise austere world. Consequently, I felt damn bad. Corky took it well, however. I offered him my air mattress but didn't insist when he initially refused. I sure as hell didn't want to sleep on the hard ground. A new mattress would come in on the next resupply. Until then, I would stay out of Corky's way as much as possible.

That the air mattress incident has stuck with me over the years is an indication of just how primitive life was in the boonies. We lived in dirt and grime, and the pleasures were simple. If someone had popped my mattress, I would have been despondent. Corky was a better man than I was.

Lima's mission for the night was to spread around the whole company perimeter. Mike and November were to depart for platoon-size ambush sites. Occupying the whole perimeter meant in essence seven or eight unoccupied positions. We could only man every third or fourth hole. Since most of the laager site was in deep bushes, no line of sight contact was possible with the next manned position. This arrangement was fairly common but always seemed to me to be tempting fate. A sizeable enemy attack would have easily overrun the spread-out defense.

But sizeable enemy attacks weren't frequent. As I have stated before, actual combat in Vietnam wasn't the norm. Weeks, often months, could pass without an infantry company doing anything more than stomping through the weeds. Violations of security principles could go unpunished for long periods. Bad habits did not necessarily have negative consequences. It was easy to be lax, to do stupid things. So the night passed uneventfully. I made an early evening check of positions but sure as hell wasn't going to do any moving after dark.

The company's mission the next day was more of the same: day-time patrolling and night ambushes. Lima was to check out the area between the company's laager site and the hilltop and select an ambush position for the evening. We wandered over the terrain for several hours. It was crossed by a number of well-used trails. Taking my cue from the trail junction ambush site that Sgt. Hikaey had selected several weeks earlier and that had been so productive—measuring productivity in terms of dead bodies—I settled on a trail junction. We returned to the company laager site in late afternoon. After a meal of Cs, we made it back to the ambush position just before dusk. The ambush was maybe a click from the laager site.

My plan was simply to set up in a platoon perimeter around the trail junction, with machine guns aimed down two of the three joining trails and M-16s aimed down the third. Since the third trail was in the direction of the company laager site, I expected it would be the least likely approach for Mr. Charles.

The problem with my plan was the vegetation. Many of the clumps of bushes that were the principal growth on the slope were well-nigh impenetrable. A number of clumps of various sizes were in the vicinity of the trail junction, several of them right at the junction itself. Consequently, an even perimeter was impossible.

I ended up with a squad and an M-60 on one side of the main trail, and with the second squad, the second M-60, and the platoon headquarters on the other side. The two fire teams in this second squad were oriented in almost completely opposite directions. An extremely thick clump of bushes was squarely in the middle of the platoon's position, making movement and coordination within the perimeter difficult. In fact, one of the fire teams in the second squad was a few meters ahead of the M-60 on the other side of the trail. Fortunately, the fire team was not directly in front of the gun but off to the side.

The grass between the clumps of bushes was short, no more than ankle high. Since we weren't dug in, the fire teams and the platoon headquarters in the open were really in the open. It was like lying on an athletic field. The M-60s and the first squad had more cover and concealment. Indeed, Lopez's M-60 on the far side of the trail was behind a small mound.

Shortly after we set up, I walked around the clump in the middle of the platoon's position and up the few meters to Lopez's gun. Sgt. Hikaey and Lopez were squatting down, peering over the mound. I was blithely standing in the middle of the trail. "Everything under control?", I asked with a grin.

"Get down, Sir! Something's out there!", one of them whispered.

I quickly moved off the trail and squatted with them, "What is it?"

"Don't know. Just saw movement up the trail."

It was still light enough to see across the adjacent open space to the next clumps of vegetation. I looked for a few seconds but saw nothing. I said: "Be sure you got something before firing. We're a little bit in front of you beyond those bushes. Don't fire us up. I'm goin' back to warn 'em."

I hunched over and moved back down the trail and around the clump, warning the other M-60 as I went by. Once on the far side, I crawled up to the forward fire team. "First squad's got movement up the trail. Keep a look-out." As I said it, I became even more aware of how out front the fire team was. I wasn't sure where the M-60 team had put the claymore, but there was a chance the fire team would catch some shrapnel if it were detonated. I started crawling back to go around the clump again to ask about the claymore. Just as I got to the platoon headquarters group, which was only a few meters behind the fire team, the claymore exploded, the M-60 commenced a prolong burst, my heart rate instantly accelerated, and my adrenalin pump immediately began hitting on all cylinders.

When the M-60 stopped, I hoarsely whispered up to the fire team, "Everybody okay!?"

Before anyone answered, several loud moans came from beyond the fire team's position followed by, holy shit!, incoming automatic weapons fire. The distinctive crackle and pop of incoming bullets is a sound that tends to stay with one a long, long time. The M-60 answered with a burst, and there were several grenade explosions. And here came the inevitable call for information: "Sir, Six wants to know what's happening," Baum whispered from a couple of meters away.

Well, at this point I sure as hell didn't know. Incoming and outgoing fire were continuing. Fortunately, I had given Sgt. Brown's radio to Sgt. Hikaey, so in theory I had communication with the other side of the clump of bushes. Unfortunately, Sgt. Hikaey wasn't the most communicative of individuals. "Lima One, this is Lima. What's happening?"

After a bit a response came: "Lima, this is Lima One. They walked into the ambush."

Well, I had that part. "Anybody hurt?"

"Negative, Lima."

"Remember, we're ahead of you on your right." I was still damned afraid of shooting each other up.

"Roger."

"Six, this is Lima."

"This is Six."

"This is Lima. We got some in our ambush. No casualties on our part, I think. We're taking incoming fire and hear moaning from the ambush site."

"Roger, Lima. We'll be adjusting some artillery. Let me know where it lands."

80   Vietnam, A Memoir

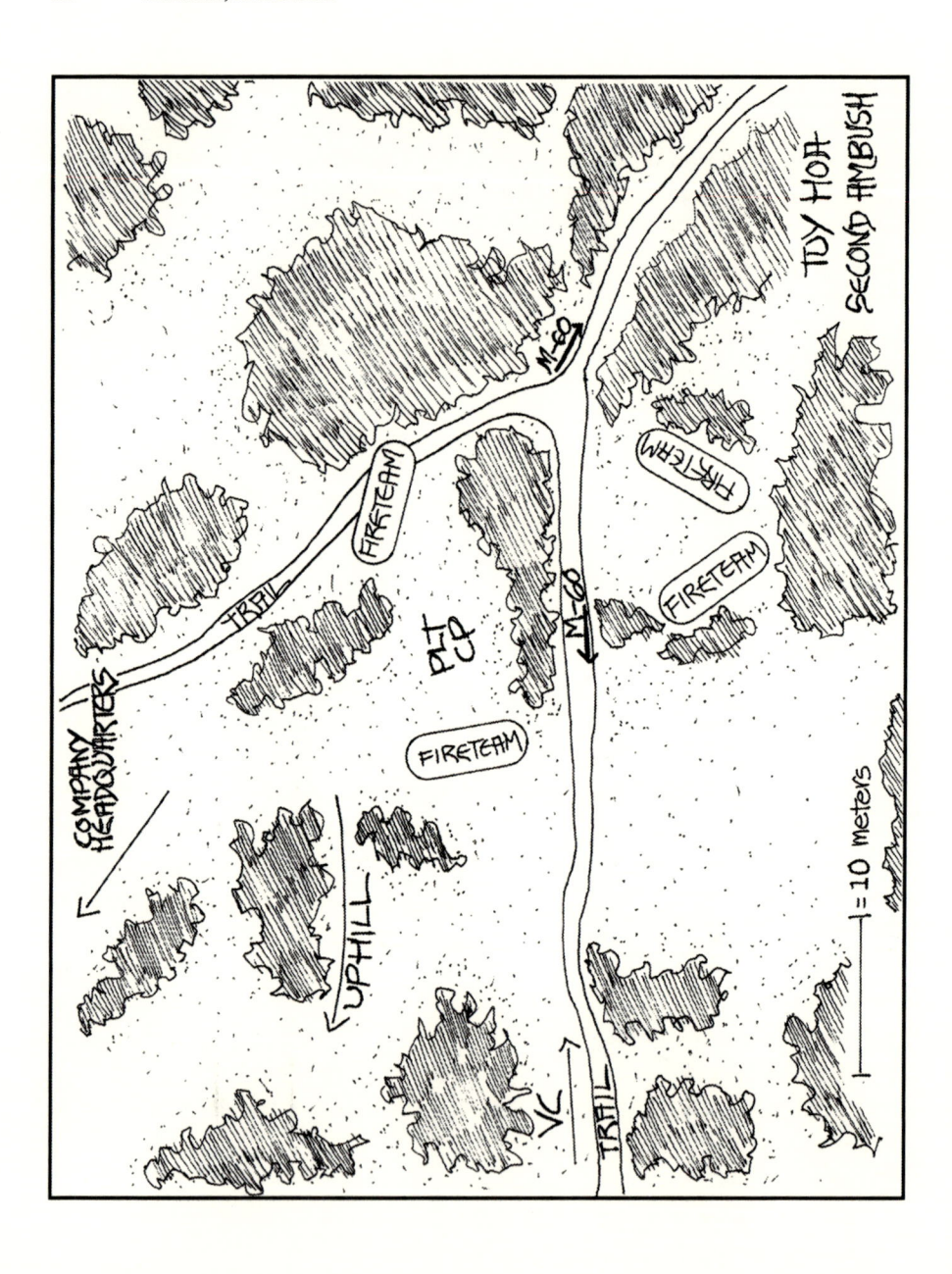

Great. Now I had to worry about shelling myself. As I was having this conversation with Jerome, I could hear close by the company's four-deuce forward observer, Sgt. Cooper, who was with Lima for the ambush, calling for fire from the battalion's four-deuce mortars. It would be only a moment before beaucoup steel would be raining down in our vicinity—I hoped like hell not too much in our vicinity. As I waited, I loudly whispered up to the exposed fire team: "Hey, everybody okay up there?"

"We're fine so far."

"Brace yourselves. Artillery's on the way."

Shortly after, the first rounds landed about a click away, on the other side of the Victor Charlies.

"Lima, this is Six. How was that?"

"Not too bad."

"Can we bring it closer?"

"Yeah, a bit. But not too much."

So over the next fifteen or twenty minutes, Blake walked the artillery gradually closer. Sgt. Cooper was doing the same with the four-deuces. Flares were also fired, but they didn't help much with visibility on the ground, just giving the sky an eerie, surreal glow. I was answering Jerome's inquiries about the impact of Brooks' artillery, but in fact I was relying on Sgt. Cooper. I really had no idea how close the stuff was getting. I just knew that the ground was shuddering from the impacts, and that the very air seemed to be in motion.

All the while the artillery was being moved in, an intermittent fire fight was taking place. Every few minutes a prolonged burst of outgoing M-60 or M-16 or incoming AK-47 or RPD fire would rend the night. On our side, the main firing was coming from Lopez's M-60 and from the M-16s of the fire team to my front. The M-79 grenade launcher in the fire team also popped away every now and then. In addition, the members of the fire team were occasionally flinging hand grenades. And the moans from the direction of the VC were continuing.

Finally, Sgt. Cooper and I decided that the artillery and the four-deuces were close enough. "Six, this is Lima. That last burst caused a high pucker factor. Don't bring it any closer."

"Roger, Lima. Are you still taking fire?"

"That's affirmative. But not heavy."

"Okay. We'll fire one more cluster and then just register it."

Lying on the open ground in the short grass, I was feeling damn exposed. A hole seemed like a nice idea. I whispered up to the fire team: "Hey, we've got a long night here. And we may get a charge at some point. You guys ought to scoop some holes if you can."

I turned my head in the general direction of the other members of the headquarters group—Sgt. Brown, Washington, Baum, Doc, Sgt. Cooper, and his RTO—and said: "You guys ought to dig in too."

We in the headquarters group were all within a rough six- or seven-meter circle, flat in the open. Despite the enemy fire, however, not everyone was enthralled with the idea of digging in. When you dig a hole every night, you develop a distaste for the chore that not even the face of death can overcome. If choice in the matter existed, some troopers were just not going to dig. I was not one of those, nor was Sgt. Cooper. From almost a horizontal posture, he and I began scrapping a common depression. We used an entrenching tool, taking turns pulling on the hard soil. Eventually we had a slit trench about four or five inches deep and wide enough for both of us to squeeze in.

Meanwhile, the bursts of both incoming and outgoing fire gradually became less frequent. At one point, a grenade exploded close to the exposed fire team. I whispered, "Anybody hurt?"

After a pause, there was an answer: "Shipley's hit a little. He's coming back."

A moment later, Spec. 4 Shipley, a rifleman, came crawling back. He seemed in good spirits. "Just got a small pain in my back," he exclaimed with almost a note of glee in his voice.

Sgt. Cooper and I crawled out of our depression. Shipley crawled in, and Doc came over. We draped a poncho over Doc and Shipley's back, and Doc took a look at the wound. Presently a muffled voice came from under the poncho: "Nothing serious. A cut and some blood. I don't see any metal in the wound."

Doc put a bandage on the wound, and Shipley crawled back to the fire team. He was obviously happy as all get-out that he would be sporting a Purple Heart, and at such a cheap price. I called Jerome: "Six, this is Lima."

"This is Six."

"This is Lima. We had one man hit. Just a minor wound in his lower back. He's now back on the line."

"That sounds good. It's hard to get a feel for your situation out there, but do you want to return to the laager site?"

Moving at night did not appeal to me. Moreover, we were in a sporadic firefight. I could envision losing half the goddamn platoon trying to get back to the company. I was content to stay put, keeping in close contact with the comforting ground. I told Six: "No. I think we're better stayin' put. We could get our butts shot up tryin' to get outta here."

I was to find out the next morning that more was behind this conversation than simple tactics. Indeed, I was to conclude it was one of Jerome's finest moments. But the full story was some hours away. Lima had a long night to get through. The unknown was whether the sporadic fire from the VC was merely an effort to extract themselves and their wounded, or was the prelude to an assault. My decision to stay put made the platoon a fixed target, but in view of the alternative, I was willing to take the risk. The thought of an unrehearsed night move back to the company scared me a lot more than did the thought of a VC human wave.

Sgt. Cooper and I settled into our depression. He was holding intermittent conversations with the fire control section at battalion's Four-Deuce Platoon. I was talking intermittently on the radio to Six and to Sgt. Hikaey, and by whispering was keeping in touch with the forward fire team and various members of the headquarters group. In between these conversations, Sgt. Cooper and I, mostly Sgt. Cooper, talked a little on the personal side.

"Damn, Sir. This ain't like Ft. Bragg. Them training aids is real."

It was a version of a common Vietnam saying. Training aids referred to any piece of equipment that was used stateside to make training more realistic: pop-up silhouette targets, for example. In Vietnam, the training aids shot back.

"Yeah," I replied, preoccupied with the immediately surrounding 25 meters and unable to comprehend Ft. Bragg 12,000 miles away. Sgt. Cooper continued with occasional witticisms as the hours went by. He also discussed his family—a young wife and two small children—not in fear or morbidly but with pride and affection. It was a conversation that two guys at the local auto body shop, or two guys in the accounting department, could be having. Only we were lying in a shallow depression deep in the coastal mountains of Tuy Hoa Province, Republic of Vietnam, with automatic weapons fire tearing the air a few feet over our heads, grenades occasionally thudding within shrapnel range, and flares creating eerie shadows.

About halfway through the night, I again made the journey to Sgt. Hikaey and Lopez's machine gun. This required backing up seven or eight meters, going around the clump of bushes, and crawling up the trail seven or eight meters. In proceeding around the clump, I passed by the other M-60 machine gun position. Although only a few short meters from Lopez's gun, PFC Henderson, the Indiana farm boy, hadn't the foggiest notion of what was going on. This was partly due to his squad leader, and ultimately me, not keeping him informed and partly due to his own lethargy. I briefed him, his assistant gunner, and the nearby fire team on what was transpiring and warned them to be on the lookout in case the Victor Charlies attempted to work their way around us.

Sgt. Hikaey and Spec. 4 Lopez were focused on the trail. I reiterated the concern about the forward fire team on the other side of the bush. The two, especially Lopez, seemed to have the situation under control, so I didn't stay long.

The night passed with excruciating slowness, a kaleidoscope of flashes, and a cacophony of sound: occasional bursts of incoming and outgoing automatic weapons fire, some of it tracer rounds, with the incoming fire becoming less frequent as dawn approached; flares from the artillery and the four-deuces; periodic H and I rounds from the same guns, impacting mainly in the area where we had stopped walking the steel toward our position; sitreps on the radio; snatches of other worldly conversation with my hole-in-the-ground companion, Sgt. Cooper; moans, gradually fainter, from the direction of the VCs; and one or two bursts from Henderson's position as he tried to get in on the action. I felt certain that the VC hadn't gotten behind us and that Henderson was just shooting at shadows. I whispered a message back for him to be sure he had a target.

I felt no need to stay awake the whole night. Enough of the platoon was going to be wide awake to prevent us from being overrun in a collective sleep. And I never was one for all-nighters, either in college or as an MP on the graveyard shift in Saigon. So I managed a few periods of sleep, probably no more than forty-five minutes total.

As morning approached, I decided that the forward fire team should be moved back. With the fading of darkness, the five or six troopers would have zero concealment. So when the blackness began to ease into the pre-dawn grey, I ordered them back. They obeyed, and more so. I intended that they would stop abreast of our position, but they kept going to the trail and the bushes a few meters behind the headquarters group. Suddenly, Sgt. Cooper and I were the point! Muttering under my breath about how difficult it was at times to get across what I wanted, I had the headquarters group crawl back also. I went around to Sgt. Hikaey's position to see what daylight would reveal.

Dawn does not break instantaneously in the tropics, but it doesn't amble in, either. Very soon, the light was sufficient to see up the trail, and to discern the gruesome effectiveness of Lima's efforts. From my position by Lopez's M-60, I could make out four or five bodies, with the first one being not much more than fifteen meters up the trail. Sgt. Hikaey hissed at me to get down, but I was too anxious to get the score. Besides, I felt pretty certain the live Victor Charlies had di-di-maued before daylight.

Sgt. Hikaey sent a fire team out well to the left of the trail. The team was to sweep over the ambush site from the flank, where a number of clumps of bushes provided an avenue of approach with a fair amount of concealment. Soon the troopers appeared up the trail in the ambush location, and the rest of the platoon moved to join them and see our handiwork.

There weren't nothing pretty about it. The first VC had caught the full force of the claymore. One of his legs was blown off near the hip and lay at an odd angle to the body. A bit of intestines protruded from a hole the size of a half dollar in his stomach. Holes from the claymore pellets and M-60 and M-16 rounds studded his body, although I was surprised the holes weren't oozing much blood. The ground underneath him was blood-soaked, however. He must have drained from holes on the back side of his body.

Lima's immediately apparent score was five dead VC. The first was the most mangled, but all of them had multiple wounds. And all had the pasty grey color of hours-old death. Blood trails indicating more casualties led in various directions. Unlike the victims of Lima's previous ambush, these VCs had been armed. We policed up seven or so weapons, mostly AK-47s but also two RPG rocket launchers. As we were completing our inventory, a chopper buzzed the ambush site. It was the battalion commander wanting a first-hand glimpse of the gore.

Jerome sounded more than happy with my report on the number of dead and the number of weapons. He instructed us to return to the laager site with the weapons. While we were enroute, he called again: "Lima, this is Six."

"This is Lima."

"This is Six. If you're asked when you get here, say that you found the bodies in the bushes this morning."

"Say again, over?" I asked, not understanding the request.

"If you're asked by Big Six, say that you searched last night but didn't find anything. You found the VCs in the bushes after daylight. I'll explain later."

I didn't know what was going on, but I did know that the battalion commander was not likely to buy this. He had, after all, flown over us as we were admiring the bodies on the trail. But this didn't seem to be the time to argue. "This is Lima, roger."

"Six, out."

We arrived at the company laager a little after the battalion CO. I braced myself for whatever was up, but fortunately he did not acknowledge my existence. He and Jerome went directly to the troopers who were carrying the weapons. After some ooing and ahhing, the battalion CO had the weapons placed in his chopper and was off, spit-shined boots gleaming and pressed fatigues looking sharp. Jerome approached me.

"He wanted the ambush site searched last night. He was insistent as hell about it. Finally, I told him you searched but didn't find anything. That's why I wanted you prepared with a story."

"Jesus fuckin' Christ. Didn't that sonuvabitch know we were getting shot at, in a fuckin' fire fight?"

A successful ambush, and the damn battalion CO was playing Ft. Benning. He wanted to follow the book that said you trigger the ambush and then immediately sweep over the site. Only the fucking book didn't have ambushes shooting back.

"It didn't matter to him," Jerome said. "He wanted it done by the book. But don't worry about it. He was happy as a clam with the outcome. A good body count."

In the front of my mind was astonishment and incredulity at the denseness of the battalion CO. But in the back of my mind was also the realization that Jerome had put himself on the line. He could easily have succumbed to the battalion CO's demand and ordered us to make a nighttime sweep in the face of enemy fire. Maybe it would have been successful and maybe we would have gotten our clocks cleaned. Jerome hadn't outright refused to relay the order. But he told a lie, didn't relay the order, and consequently didn't present the platoon, and me, with an absurd mission.

Just as I was beginning to feel good about Jerome, however, he put me in a funk. I assumed that since the whole damn platoon had gotten practically no sleep, we would not have much to do for the day. Maybe we would guard the laager site while the other platoons patrolled.

Sorry 'bout that.

The orders for the day were for the company minus Oscar, a fire team from each rifle platoon, and a few headquarters flunkies to patrol in the direction of Lima's first successful ambush a bunch of days previously. The battalion's Recon Platoon was to land shortly and was to patrol in the vicinity of Lima's ambush of the night before. Despite its adventuresome sounding name, the Recon Platoon's usual mission was to be part of the fire support base palace guard. Most of the platoon welcomed any opportunity to escape this deadening duty. Thus they arrived primed for action.

Lima was primed for sleep, but we trudged off, fortunately at the rear of the company column. The line of march was parallel to the sizeable trail that passed through the first ambush site to near our current laager site. The trail was the one on which Mike had conducted its ambush several day previously. The journey through the bushes wasn't easy, but at least we didn't have rucks.

I did not have the foggiest notion as to what the mission was—probably another one of those wild goose chase intelligence reports. The battalion's Recon Platoon seemed to have a more meaningful mission: to work outward from Lima's ambush site, following any interesting blood trails or the like. In fact, after we had been out for a few hours, the Recon Platoon leader reported over the company net another body and an AK-47. Jerome called over the radio to me: "Did you hear that Lima? You got another one."

"This is Lima, roger." I was too tired to care, but I relayed the news to the platoon. The long hot day dragged on. We eventually reached the destination, a patch of jungle close to Lima's first ambush site. It was like all the other patches of jungle and had zero signs of habitation. So we started back.

By this time, it was past 1500. Jerome chose to return on the trail, and the company took off, lickety-split. All the care exercised on the trip out was long gone. The evening meal and a soft air mattress beckoned. None of the company had gotten much sleep the previous night, so the thought of finally getting some rest was all-consuming. I was at the head of Lima, which was still bringing up the rear. It was an effort to keep up with the rear trooper of Mike, the platoon ahead of us.

Suddenly from the head of the column came a sustained burst of automatic weapons fire. It sounded like outgoing but I couldn't be sure. The radio crackled with hard-to-understand yelling. I paused a moment to try to decipher what was being said, and when I turned forward again no one was in sight. I looked back at the troopers behind me. They were no longer showing exhaustion. The blood lust was up. They wanted to get into the fight and were crowding forward.

I wasn't so sure. I had read too many accounts of gung-ho soldiers being lured into an ambush. The fact that we were diddle-bopping along a trail was a particular cause for concern. A late afternoon thrashing of a tired and careless U.S. or South Vietnamese unit rushing along a trail toward home happened all too frequently. I had a great fear of charging into the kill zone of a massive VC ambush. I dallied for a moment, then said:

"Okay, let's spread out. We're too close together. We're goin' forward slowly. And watch the goddamn bushes. We could be movin' into some deep shit."

So we began moving cautiously forward. I peered intently into the thick foliage on either side of the trail, braced for the sudden burst of automatic weapons fire that would signal our doom. Occasional shots still sounded from up ahead. The trail dipped and bent, zigged and zagged, rarely allowing a view to the front of more than ten meters.

88   Vietnam, A Memoir

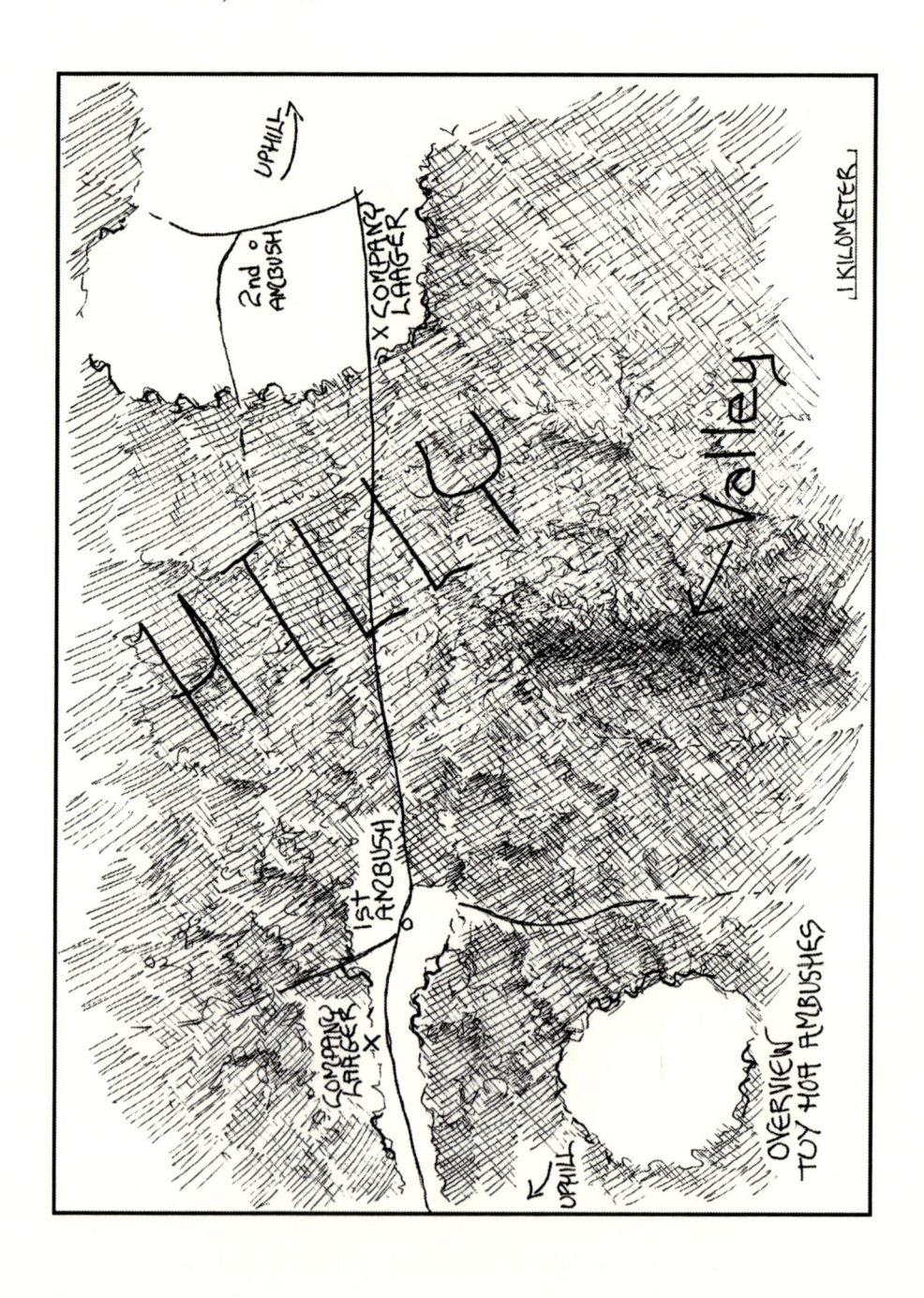

It was at least a hundred meters—a hundred lump-in-your-throat meters—before we caught up with the tail of the column. The other two platoons and the headquarters group had rushed forward with great abandon. If a VC ambush had been in place, it would have been immensely successful. The shooting, however, was only at a couple of stragglers in the vicinity of Mike's ambush of several days previously. Our side had no casualties, and the bad guys had none that we knew of.

The incident was a small one, but it was an example of the dangerous enthusiasm of the paratroopers. And not only paratroopers were guilty of such exuberance. Many "leg" units, particularly in the early years of the war, were also anxious to meet the enemy and were similarly prone to rushing unthinkingly into uncertain situations.

Lima caught up with the column just as the action, what there was of it, appeared to be over. The disappointed company resumed its move along the trail to the end of the heavy underbrush, the start of the open area on the hill's slope, and the laager site. We passed the body that Mike had created, the headless guy whose last conscious sight was a claymore a foot from his face. The laager site was reached shortly thereafter, and the company quickly spread out over the positions.

Jerome shortly called a briefing. The whole company, with the exception of an outpost per platoon, would be in the laager site this night. Given the general condition, we would be sleeping the sleep of the exhausted. The outposts would be cutting ZZZs also. Ideally, one person per position and outpost would be awake, but after thirty-six hours of close to no sleep for the majority, all bets were off. The Recon Platoon was to set up an ambush a short distance up the trail from Lima's slaughter of the previous night. The Recon Platoon leader, a gung-ho West Pointer with a ranger tab and impeccable web gear, immaculately arranged, stated his theory of ambushes: all troopers would be awake all night.

I did the mental equivalent of rolling my eyes. All troopers awake all night was the Ft. Benning solution. It didn't comport with the reality of living permanently in the bush, of having to do a full day's work the next day, the next, and the next after that. But this was recon. Its normal next day was guarding the battalion fire support base, usually in a deep sleep.

Then Jerome produced his real news. The company was going back to Tuy Hoa the next morning for a two-day stand-down. Although brief, the rest would be the company's first in months, since long before I had arrived. I was ambivalent about it myself, having just returned from my two-day medical R&R. The troopers seem pleased with the news, but not really ecstatic. Their exhaustion was undoubtedly a factor in their lack of overt enthusiasm.

A Small Break, Leeches, And Snakes

Thus bright and early the next morning, after a deep and thorough sleep, we were on our way toward the coast. The greens of the jungle-covered mountains gave way abruptly to the rice fields of the coastal plain. Beyond lay the 173rd's compound, a wide beach, and the azure blue South China Sea.

The stand-down was an organized affair, not the drunken debauchery that is often depicted in the movies. A drunken debauchery, for me at least, was in the not-too-distant future, but this brief pause in the war was sedate. No barracks or even webtocs—large tents draped over wooden frames—were available. We simply constructed our poncho hooches in a line in a sandy field. The two days were spent in showering, a trip to the PX, and in the afternoon of the second day, a steak and beer barbecue on the beach.

A leadership change was made during the two days. Lt. Monroe, the Weapons Platoon leader, was moved to the battalion staff. As I have noted, company-grade officers rarely spent a full year on the line, a state of affairs welcomed by some, disliked by others, and universally and rightfully resented by the EMs. Monroe was now the S-3 Air—an assistant to the battalion S-3—and Oscar was in the hands of an E-7 platoon sergeant.

The steak and beer barbecue was a tame affair. The troopers splashed in the surf and sat on the beach, some in shorts, some in jungle fatigue pants. Jerome made the rounds. After months in the humid, hot, claustrophobic jungle, the company luxuriated in the wide expanse of warm dry beach and the softness of the ocean breezes.

But the respite was soon over. As evening fell, we were transported back to our little line of pathetic hooches. For some of the troopers, it was their last ever visit to an ocean beach.

A chopper assault returned A Company to the field. We were up with the sun. Rucks were packed. Soon the distinctive whump-whump of the Hueys could be heard. They landed, we loaded up, and off we went, winging back to the mountains.

Preparation on the LZ was heavy. The Air Force hit it with napalm and 750-pounders. The gun ships shot the hell out of it. Artillery added to the smoke and destruction. And as we came in, the door gunners unloaded with a vengeance. All the activity had my adrenalin pumping. The LZ was a small field of waist high elephant grass. Lima was to be the lead platoon for the day, so we were in the lead lift. The choppers barely touched down before they were zooming out. In fact, they zoomed out so fast that one trooper, PFC Montdragon, didn't have time to get off. Jerome was to use the incident to give me his idea of a leadership lesson.

As soon as we unloaded, we made for the tree line about 30 to 40 meters away. After two days in the dry pleasant breezy heat of the coastal area, we were smacked by the stifling hot humidity of the jungle-covered mountains. Even before the second lift arrived, about three minutes later, we were back to being dripping miserable line doggies.

The general mission for the day was to hump through the jungle away from the LZ, searching the base of an alleged mountain. We would then return to the vicinity of the LZ to laager. Even though we would be returning to the starting point, we would carry our rucks. Don't want Charlie to get those things.

Lima was in the lead. The terrain was pretty much featureless. The alleged mountain was off to our left but couldn't be seen due to the thick vegetation. I was attempting to follow an azimuth, sending the point out 100 meters or so, having them cloverleaf, and then moving up with the main body. Only I couldn't keep Jerome happy. He kept seeing terrain features on the map—small hills and valleys, trails, and the like—that I sure as hell wasn't coming across on the ground. Also, he kept giving me compass corrections, contending that I was drifting to one side or the other. Because the company had been operating mainly in platoon-size increments for several weeks, it had been some time since Lima had been the point platoon in a company move, and we weren't doing very well.

Eventually we made the turn to get back to the LZ. I was still looking for the alleged mountain when suddenly we were climbing a steep hillside. The going was rough. Lima was fully on the jungle-covered slope when Jerome came to it. He went ballistic: "Lima, this is Six. You're on the hill!"

"This is Lima, roger." I suppose I knew it, but the fact hadn't risen to the level of a conscious thought. I was intent on plowing upwards.

"Well, Lima, how about turning? You're not supposed to be climbing the goddamn thing."

Jerome rarely cursed on the radio, so I knew he was pissed. "This is Lima, roger."

So I turned the point, and then the platoon. The company followed. We struggled sideways along the steep slope, grasping at trees and bushes to keep our balance, wait-a-minute vines catching our rucksacks. It was a while before we found our way back to flat land. The hillside traverse at the end of a long day pretty much sapped everyone's strength. Fortunately, we made quick time getting back to the LZ and the comfort of a laager site. The air mattress was especially welcomed that night.

Before dusk, a chopper brought in one of the brigade's chaplains. I never much cared for chaplains, or for military religion in general. The saying is that there are no atheists in foxholes. Well, I didn't, and don't, buy that. The carnage of war, the blood, gore, and suffering, the inhumanity, these things seem to me to be reasons to question the existence of a benevolent god. If the supreme being is such a cool guy, gal, or it, why does he, she, or it allow the horror? And why does he, she, or it permit the existence of war lovers like myself, people who enjoy, revel in, the horror? If I have to classify my religious beliefs, I would call myself some sort of deist. Thomas Jefferson and others among the Founding Fathers were reportedly also of this persuasion, so I guess I'm not keeping inappropriate company. Anyway, the bottom line was that I never felt comfortable around military chaplains. Jerome spoiled my evening by announcing that the chaplin, a major, would accompany Lima the next day. Great. The mission for the morrow was for the company to move from the LZ in the direction opposite to our route of this day. The move was to be with platoons abreast. The vegetation seemed more open, patches of jungle broken by clearings and fields.

It rained during the night, not hard just steady and soaking. The next day was drizzly. The company started off with Lima as the middle platoon. November was on the left followed by Jerome and the headquarters group. Mike was on the right. The platoons were out of sight of each other, a half click to a click apart. Lima moved in a column, my standard formation. Nothing fancy for this child. I was behind the lead squad and the chaplain was to the rear of the platoon headquarters. He was innocuous enough, just a nice middle-aged guy, but I did my best to ignore him. His presence was definitely an irritation.

The day's effort was without hostile encounters. Lima's area was flat and relatively open, with numerous clumps of bushes. November and the company headquarters were having a much more difficult go of it. The vegetation in their area was apparently thick, and the footing was swampy. Jerome and Lt. Kline bickered constantly over the radio. At least I wasn't the only one Jerome could find fault with. Kline gave as good as he got, however. He seemed to enjoy the verbal sparring. Jerome tried to keep the three platoons in line by having us radio a sitrep every 200 meters. Terrain features were few, so locations were guess work, and I was still a lousy guesser. At one point, Jerome even had November fire a shot so that Mike and I could orient ourselves. It didn't help much.

Lima eventually reached a large open area. The expanse covered a small valley and the high ground on each side. The valley was about 100 meters across, and the hillocks on each side were about 15 meters above the valley floor. The whole area was covered with knee-high grass. We stopped there to keep from getting ahead of November. Jerome finally decided he had enough of the swamp and settled upon Lima's location for a laager. Consequently, Mike and November turned toward us, closing on the valley and hillocks in the middle of the afternoon. The position was far from ideal. The company was spread out over the valley and the small hills, with lots of space between positions. And to conform to the terrain, the perimeter was considerably more jagged than round. It rained a bit in the afternoon, so walking around in the high grass soaked one's legs, making for a damp night on the air mattress.

Next day's mission was more of the same. At least the chaplain wouldn't be with us, having been extracted shortly after we laagered. The company was to advance with platoons abreast, again with Lima in the middle. After a quiet night and breakfast, we were off. My standard breakfast was coffee and a C-ration pound or fruit cake. It was a simple pleasure spoiled each day by the speed with which Jerome wanted us to be on our way.

Lima's route this day started with a stretch of calf-deep water. The vegetation was thick. After this slog, we broke into intermittent jungle and open areas. At one point we came upon a hole in a field. The hole went down at a very steep angle and was about two feet in diameter. In many areas of Vietnam, the VC made extensive use of tunnels, hiding, living, eating, and dying in them. We hadn't had much experience with tunnels, and some members of the platoon were convinced this was a VC-constructed facility. I thought it was more likely a hole made by a dud, or unexploded, bomb. It didn't appear to have any shovel or digging marks. A one or two thousand pound bomb slamming into the soft earth at tremendous speed would burrow a considerable distance. A light shown down the hole revealed nothing. We dropped a few stones—probably not a smart thing to do if a dud explosive was indeed down there—but couldn't hear them land. One of the smaller troopers even wanted to be lowered down but I decided not. I was not persuaded the hole was of any significance and was concerned that anyone lowered into it would suffocate.

The three platoons found each other in the evening. The chopper that had extracted the chaplain the previous afternoon had returned Montdragon, the trooper who had been unable to get on the ground when we air assaulted two days before. Jerome had been making a big deal of the matter, threatening punitive action against Montdragon. I couldn't see what the problem was and said so, but Jerome wasn't to be swayed. Shortly after we laagered, the company RTO called for me to report to Jerome with Montdragon. As we were going over, I warned Montdragon that for some reason the CO was really pissed about his, Montdragon's, failure to unass the chopper. Montdragon was a short perpetually happy guy and didn't seemed phased by the prospect of having to appear before the company commander.

I reported to Jerome at the company CP. "Sir, I've got Montdragon."

"That was a damn inexcusable thing, Lieutenant, him not getting off the chopper."

"Ahh, come on, Sir. What was he supposed to do, jump fifteen feet? The damn thing was way up in the air before he got to the door. It wasn't his fault the chopper pilot was a lily livered shit."

"Maybe. What d'you think I should do?"

Now what the hell was going on? I thought Jerome had made up his mind to hit Montdragon with an Article 15. Now he was asking my opinion. "I don't think you outta do anything, Sir. It was just an unavoidable thing. It should just be forgotten."

"Well..., alright. But make sure it doesn't happen again."

"Right, Sir."

So Montdragon and I departed. He had been a few feet behind me and heard the whole exchange. It occurred to me that Jerome's performance was a charade. He simply wanted to put me in a position of defending my men, and especially of having my men see me defend them—perhaps create some good feelings on the part of the troops for their platoon leader. It seemed to me to be too contrived to really be accepted by the troops, but who knew? Anyway, Montdragon and I returned to the platoon, he seemingly oblivious to what had transpired.

That evening choppers delivered a hot meal and mail. I received a letter from home. It was the first one since they had learned of my new status. I had told them a number of months before leaving the 716th that I would be staying in Vietnam another six months. After my move to the 1/503rd, 173rd Airborne Brigade, I gave them my new address but didn't give much in the way of details. Finally, I had explained the change. It was a short letter. I simply said that I had transferred to the infantry and was now an infantry platoon leader in a paratrooper unit. I made the change because I wanted to experience what the ultimate soldier, the line soldier, experienced. I also asked for aid packages. I was now living in the jungle, sleeping on the ground, and could use items like kool aid mix, ice tea mix, and hot sauce to spice up the C-rations.

The response I received that evening was accepting, but I got the impression my mother didn't really comprehend the meaning of the switch. I was now in close daily proximity to death. If she realized that, she hid it well. She did say that an aid package was in the mail, which was welcome news.

About this time I also made a significant decision. I decided to put in for another six-month extension in Vietnam. This would give me two years, the maximum consecutive period that an officer was normally allowed to stay in Vietnam. My present DEROS was in February, which would give me about five months on the line as an infantry platoon leader. Even though I had experienced the field, had a small taste of combat, I was not satisfied. I wanted more. Another six months would give me that more. At the completion of the time, I would still have six months left in the Army to the end of my 18-month active duty extension, which I had received while in Saigon.

I told Jerome and First Sergeant Duckett of my desire for another six months. In due course, the paperwork dribbled out to the field. I affixed the required signatures and thus committed myself to an additional half-year in the 'Nam.

The mission for the next day was to conduct a chopper assault and then patrol. The laager site was fairly open and an open field was nearby. It was our pick-up zone. The choppers descended in a fog and fine drizzle. The flight to the LZ was short, but the sun had broken through by the time we started in. The LZ was a field on a small bluff beside a sluggish, muddy river and could accommodate about three choppers.

Lima was given responsibility for the side of the LZ away from the river. The tree line was only about 20 meters from where we landed. But tree line was a misnomer. It was an extremely thick line of bushes with just a few small openings to the jungle beyond. As was the standard procedure on an LZ, I hurried the troops off and into the tree line. Only it wasn't easy to get into the bushes. One trooper, a black PFC named Randolph, in particular seemed to be reluctant to venture from the open. Noticing him hesitating, I ordered him in. He inched his way forward but with no discernable progress. I trotted on to another sector. When I returned a few moments later, he was still standing a few feet away from the bushes.

"Randolph, in the woods! What's the problem, anyway?"

"Leeches, Sir. I ain't goin' in them leeches. They's all over."

I looked more closely at the bushes a few feet away. The damn things were alive with leeches, little half-inch to two-inch bloodsucking worms. Many of them were attached to a leaf or a branch by only one end. The other end, apparently sensing din-din, bobbed and weaved in the air, looking for red meat to latch onto. Both ends of the varmints looked like tiny suction cups. I glanced at the ground. It was alive with the critters also. A few of them had started up my boots.

The LZ had apparently been a cultivated field in the not too distant past. The loose soil was muddy from recent rains. Grasses and small shrubs dotted the ground. The vegetation reminded me of the kinds that sprang up in soybean fields back in Virginia. In fact, that's what came to mind as I stood there: a wet, unweeded soybean field in Virginia in mid-July. Only the mud, wetness, and plants took second place in my thoughts to the leeches.

It wasn't long before the whole company was on the ground. We established the outline of our laager site, dropped the rucksacks, and set off on patrols. Lima was to work its way along the river for a couple of clicks or so. By this time, leeches had found bare skin on most troopers. Anyone who didn't have trousers tucked into their boots had leeches on their legs. Leeches on arms and under belts were common. The little slimes didn't need much time before they were drawing blood. They could be pulled off but the instructions were that this risked leaving the heads attached. Smokers could use a lit cigarette to get a leech to undo quickly. The Army's insect repellant—bug juice—had the same effect.

Incidentally, bug juice could be the difference between maintaining one's sanity and going berserk. The powerful stuff the Army gave out could, if liberally smeared on exposed areas, keep the mosquitoes at bay. They would still be within hearing distance, but the constant whine could be endured. The biting that took place without the bug juice was another matter.

As we moved along the bank of the muddy sultry river, the troopers quickly discovered that squirting bug juice on boots and clothing helped in leech control. All leeches weren't deterred, but many were. Buoyed a little by this discovery, Lima completed its patrol. Back at the laager site, we dug holes and set up hooches. After I blew up my air mattress, I sprayed the outer edges, and the adjacent ground, with bug juice. Leeches were everywhere. I noticed an itching between my belt and pubic region, dropped my pants, and found three of the rascals digging in. I gave them a squirt of bug juice. They shriveled up and let go but left a bloody residue. I found a few more on my lower legs.

A hot meal was delivered that night, and I got into a small pissing contest with Jerome. Hot meals were served out of mermac containers—insulated containers the size of suitcases. Each container had one item: meat, potatoes, vegetable, ice tea, whatever. The containers were set up about five meters apart and manned by troopers from one of the platoons, on a rotating basis. The other platoons took turns in the chow line, which had to be spread out to reduce the possibility of casualties from incoming mortar or small arms fire.

Lima was first in line this evening. The troopers were fairly well spread out, the line stretching most of the length of the field and into the woods, but still within the company perimeter. I spread them out a little more. Then just as we were about to start through the line, Jerome piped up: "You're too damn close, Lima. Spread it out."

I waved the line back, and the troopers shuffled a bit, but not enough to satisfy Jerome: "Lima, you're not gonna eat until you're spread out."

"Sir, we are spread out. Look at 'em. Five meters apart."

"They're not spread enough, Lieutenant Holland. And you're not gonna eat 'til they are."

A rifle company in the field was like a close-knit family. And sometimes family members get on one another's nerves. I and Lima were evidently on Jerome's nerves this day. I walked back along the line, physically moving each trooper back a few feet. Finally we were spaced out enough to satisfy the company commander, and the chow line began moving.

One of the most sought after items in the chow line was near the end. This was usually a mermac container with ice tea or kool aid. The thing that everyone craved was what kept the liquid cool: ice. Rarely was there more than ten or so fist-size lumps, so only a lucky few troopers got a brief antidote to the always present heat. Occasionally, however, some perceptive guy in the rear sent out a mermac filled with nothing but the cold stuff. A canteen cup of ice was heaven in a very small container.

I usually welcomed night. Most of the time, it meant at least a little sleep. A precious commodity in the field, sleep was something a grunt never could seem to get enough of. Partly it was the exhausting effort of the days. Partly it was that a full night's sleep was rare. The general situation and the noises of the jungle at night interfered with prolonged sound sleep. Usually troopers pulled a one to two hour shift on guard, either at a perimeter bunker or on radio watch. Even platoon leaders and platoon sergeants participated, although the level of participation varied from unit to unit. As I've noted, Sgt. Brown hadn't been a regular on radio watch when I arrived. Having played the game for a long time and being unencumbered with the enthusiasm of youth, most platoon sergeants were not anxious to lose sleep and would readily pawn radio watch jobs off on the other members of the platoon headquarters. Being an FNG without infantry experience, I was reluctant to counter Sgt. Brown's procedure. I eased myself into the watch at times, however, and later when I had my feet more solidly on the ground, became almost a regular. But radio watch or not, a full night's undisturbed sleep was pretty close to unheard of. Nevertheless, night presented the best opportunity for at least a little sleep.

But sleep on this night was not a pleasant prospect. The leeches were on the make. The field was alive with them. Whenever you stayed in one place for more than a moment, you became aware of dozens of weaving, bobbing worms, tails attached to the ground, suction-cup heads looking for flesh. Through the late afternoon and into the evening, I plucked a few more off me. Before retiring, I refurbished the ring of insect repellant around my air mattress. And when I retired, I curled up in the fetal position, trying to keep any portion of my body from hanging over an edge of the mattress.

The night passed slowly. I awoke frequently, going back to the fetal position whenever I realized I was tempting the worms. Only a couple of the creatures found their way through my defenses. I picked them off in the morning, this time from my lower legs. Most of the troopers looked bedraggled in the early sunlight, all but a few having suffered physically, mentally, or both from the creatures.

A hump to some higher country was the mission for the day. Usually at least a few troopers required some chewing on to get out of the laager site in the morning. Not this day. The leeches put a little speed into even the slowest poke. The laager site was cleared in record time. The leeches commanded our attention for the first half of the day's walk. For once, the travails of the slippery mud, the wait-a-minute vines, and the rucksacks biting into the shoulders took second place in our concerns. The leeches weren't really noticeable until we paused. Then one quickly became aware of dozens of bobbing, weaving suction cups looking for a feed. The usual procedure when we stopped as the point clover-leafed was to drop to a sitting position, leaning back against the pack. But this day many troopers just bent over, resting the pack on their backs and warily watching the undulating ground.

Eventually, after a few clicks, the leeches gradually became fewer. By the time we reached the destination, the bloodsuckers had all but disappeared. The laager site was another recently—maybe a year or two previously—abandoned field. We arrived about mid-afternoon and so had plenty of time to construct bunkers and inspect our personal parts for still feeding leeches. The company perimeter was partly in the field and partly in the bordering jungle. A fairly large grove of trees sprawled in the center of the field, which was probably two acres in area. Lima's portion of the perimeter was in the field, and the platoon headquarters bunker bordered the grove of trees in the perimeter's center.

The mission for the next day was to stay put and explore—day-time patrolling. Lima's task was to descend to a river valley, do a little circling, and return. We pushed off about 0830. Initially, the route wasn't too difficult, but then we started descending. The slope wasn't quite a cliff, but on the other hand, the best means of locomotion was to sit on one's butt and slide. We found an old trail and some very old small caves, no more than indentations, in the side of the hill. We worked our way downward, finally coming to a wide wet valley. The orders were to make our way to the river bank and check it out for a click or so. Between us and the river, however, was a swamp with saw grass eight or more feet high.

Despite the troops' obvious reluctance, I ordered us to plunge in. After a few meters, however, it became apparent that the grass was alive with leeches. I said the hell with this shit and directed a retreat. We made it back to the base of the hill and started climbing. I decided to get to the top of the slope, circle a little more, and return to the laager site from a different angle. We found the abandoned site of a few thatched buildings and a small garden. Nothing was left of the buildings but the framing poles.

From the abandoned habitation, we set our course for the laager site. An old trail aided our progress. The growth on each side was thick up to knee level. Small and large ferns and other shrubs completely obscured the ground. We were making good time. I was behind the lead fire team, and we weren't stopping to cloverleaf, just chugging along. The trooper in front of me stepped over a log across the trail, as had the four or so in front of him. As I approached the log, which was about a foot in diameter, the sucker moved! The damn thing was crossing the trail! I realized I was looking at a small portion of one humongous snake.

With great alacrity, I advanced to the rear, trampling Baum and several other troopers in the process. The trooper that was ahead of me turned around at the commotion. When he saw the moving log, he also did a fast shuffle away from the activity.

The platoon stood and gawked at the moving monster. All that could be seen was the three-foot section on the trail. Where the tail was, and of more concern where the head was, were not initially discernable. The ferns and shrubbery on each side of the trail hid the beast. With the ground vegetation thinning out at about knee level, however, we could see about 25 or 30 meters into the trees. I noticed a large stump off to the right, maybe eight feet high, three feet in diameter, and fifteen feet from the trail. The end of the snake finally crossed the trail, and almost simultaneously I saw movement at the tree stump. The snake was climbing the trunk and descending into its hollow interior. I never did see its head. Its body was coming up the far side, so all we really saw was a foot-in-diameter glistening body going over the top and down into the hollowness.

After the trail was clear, we cut a fast choggy out of there. The unknown terrors hidden in the ferns and shrubs on each side of the path put a little something extra in our pace, and the trip back to the laager went quickly. When we arrived, we learned that another platoon had also found a snake, a python probably, about twelve feet long. He, or she, was right outside the perimeter. The troopers were less skittish than Lima about snakes and actually brought the thing into the perimeter for all to admire. He, or she, was eventually turned loose—outside the perimeter—and was last seen slithering into the undergrowth.

Talk of snakes occupied the remaining few hours of the afternoon. Talk and sleep. The laager site was actually a pleasant spot, particularly when compared to the leech palace of two nights before. The temperature was comfortable when one wasn't moving, maybe in the middle 80s. And the humidity was actually palatable and not overbearing. So curling up on a nice air mattress was pretty close to a luxurious experience.

The next day's mission was a chopper assault into a different area. We would spend the first night as palace guard at a new fire support base. But initially there was the matter of getting picked up from the current laager. Usually a PZ extraction was no big deal. For the last chopper load from this laager, however, the extraction was memorable.

Lima was the trail platoon, the last one to be extracted. That meant that the Lima platoon leader, me, was to be on the last chopper. Because of the sloping terrain, the PZ could handle just one chopper at a time. A chalk—one chopper load—would be picked up, the chopper would circle while succeeding chalks were picked up, and then the flight, about two platoons' worth, would depart for the LZ. Thus two flights, or lifts, would get the whole company.

The extraction went without incident until the last chopper came in. Ten of us were left, usually too many for one Huey. Since it was the last chopper, however, everyone had to get on. Otherwise three or four troopers, including me, would have a long wait for another ride. You just didn't leave a handful of troopers behind for the next bus. In addition to the general principle of not being in Indian country with inadequate forces, there was the fact that U.S. laager sites were an important part of the VC supply system. Rations, batteries, equipment were all available at zero cost. Even in apparently VC-free areas, a laager site could very well be subject to a VC search within a few minutes of the troops' departure. So when a unit was extracted, every effort was made to get the last group out quickly and in as large a body as possible.

Thus ten troopers with full packs piled on the last chopper. The pilot applied power and the machine chugged a few feet into the air. The normal way a chopper took off was to get a little bit of altitude and then proceed horizontally, gaining speed which in turn helped it gain more altitude. We began moving forward, but the heavy load prevented us from rising much. The tree line was less than 100 meters away. The chopper groaned toward it, the whipping blades clawing for height. An emptiness rose in my stomach. The trees were fast approaching. We weren't going to make it!

The other faces in the chopper echoed my fear. The sluggish machine staggered forward. The tree line was getting close enough for individual branches and leaves to be discernable, and we seemed to be on a direct line for them. Gradually, almost imperceptibly, we inched upward, the chopper shaking and resisting. Then we were at the trees. The Huey's skids plowed through the tops, slowing us down dangerously. Fascinated and horrified, we looked at the leaves just beneath us. The tree line was on the edge of the hilltop. After about twenty meters, the ground fell away sharply and for several hundred feet. The drop-off was what the pilot was striving for. It would enable him to dive and pick up speed.

And dive he did, like a rocket. As soon as he hit the drop-off, which was not a moment too early because the grasping branches were bringing us close to the stalling point, the pilot pointed the sucker at a 45-degree angle and headed for the valley. The acceleration pushed us against each other and towards the rear. Having survived the fear of crashing into the trees, we now had to deal with the fear of plowing into the ground at 100 or so miles an hour. Some might survive a crash into the trees at slow speed. Slamming into the earth at dive bomber speed would have left no survivors. We held on, watching the tree tops on the hillside whizzing by. The upcoming valley floor was visible through the front bubble of the chopper, past the pilot and copilot. Our lives were in the hands of some unknown chopper jockey. Was he a rookie or a veteran? Had his time come, and ours with it?

After excruciating seconds, whoever he was began pulling out of the dive. He had the machine under control. Whether it was ever out of control, whether the pilot viewed this as a near-death experience as did his passengers, was something we didn't know. In the years since, I've often wondered.

We married up with the rest of the flight and made the LZ, a large open plain. Half the company was already there, as were elements of the battalion fire support base apparatus. The company's mission for the rest of the day was merely to establish the base perimeter. We dug our bunkers, put out the claymores and tripwire flares, and relaxed. The four-deuce mortars and 105-mm howitzers were soon in place and firing away at imaginary troop concentrations. The day was sunny and pleasant, the grass soft and inviting. Much napping was done.

The Delinquent Defecator

Alpha Company had only one night as palace guard for the fire support base. The next day the company departed for what was to be a little over two weeks of bushwacker operations—platoons operating for extended periods in their own AOs, patrolling, ambushing, and generally marauding. The first day's movement was a short one. To the north of the base was a mountain, and we simply walked around the mountain, setting up a company laager site on the other side. The laager site was four to five clicks from the fire support base.

The laager site was in a patch of irregularly shaped woods. The perimeter in Lima's sector followed the edge of the woods. The edge was in the shape of a rough V, with the open end of the V facing the interior of the perimeter. The fact that the interior of the perimeter was woods and the outside was an open field led to an incident that became part of my permanent military record. Moreover, I was not to discover this little tidbit in the files for almost twenty years.

What the perimeter situation led to was Lima's troopers, including myself, defecating inside rather than outside the company's lines. Normally, we sought a place outside the perimeter to crap. But when the outside offered no concealment and the inside did, the inside was tempting, particularly if the perimeter covered a large area. No one wanted to get greased by a sniper while taking a dump. If you had to die, you should at least have your pants pulled up. So Lima crapped inside the perimeter that afternoon and evening. Big deal. We thought nothing of it.

The next morning the three platoons set out for their AOs. The company headquarters and the Oscar stayed behind, spreading out to occupy the entire company perimeter of the night before. It was to be five days before we learned of the anguish suffered by these stay-behinders, who did nothing but sit on their butts.

Those five days were spent in our AO, an oblong area about two kilometers by three kilometers. The overall mission as we understood it, and rarely did we have much understanding of the big picture, was for the battalion and several other large units to serve as a buffer between the interior mountains and the rice paddies of the coastal lowlands. The purpose of the buffer was to allow the peasants on the coast to harvest the rice crop without being harassed by the bad guys. In theory, we would interdict the bad guys and generally make their lives miserable. We were to play Mr. Charles' own game—sneak around, ambush, make like Indians (before that characterization became politically incorrect).

The area had previously been inhabited by peasant farmers. It contained open fields, some of them with growing crops—corn, squash, and the like—a number of crisscrossing trails, and abandoned building sites. Practically all the buildings had been dismantled or otherwise destroyed at some point in the recent past. The area also contained patches of jungle and a mountain or two. The mosquitoes were the worst of any place I encountered in Vietnam, with the exception of some houses of ill-repute in Saigon. Usually, liberal doses of the Army-issue bug juice would keep mosquitoes off exposed flesh. The varmints in this area, however, were particularly fierce. The bug juice was strong stuff and tended to sting or numb sensitive skin, such as the lips. Consequently, I usually left the stuff off my lips. But during the first night in the AO, my lips were set upon with a vengeance. In the morning, they were swollen and itching, as were my eyelids. Thereafter, I liberally doused every bit of exposed skin.

During our stay in the area, the happy family that was the platoon experienced a few family squabbles. We began to get on each other's nerves a little. Several incidents, none major, indicated conflicting personalities and underlying tensions. One focus of these minor family spats was new Sergeant Baum, formerly Spec. 4 Baum, my RTO. He had received a promotion—it had been in the works when I arrived—and been given a squad. The squad members were the boisterous bunch of PFC Moste, the trooper who had showed his manhood by taking a machete to dead Victor Charlies several weeks before. Our first night out, we established our laager in a grove of bushes and underbrush on the edge of a field. We didn't dig in with overhead cover, but I did order shallow holes. I felt safer with a little dirt around me. The troops weren't too happy with the digging, but I insisted.

Baum's squad was giving him a particularly difficult time about digging. They were being humorous, but with a hard, defiant edge. We were fairly close together, and the rest of the platoon was increasingly aware of the difficulties Baum was having. Finally, I intervened: "Hey, knock the fuck off. Your squad leader said dig, so dig."

"Aww, Sir. We're just having a little fun." It was tough guy Moste, pushing the edge.

"Yeah, well, it sounds like too much fun to me."

They toned down a little and commenced to work, but Baum was not destined to have an easy couple of weeks.

One notable event during these first few days was the loss of Sgt. Hikaey's pig. The instructions were to destroy any food supplies, livestock, and crops that we came across. The area was not supposed to have any friendlies in it, or civilians at all. Everyone had allegedly been evacuated or driven out. It was officially a free-fire zone.

Sgt. Hikaey had come upon a small pig during the first day or so. In one of the periodic sitreps over the radio, I had somewhat humorously reported that we had captured a pig. I didn't take into account two facts. Sgt. Hikaey had become attached to the damn animal. And the battalion commander, not having enough to occupy his time, had developed a hankering for a pig roast.

With the pig, we found several containers of rice, each about the size of a wastebasket. I had reported these also and asked what we should do with them. That was a mistake. I should have just left the small cache unreported, but I was still having difficulty identifying things that in theory I was suppose to do but in practice I would be best off not doing. Initially, I was told that a chopper would be by to pick up the rice. After some hours, however, I came to the conclusion this wasn't going to happen, so I decided to bury the stuff. That way if battalion ever wanted to get the rice, we could dig it up, but in the meantime it would be denied to the VC. Thus we dug a pit in the field in front of the laager site. The rice didn't go in right away; I still had visions of it being picked up. But Sgt. Hikaey put his new companion in, as a temporary holding pen.

A complicating factor in this little melodrama was malaria. For several weeks, the malady had been claiming more and more of A Company, and by this time probably thirty troopers had been evacuated from the field, maybe eight to ten of those from Lima. We were supposed to be taking malaria pills—a small one daily, and a large one weekly. Whether faithfully taking the pills would actually prevent one from contracting malaria, I don't know. The suspicion on the part of some higher ups was that the troopers were purposely not taking the pills in order to get out of the field. A bout with malaria was at least a 30-day hospital and convalescent stay, a month of not humping the boonies. Not taking pills was not a sure way of getting malaria—I only took mine haphazardly, partly because the big ones upset my tummy—but it was a tempting avenue for anyone tired of living like an animal. Malaria casualties had become so common in the battalion over the previous few weeks that for a time each trooper was required to swallow his pill in the presence of an officer. Company commanders were threatened with relief from command for having too many malaria casualties—sort of like firing the coach of a poorly performing athletic team.

Anyway, on that day when we had a captured pig, we also had a trooper with a fever of 102 degrees and hot and cold flashes—an obvious malaria case. He had been getting sick for a day or so, and I had tried to have him evacuated the previous evening. Jerome was giving me a hard time, however, undoubtedly because Battalion was giving him a hard time. Jerome wanted me to be sure that the guy was sick enough to leave.

I had no doubt that afternoon. The trooper had malaria and should be extracted pronto, and I told Jerome so. Somehow, however, the request for a medevac and the report about the pig became connected. Jerome was on the radio: "Lima, this is Six."

"Six, this is Lima."

"This is Six. Higher wants to know how big your pig is."

What the hell was this? "Six, this is Lima. He's about 25 pounds." That was a lousy estimate. Ten pounds was more like it. After about 15 minutes, Jerome called:

"Lima, this is Six."

"Six, Lima."

"This is Six. A chopper is on the way to get your medevac and the pig."

"The pig?"

"Yeah. The battalion staff wants a roast."

Shit. What the hell was I to tell Sgt. Hikaey? He and I did not have the best of relationships anyway, and here I was being required to turn over his new-found pet for a meal. On the other hand, I had begun to suspect that he had visions of carting the pig around for a long time. The animal would be a substitute for the mongrel dog that we could never adopt—like they do in war movies—because we could never find one. Dog meat was standard Vietnamese fare, which meant stray dogs were rare. Giving the pig to battalion would preclude it becoming the burden that I envisioned it could become.

"Sergeant Hikaey, the battalion CO wants your pig."

"What, Sir? My pig!?"

"Yeah. He wants it."

"But Sir. I wanna keep it. Why does the CO want it?"

"It's war booty. We're suppose to turn over war booty." I didn't have the heart or guts to say that the oinker was destined to be food, although you had to be pretty damn dense not to figure out what was going on. The chopper was soon within hearing, which brought an end to the conversation. Sgt. Hikaey, realizing I meant business and not having enough time to think up further arguments, got his pig. The malaria trooper got himself together. He was zombie-like at this point, getting pretty close to delirium. The chopper landed, and both the pig and the trooper were put on board. After it departed, I figured no one was ever coming for the rice, so we put it in the pit and piled on the dirt.

Jerome called a short time later: "Lima, this is Six."

"Six, Lima."

"Lima, Six. I thought you said the pig was 25 pounds. Big Six says it's only a pup."

"Six, this is Lima. Well, it sure seemed big to me." What the hell, I didn't have scales; another black mark in my book. But at least the malaria trooper got out of the field.

The next few days passed uneventfully. Mostly, we wandered around the northern half of the AO. We did make one penetration of the southern half, which led to another run-in between myself and Sgt. Hikaey. The penetration came as the result of some prompting from Jerome—the troops and I were content to laze around the fields and open spaces in the north. But following Jerome's direction one morning, we headed south. After struggling through some fairly thick vegetation for several hours, we arrived at a hill covered mostly with grass. On the far side was a bit more jungle, and then a wide, open plain. Beyond the plain, which was about two clicks across, were hills and more jungle. Indeed, the area on the far side was where we had been several weeks before. The hilltop laager site where the trooper with the severe case of jungle rot was refused evacuation was directly across the way.

We were in the process of establishing a small perimeter on the grass-covered hill when a call came over the horn: "Lima, this is Six."

"Six, Lima."

"Lima, you need to send out an ambush patrol tonight. Let us know the location."

Damn. We were to divide ourselves even more.

"Six, this is Lima. You want us to split ourselves in two?"

"That's battalion's orders. They want to be sure we're blocking all routes to the lowlands."

"This is Lima, roger."

"Six out."

So I informed Sgt. Hikaey that his squad would have to establish an ambush that night. We had crossed a trail about a click back. His boys could just set out a couple of claymores and relax. He asked, "Do we have to, Sir?"

"Well, yeah."

"Do we have to, Sir?"

It took me a moment to catch his drift. He was suggesting that we pretend to send out the ambush but not actually do so. I bet that even at Ft. Benning they didn't teach this situation.

"Look. Those are the orders, and that's what we're gonna do."

"Do we have to, Sir?"

"Yeah, goddammit. Now let's get goin'!"

Reluctantly and with a display of considerable irritation, Sgt. Hikaey got his squad together and set off for the ambush site. The rest of the platoon—the other squad and the headquarters group—spread out over the gaps in the small perimeter.

Dusk had just arrived when a claymore exploded and an M-60 let go from the direction of the ambush site. I suspected immediately that Sgt. Hikaey was just looking for a return ticket. Sure enough, within a few seconds he was on the horn: "Lima Six, this is Lima One. We popped the ambush. Can we come back now?"

The sonuvabitch sure as hell wasn't being coy about his intentions. I felt he was pretty damn close to insubordination.

"Lima One, this is Lima. Did you get anything?"

"This is Lima One. We didn't get anything. Can we come back now?"

I mulled the situation over for a moment. The squad had revealed its location, which wasn't good. On the other hand, the obviousness of Hikaey's lie was too much. I finally said: "Negative on returning to the laager site. Stay in place."

"This is Lima One. Do I understand to stay in place? Why?"

Because I said so, mothafucker. "Because it's too dangerous to move at night, and it's almost night. And something might come along later on. Stay in place. That's the order."

I wasn't about to let Sgt. Hikaey ride roughshod over me. He was pushing too close to the edge. So the night passed. Just after dawn, Hikaey and his squad returned. He was an unhappy cowboy, but not at the moment a confrontational one. We didn't say anything more about the incident. It put me on notice about Hikaey, however. He required delicate handling. And the scary thing was that he was soon likely to be the platoon sergeant.

Sgt. Brown would be leaving the field within the next ten days, to spend his last months in Vietnam in the company rear functioning as a supply sergeant. He hadn't been the focal point of my relationship with the platoon since the first few days. But he had handled the logistics, the resupplies, and a number of administrative matters of which I was only vaguely aware. His desire to leave the field was evident. Almost nine months in Vietnam, all of it in the field, a family awaiting him, he'd had enough. And to top it off, the last month he had been stuck with baby-sitting an FNG infantry platoon leader. The only good thing about those weeks was that at least he finally had a platoon leader. For months before that, he was the man.

We departed the laager site, making our way just a click or so to the west. My plan was to spend the day at the point where the main north-south trail hit the broad plain in the southern portion of the AO. There, we could watch both the trail and the valley. In the evening, we would move up the trail a bit and set up an ambush.

The day was relaxing—no humping, no moving even. We just sat in the bushes in a little perimeter, sleeping and watching. At one point in the afternoon, I noticed a silhouette about a click away, in the middle of the plain. We couldn't tell if it was a bush or a person. After much discussion, I sent a fire team a couple hundred meters into the open. The M-79 grenadier lobbed a few rounds in the shadow's direction. It didn't move, so we concluded it was a bush. So much for the adventuresome life of an infantryman.

Towards dusk, we moved about a click up the trail to find an ambush site. I settled on a stretch that would give each machine gun a straight portion of trail to blast. I had each squad set out temporary security on its portion of the trail, and we began establishing positions, digging shallow holes. We had just gotten started when the security position to the south let loose with a prolonged M-16 burst, close to a full twenty-round clip. The lethargy and laziness of the day instantly disappeared. Shovels were dropped, weapons grabbed and pointed. The adrenalin pumped. A member of the two-man security team came running back: "A gook was comin' up the trail!"

"Didja get 'im?" I asked.

"Don't know."

I went with the rest of the squad down to the scene of the action. The two troopers said that the VC disappeared in the bushes to the left. We spread out in a rough line and advanced in that direction. It was inconceivable to me that so many rounds could be fired at such close range without something being hit. Consequently, I was sure we would find a trophy in short order. The vegetation was very thick, but after only about ten meters we came to another trail. It paralleled our trail for a few meters before bending to the east. The immediate area around the trail was a little more open than the thick brush we had just come through. We searched but found nothing—no body, no blood trails, nothing.

Darkness wasn't too far off, so we returned to the first trail and the ambush site. But Sgt. Brown was having none of it: "We've got to move, Sir."

"Are you sure? It's getting pretty dark."

"They know our position. We can't stay here."

I wouldn't have thought it necessary to move, but maybe he was right. If a large force with some degree of ability was out there, our position was roughly pinpointed. So we saddled up and headed north. Given the late hour, however, I was determined not to go far. We needed to get settled before darkness descended in full. After about half a click, only a quarter of a mile, we came to a stretch that satisfied my simple needs for an ambush site: straight entering trails and room for a small perimeter. Sgt. Brown seemed content with the distance we had moved. We set up shop. Expectations were high that we would get some VC, but the initial encounter was the only contact. The activity likely drove any potential nighttime travelers to ground for this night.

The next day's mission was to return to the company laager, but by way of a mountain in the north-central portion of the AO. We were to search the mountain for possible Charlies. We humped north and moved up the eastern side of the hill, which was more of a ridge than a mountain. On the northern side was a stream. We stopped there to clean up—mainly shaving, which most of us hadn't done for the five days of the bushwacker. When the company was together, shaving was generally done every two or three days, with the CO and the first sergeant keeping close tabs. Off by ourselves, however, I didn't really care and didn't insist. But now was time to get pretty.

Sgt. Brown was nagging everyone to do a good, thorough job when one platoon member bit back. Reilly had been a quiet trooper, a white guy from the rural Midwest. I had never heard him raise his voice, argue, or even say much of anything. But he started snapping at Sgt. Brown: "I'm doin' it Sarge! Don't fuckin' yell at me!"

This was pretty damn close to insubordination, and Sgt. Brown was instantly charging across the stream. He was about six feet three inches and a former boxer in the 82nd Airborne Division. Reilly was about five feet eight inches, but stocky. A large rock was between them. Sgt. Brown stopped at the rock and thundered: "Don't talk back to me, trooper! I said to fuckin' shave!"

"I said don't yell at me, Sarge!"

Suddenly, our little family was disintegrating before my eyes. "Hey," I said, "knock it off! Reilly, the platoon sergeant said shave! So shave!"

"He can't yell at me like that, Sir!"

112   Vietnam, A Memoir

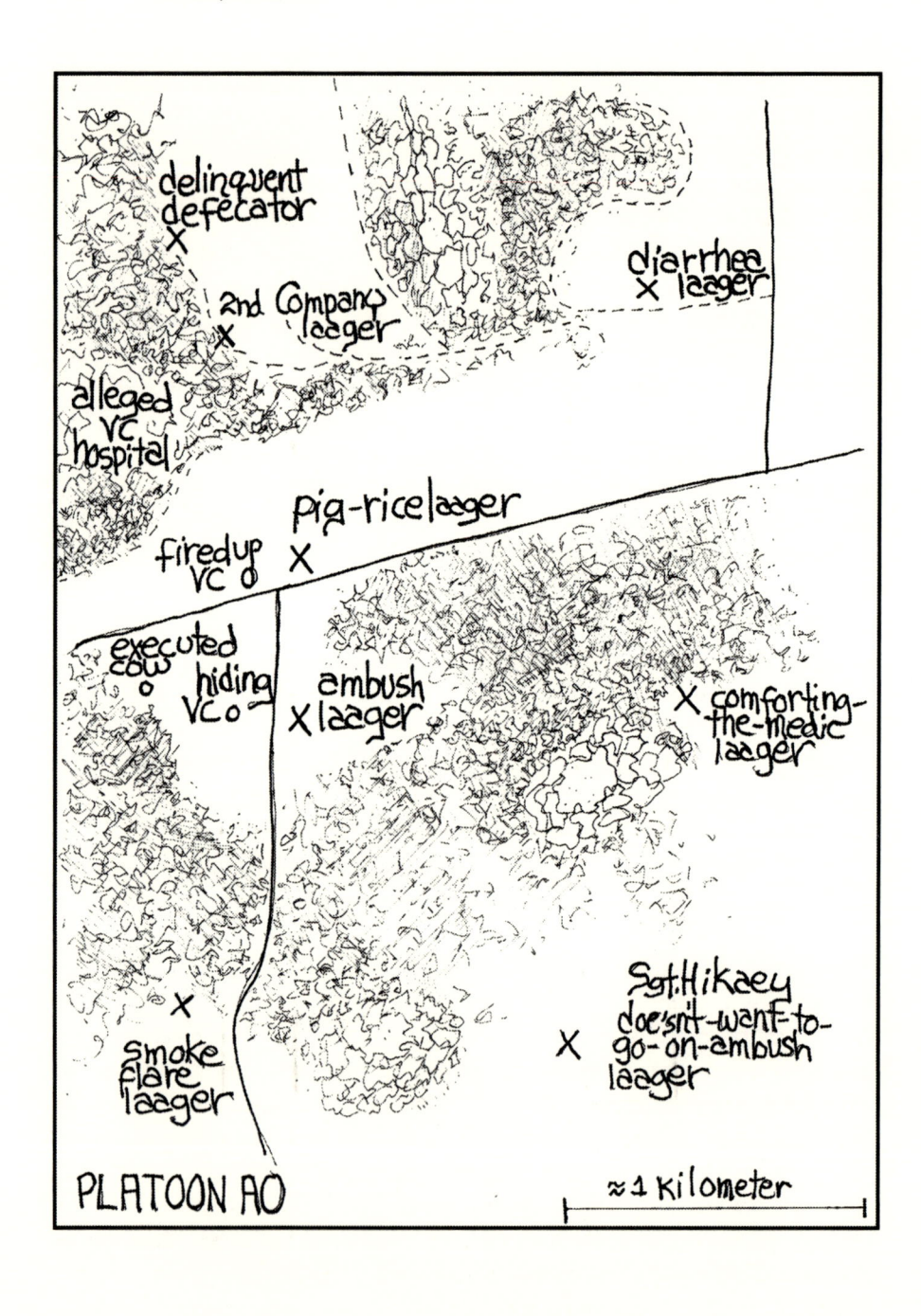

[Hand-drawn map labeled "PLATOON AO" with scale "≈ 1 kilometer". Marked locations:
- delinquent defecator
- 2nd Company laager
- diarrhea laager
- alleged VC hospital
- fired up VC
- pig-rice laager
- executed cow
- hiding VC
- ambush laager
- comforting-the-medic laager
- smoke flare laager
- Sgt. Hikaey doesn't-want-to-go-on-ambush laager]

"Hey, c'mon! The sergeant said to shave! What the hell's the problem?" I felt like I was getting into an argument that I shouldn't be getting into. Of all people who might have approached insubordination, Reilly seemed the least likely. I had no idea what set him off, but it must have been festering for some time. Fortunately, he appeared to have exhausted whatever was ailing his psyche. He didn't say anything more, just grumbled. Sgt. Brown let the matter drop, although he would have been justified in making an issue of it.

The troopers went back to their cleaning. That task completed, we started up the ridge we were to check out. It was jungle-covered and showed little sign of recent activity. We tramped the length of it and then headed off the west side to the company laager.

I expected a friendly greeting from Jerome. After all, we hadn't seen each other for five whole days. But he had apparently spent the five days fuming and building up a load of bile. I approached with a friendly, "Well, here we are, Sir."

"Goddamn Lima! Don't you know about shitting?"

"Sir?"

"Shitting, shitting, don't you know about shitting?"

"Well, uh, yes Sir. I, uh, don't understand."

"Your goddamn platoon shit all over the place. You're supposed to shit outside the perimeter."

The story gradually emerged. After the three platoons had departed the laager site, the Weapons Platoon and the headquarters group had spread out to occupy the entire perimeter. Lima's egregious error of shitting inside the perimeter was discovered. The discovery must have been in dramatic fashion, but I never learned the details. In a few months, I was to have my own run-in with misplaced shit, so I can appreciate Jerome's unhappiness. Still, he did seem to be overreacting, particularly in view of the very tactical fact that we had chosen to shit inside the perimeter because shitting outside, in the field, would have exposed us to possible sniper fire.

But it was to be two decades before I comprehended the deepness of Jerome's unhappiness. After Vietnam, I remained in the Army Reserve, for the first few years in an inactive status but later, as bad memories faded a bit and nostalgia set in, at an increased level of participation. At one point in the mid-1980s, I was given a microfiche copy of my cumulative Army record to review for a promotion board. There, buried in history, was the Officer Evaluation Report that Jerome had written on me twenty years earlier. Overall, it was about average, but included in the narrative was one damning sentence: "On one occasion Lt. Holland had to be counseled about the sanitary habits of his platoon."

Damn! My permanent military record, which might survive as long as the nation itself, condemns me as a careless shitter. What a legacy. Actually, I have to admit to a perverse sort of pride. Being branded in the nation's archives as a delinquent defecator has a certain uniqueness, a panache, your ordinary citizen would have trouble matching.

But this revelation about the extent of Jerome's displeasure was a long way in the future. At the time, his anger seemed to abate after the initial blowup. We received a resupply that night, and a hot meal. Mail was also delivered, and the newspaper *Stars and Stripes*, the soldier's source of events in the world beyond his immediate vision.

We returned to the AO the next day. The company headquarters and Oscar followed for a click or so to set up a new laager—too much human residue at the old place. I took the platoon back to the center of the AO for the first night. We laagered in the same spot as we had buried the rice and surrendered the captured pig to battalion—not necessarily a good idea but carelessness is easy to come by.

The next day we took on another piece of livestock, a cow. The episode was one of the more regrettable ones during my Vietnam years, which probably says something about my distorted sense of values—dead humans are okay, dead animals are a tragedy. We moved a little to the west in the morning, and there was a cow, more like a water buffalo cow than a good ol' American cow. The instructions were to destroy all crops and livestock, so after checking on the radio with Jerome, I ordered the animal executed. We could then eat the deceased. A few of the Midwest farm boy troopers in the platoon proclaimed a knowledge of how to butcher beef.

Only the cow wouldn't die. We must have put 30 rounds in the thing over a 15-minute period, and it just stood there. Jesus Christ, why wouldn't it go down!? The M-16 was supposed to be a destroyer, but the damn cow hardly seemed phased. I asked the troopers doing the executing: "Why isn't it going down?"

"Don't know, Sir."

"Where are you shooting it?"

"We're trying for the heart."

Blood was streaming from holes in the sides and chest, but the heart itself must have escaped a direct hit. "It'll go down soon, Sir," one of the troopers said, a little uncertainly.

I couldn't watch anymore and walked off. The rest of the platoon was in a grove of trees some distance away, not having much taste for the proceedings.

The executioners didn't seem to be enjoying their task, either. All those hardened paratroopers were acting like a bunch of patsies. I suppose someone could have shot it in the head, but nobody seemed up to dealing with those moon eyes.

Finally, agonizingly—for both us and the cow—the thing went to its knees, tottered for a bit, and keeled over. Then Henderson, the M-60 gunner from Indiana, stepped forward to cut some steaks. It was quickly apparent that he had no more idea of how to butcher a cow than I did. Again, I retreated. A fire was started and eventually one of the troopers brought me a grisly piece of bloody meat. I skewered a bit on a stick, held it over the fire until it was charred, and made a pretense of eating. I didn't see anyone else digging into a steak dinner with great gusto. After awhile, we departed the area and the bloody carcass for a laager site a few hundred meters to the east. That evening, I noticed the platoon members dug into the much maligned C-rations with little of the usual gripping.

The next day we moved down the main trail to the south, past the site of our ambush of three nights before. Near the southern exit onto the open plain we established a laager, spending the rest of the day watching the trail. The following day, I sent Sgt. Hikaey's squad on a patrol to the east, through the thick jungle in that section of the AO. Shortly after the squad left, one of the troopers in the stay-behind squad hit a trip-wire on a flare that had been set out the night before. The laager site was in the woods, but the flare set off considerable smoke that penetrated the jungle canopy. A "bird dog", a piper cub, with an aerial artillery observer was flying in the vicinity, saw the smoke, and thought he had found Charlie. Suddenly I was aware of a plane buzzing the trees just over our heads. I quickly got on the horn: "Six, this is Lima!"

"Lima, this is Alpha One." One of the company RTO's answered. Jerome was asleep, taking a dump—outside the perimeter, certainly—or otherwise occupied.

"Alpha, this is Lima. We're getting buzzed by some plane. I assume its one of ours. How about seein' if you can call the dog off before he blows us away?"

The bird dog had a few rockets that he could fire his own self. Of more concern, he could call in artillery or even air strikes. A few minutes later Jerome called. "Lima, this is Six. The bird dog thinks he's got some Charlies. Are you sure it's you?"

Sgt. Brown was nearby the radio. His few days left in the field were weighing heavily on him. "Goddamn, Sir! That dumb sonuvabitch's gonna fire us up!"

"Six, this is Lima. That's us. I say again, that's us he's spotted. We accidently popped a flare that sent smoke through the trees. Request you get him outta here before we're dead meat."

After a few more tense minutes, Jerome called: "Lima, this is Six."

"Six, this is Lima."

"Lima, Six. We called him off. Just be careful of your flares."

"Six, Lima. Roger, out." Right. It was our fault that some damn flight jockey was trigger happy. All of those assholes should have to spend a month humping the boonies before being let loose in the wild blue yonder.

The morning was passing slowly and drowsily. At the platoon laager, we were watching the trail. Periodically, Sgt. Hikaey would call in with a sitrep from the patrol. The peace was disrupted a little after noon, however. A rattle of automatic weapons fire came from the direction of Hikaey's patrol. It was followed after a short pause by several more bursts. I waited a long minute and then called: "Lima One, this is Lima."

There was no answer. I called again: "Lima One, this is Lima Six, over."

Finally came a response: "Lima Six, this is Lima One."

"This is Lima Six. What's goin' on?"

"This is Lima One. We got a big'un. The biggest damn slope I've ever seen."

"Is he dead?"

"Not yet."

"This is Lima Six. D'you want a medevac?"

"No. He's dying. He won't last."

"Are there any more?"

"No. I don't think so."

I relayed the news to the company. There was no more activity, and Sgt. Hikaey was back at the laager by mid-afternoon. He and several of his men were full of stories about the big dead VC, but I noted that they didn't have any weapons or booty. Also, not everyone seemed to be telling stories about the encounter. And finally, Sgt. Hikaey seemed a little vague as to where the incident occurred, not being very precise as to grid coordinates or description of the area. I was a little suspicious, particularly in view of Sgt. Hikaey's recent bout with the truth at his nighttime ambush, but I didn't press it.

The next day, however, I decided to move in that direction. The map showed a stream source, or spring, that might be a good spot for an ambush. So the following morning, I gave the order to move to the spring, and "Oh by-the-way, Sgt. Hikaey, let's take a look at this enormous dead Victor Charlie on the way." As I suspected, we didn't find the body. At the spot of the alleged encounter, there was zero evidence that I could see. Sgt. Hikaey opined that the VC must have hauled the body away. I didn't publicly call him a liar, but I did file another incident away in the ol' memory bank.

The Delinquent Defecator   117

That night at the spring I tried dealing with another problem. We had a new platoon member. Doc, the unwashed medic who had attempted ineffectively to slice my infected finger, had returned to the rear. The medics were not permanently assigned to companies, being run out of the battalion headquarters. A medic could stay with a company for his whole tour, but more likely he would be rotated between a company and the battalion rear, sometimes returning to the field with a different company.

So Doc was replaced with Doc. The new Doc was cleaner than his predecessor, but he had another problem. He was afraid of the dark.

Under Sgt. Brown's regime, as I've noted, the lower ranking members of the headquarters group—the two RTOs and the medic—had conducted a sort of collective radio watch in which in fact everyone mostly slept. I was gradually and not very systematically instituting a more structured approach. A single individual was to be on radio watch at any particular time. The two RTOs and the medic had shifts, and I was beginning to take one myself. In a bow to Sgt. Brown's longevity and shortness, I didn't insist that he get in the rotation.

Unlike guard on the perimeter positions, radio watch did not entail actually watching and listening for the enemy. It merely involved listening on the company net and responding verbally or breaking squelch when we were ping-ponged: "Lima, this is Alpha Romeo. If you are ping-pong, break squelch twice, over."

"Skitchree, skitchree."

"This is Alpha Romeo. Roger, out."

If Lima had an outpost or ambush out, the Lima radio watch would periodically ping-pong it.

Thus radio watch was not a very demanding task. The main requirement was to stay awake. The platoon's new Doc, however, was having difficulties. He claimed he couldn't handle the task. He buttressed his position with the assertion that medics weren't supposed to stand guard. My response was, "Look, you're not standing guard. You're just listening to the goddamn radio. Are you a conscientious objector or somethin'."

"No Sir."

"You even carry a .45. Who says ya don't hav'ta pull radio guard?"

"The battalion medical officer, Sir."

"I sure as hell never heard it. We'll check it out when and if we ever have a stand-down. 'Til then, you're a warm body for the radio. If you don't do it, it puts a burden on everyone else."

"I just can't handle it, Sir. It scares the hell out of me. I'm terrified of being awake at night."

So the argument had been going for several days. Finally on this day, I said: "Look. I'll sit up with you tonight. But you're not gettin' out of this. You've got to stand radio watch."

Before evening arrived, however, I sent Baum's squad on a patrol, going southwest, then east, and then returning northwest to the starting point. For want of nothing better to do, I went along, actually running the thing and not letting Baum exercise any judgment. It was an uneventful stroll through the bush. I wanted to see if any of those VCs Sgt. Hikaey kept seeing would turn up, but none did.

Evening came, and with it pitch darkness. The laager site was in a dense patch of jungle. The spring was just below the laager, which was on a relatively flat piece of ground. A steep incline about ten feet in elevation was what put the spring below the laager site. No moonlight penetrated the thick foliage.

The RTO on radio watch, PFC Jensen, who had been selected by Sgt. Brown as Baum's replacement, awakened me about 0200. I hissed at Doc, who was a few feet away: "Doc, get up. You and I are on." It took a few tries, but eventually Doc was crawling toward the log where I was sitting. For a guy supposedly afraid of the dark, he was one heavy sleeper. Maybe the real problem was that radio watch interfered with his deep slumber.

He located the log and heaved himself up into a sitting position. The blackness was absolute. We could see nothing. The troopers watching at the four platoon positions were in the same boat, but so were any VC that might be in the vicinity. The utter blackness and lack of visibility exacerbated the night-time noises of the jungle. Rustling, chirping, moan-like soft wails, all assaulted the ears. After a short period I became aware that the log was shaking. To distract Doc, I whispered, "See. Nothing hapnin'. All you got to do is sit. No big deal."

"I don't like this, Sir," said a quavering voice.

"Hey, c'mon. You're a paratrooper. You can handle this."

But Doc was having none of it. We spend the two hours with him shaking and whispering in a quavering voice and me trying to instill some backbone. The training session ended, but it was obvious Doc was far from cured. Maybe we should avoid pitch dark laager sites. But I was determined Doc wasn't going to weasel out of this duty. He would have to make an effort. And in truth from then on he did handle radio watch, not with great elan but adequately, although I suspected that the two RTOs covered for him a bit.

Buck Fever

The next day was to be a return to the company laager site for resupply. My plan was to push to the west through the woods and on small trails, intersect the main north-south trail, head north past our pig-rice laager site of the first night in the AO, and find the company. The trip went without incident until we neared the pig-rice laager site. The north-south trail intersected the main east west trail through the AO just below the site. For the last 100 meters, the north-south trail was pretty much in the open. A field lay to the right. A narrow band of trees and bushes paralleled the left side of the trail. The trees and bushes grew from a trench and adjacent earthen mound that extended for several hundred meters and that we had not checked out thoroughly in our travels. The old pig-rice laager was in a small loose thicket in the middle of an open expanse. Some of the expanse was semi-cultivated crops. An overgrown corn field lay to the left of and a bit beyond the thicket.

Just after we hit the trail junction and as the point was about to reach the old laager site, I spotted an individual in black pajamas at the edge of the corn field, about 100 meters from us. A bandoleer was clearly visible over his right shoulder and across his back. He appeared to be picking corn.

A goddamn Victor Charlie! Right there! The first live VC most of us had seen! Smack dab in the open! And the sorry sonuvabitch hadn't seen us although we were as much in the open as he was. Most of the rest of the platoon saw the guy at about the same time, and to a man we were frozen. The first thing that went through my mind was, ambush. A standard VC ploy was to give you a look, luring you into a chase. Most of the platoon was already in the open. Only the last few troopers were still abreast of the line of trees that paralleled the north-south trail. We might already be in a kill-zone. Charging across the field could be just what someone, someone with an itchy finger on a Chicom machine gun, was hoping we would do.

In hindsight, what I should have done was to order everyone to drop where they were. Then I should have sent the rear-most fire team way round to the left. The fire team could make its way to the woods about 100 meters to the west and follow the woods up to the left edge of the corn field, a location that would put it within about 30 meters of the guy.

But hindsight is hindsight.

What I did was to order the platoon to shoot the sonuvabitch. It was a free-fire zone, he had a bandoleer of, presumably, bullets across his body, and he was wearing the standard VC uniform, black pajamas. Of course, all peasants wore black PJs, but that was their problem. There was another consideration. I had never shot anyone, and now was my chance. How could one possibly go back to the Land of the Big PX without personally killing someone, particularly if one was an infantryman? After all, that's what the whole damn thing was all about, wasn't it, killing?

So I whispered to the lead squad, which I was in the middle of, to fire the VC up. I motioned for the rear squad to do the same. And I raised my M-16 to my shoulder, clicking the fire selection switch to automatic in the process. The result was that an infantry platoon of almost 30 paratroopers took aim at a stationary and unawares VC a scant 100 meters away. The poor sap was dead meat, about to buy the farm. Hot damn!

The platoon's line of march was diagonal to the direction to the VC, so everyone had an unobstructed shot. The entire line let go pretty much simultaneously. The fusillade was deafening, with most weapons seeming to be on automatic. Assuming each of 20 troopers fired almost a full magazine, say 15 rounds, 300 bullets went zipping across the field. No one could survive that horizontal rain of death!

Mr. Charles was untouched. And he wasn't waiting around to get touched. He covered the 30 meters to the woods to our left in world record time. As he was gazelling the distance, a woman and a small child popped up at the tree line and quickly disappeared into the darkness. Mr. Charles was right behind them.

Thirty paratroopers, most with smoking guns, stood sheepishly in the field, feeling foolish. Most, however, were probably secretly relieved. Killing an unsuspecting VC in the open in front of his wife and kid wasn't the most macho thing in the world. But even given a certain degree of reluctance, how could a platoon of paratroopers miss such an open target? I don't know about the others, but I know what happened to me—a classic case of buck fever, the choking a novice hunter is likely to do the first time he takes aim at a big target. I put the weapon to my shoulder and pointed it, but I certainly did not get a proper sight picture of the target, and in no way did I go through the standard firing procedure of BRASS—breath, relax, aim, slack, squeeze. Instead of gently taking up the slack in the trigger and slowly squeezing it, I jerked that baby forcefully to the rear.

Consequently, the first round was on a trajectory probably a good ten feet over Mr. Charles' head. Since the weapon was on automatic, other rounds followed. In fact, I expended almost a full magazine without letting up on the trigger. The recoil forced each shot higher than the previous one. When I finally stopped squeezing, the damn gun was approaching the perpendicular. My bullets were like artillery shells, falling to earth way beyond the extent of my vision.

We moved on line to the location of Mr. Charles' crop-picking. As we did so, the radio crackled: "Lima, this is Six. What the hell's goin' on!?"

"Six, this is Lima. We spotted a Charlie in the open and fired him up."

"This is Six. I assume you got him with all that."

After a pause, I responded: "Well, uh, actually, he got away."

"Well, you nearly wiped us out here, Lima. Your rounds were whistling through our position."

Shit. The damn company laager site was in a line with us and the VC. The laager site was a click or so away. At that distance, M-16 rounds, even ones zipping through trees, still had plenty of oomph. "We didn't get anyone, did we?" I asked hesitantly.

"No, but it was a close thing. Alpha Six out."

Jerome didn't sound any too happy. I also detected a bit of grumbling in the platoon. The consensus seemed to be that I had made a tactical error. My new RTO even remonstrated with me gently. He was a big Jewish kid from Southern California who had attended UCLA for two years. He apparently didn't like the idea of gunning down an unsuspecting individual, forget the fact that Charlie rarely told U.S. troops, "Get ready, here I come."

The kid, Jensen, said, "We could have captured him alive, Sir."

"Maybe, but I was afraid we were walking into an ambush. Luring you into charging across an open field is a standard VC trick."

"I guess so, Sir, but I didn't like that."

Damn soft Americans. How were we supposed to win this frigging war if we weren't willing to do a little cold-blooded killing? But Jensen had a point. I didn't feel so good about the decision myself. We could have had a good chance of getting a live VC by having the rear fire team work its way up the tree line to the west. But as I said, hindsight is hindsight.

We got ourselves together and recommenced the journey to the company laager. We arrived before too long and were greeted with much ribbing about our shooting the hell out of the countryside. Lt. Roberts, who was somewhat on the serious side, had arrived with his platoon at the laager site before our little one-sided fire fight. He didn't do any kidding but told me that as soon as the firing ended he had ordered his troops to saddle up. He was convinced that Lima had walked into one horrendous ambush.

The resupply that night included an item I hadn't seen since I had come to the field, with the exception of my convalescent time and the two-night company stand-down. That item was beer. The resupply chopper brought enough for about one can per man. I scarfed mine down in nothing flat and then went prowling among the platoon for anyone who might not be drinking theirs. "Hey, any of you guys not drinkin' your beer?" This resulted in another couple of cans. I don't think any gave up his can because I was the platoon leader, but in hindsight—again hindsight—it was something I shouldn't have done. An officer asking for favors, no matter how minor, of his men is something that should be avoided as much as possible. But I did go to sleep that night with a mild welcomed buzz.

In the morning, we returned to the AO. Actually, we were already in Lima's AO as the company laager site was in the northwestern portion of it, but we split from our parent. When we left, we did so without Sgt. Brown. He was finally leaving the field. I regretted his departure, particularly since Sgt. Hikaey was taking his place. I envisioned a much more stressful, adversarial relationship with the good Hawaiian than I had enjoyed with Sgt. Brown. Moreover, I had a great deal of respect for Sgt. Brown's knowledge and instincts. My reliance on them had been a major reason that I had survived my first few weeks as a fresh-faced, minimally trained infantry platoon leader. I didn't accord Sgt. Hikaey's knowledge and instincts the same degree of respect.

We headed to the east side of the AO. The first few hundred meters were on a small trail through the jungle. We came then to a large open area. The trail went directly across it. I sent a fire team around the right side of the field, skirting the tree line, to guard against a possible ambush. When the fire team reached the point on the other side of the field where the trail reentered the woods, I led the platoon directly across the open area. We laagered that night in an abandoned housing site that had contained four or five dwellings. Only the frame poles were left.

The next day we headed southwest toward the rice-pig laager site and the scene of our fusillade at the live VC. I intended to once again go to the southern portion of the AO overlooking the wide plain. We started down the main north-south trail with the trees and hedgerow beside it when all of a sudden one of the troopers spotted a figure, a woman. We had been walking by these trees on the mound and in the adjacent trench for almost two weeks and had not taken a serious look. We did so now and discovered a whole damn clan had been right under our noses. Maybe not a whole clan, but there were at least two women and five children ranging in age from less than one year to probably about eight, and glory be, a military aged male in his late teens or early twenties. He might even have been the dude we had shot at two days before. The group had been living in underground hooches in the trees and bushes. We found enough clothes to support considerably more than the small group before us.

I reported the find to Jerome. After a bit, he instructed us to proceed toward our laager of the previous night. Near there we would meet up with a platoon from C Company and turn over the male. The C Company platoon, which was operating in an AO adjacent to ours, had a prisoner of their own. A chopper would pick them both up. We would keep the women and children for a pick-up later in the day. We packed up our entourage and headed northwest, along the main trail. For some reason, I was especially peeved at Doc this morning. The Vietnamese gave me an opportunity both to have Doc do something useful and to get him out of my immediate presence. I directed him to the rear of the column with instructions to take medical charge of our prisoners.

After a few minutes of plodding, I glanced behind me and who should be there but Doc. "What're you doin' here? I thought I told you to stay with the slopes."

"Sgt. Hikaey told me to come back up here, Sir."

Sgt. Hikaey!? As the platoon sergeant, his position was at the rear of the platoon, where the Vietnamese happened to be. But what was his problem with Doc being there? Maybe my case of the hips at the medic was contagious. "Well, goddammit, I told you to get with the Vietnamese. Now head on back there and tell Sgt. Hikaey I said so."

Christ. Dealing with this outfit was like running a family. We were definitely getting a little tired of each other. After a bit I looked back and saw that Doc was buried in the middle of the column. He either hadn't wanted to face Sgt. Hikaey again or had done so and been booted out. Whatever the case, he was trying to keep a low profile, out of harm's way. The situation was too exasperating to make an issue of, and I let it ride. We were about to make contact with C Company's platoon, anyway.

The Charlie Company platoon leader was a Lieutenant Cedric. I had never met him but had heard much. He was a ring-knocker, a West Pointer, and was highly thought of by the powers that be. He and several of his classmates had been featured in a national magazine. Jerome and Lt. Kline, November, had mentioned him in favorable terms on several occasions. Consequently, I disliked him even before I met him. And our first meeting did nothing to mitigate the pre-conceived opinion that I had formed.

We met up with Lt. Cedric and his boys in an open field. I was behind the lead fire team. Cedric came tromping down line, looking for the platoon leader. As much as it was possible to do in the field, he looked sharp. Web gear—belt and shoulder harness—were in place per regulation. He was about the only field soldier I saw in the 173rd who had insignia sewn on his uniform. Rank, infantry crossed rifles, CIB, jump wings, ranger tab, 173rd patch, they were all there. Just about everyone else had a blank uniform, no insignia at all. Approximately every three weeks, the resupply chopper deposited a pile of clean, but much worn, fatigues. We would paw through the pile to find a shirt and pants somewhat close to our size. Sometimes the shirt might have a few items on it and sometimes not. But the bottom line was that you couldn't tell from looking at a 173rd infantry company in late 1967 who had what rank.

Except for my glasses, I was especially unidentifiable. Glasses were not as common among the enlisted troopers as they were among the company grade officers—the lieutenants and captains. Must be something sociological there. Concerning web gear, I had become as experimental as the most untamed trooper. A belt with a canteen and rifle cleaning kit, a first aid shoulder bag with fragmentation and smoke grenades, and crossed bandoleers with M-16 magazines had become my standard apparel. I looked like a four-eyed Pancho Villa.

So soldierly looking Lt. Cedric came strolling down Lima's strung-out line, looking for his counterpart. He strolled by me with hardly a glance. Such an unconventional approach to Army gear obviously could not be on the person of the platoon leader. The RTO behind me and my glasses might have given him pause, but he was much too certain of what an officer should look like to suspect that this renegade was the Man. I watched him go, relishing the moment. The rebel in me reveled in not looking like an officer. I was an old Vietnam hand, and now a grunt at that. Still looking for Lieutenant Dudley Do-Right, Cedric eventually arrived at the end of the platoon. Someone directed him back toward the front. In a short time, he was hesitantly approaching me. "You the platoon leader?" he asked suspiciously.

"Lieutenant Holland here. There's your prisoner back there."

Cedric's distaste was ill-concealed. He didn't linger. The officer corps was obviously going to hell in a hand basket. Besides, I had shown him up by letting him traipse the length of the platoon without identifying myself. His troopers took control of our male VC and some documents that had been amongst the clothes we had found, and departed. Neither the departing VC nor the women and children staying with us displayed any unhappiness or fear. Maybe they were just an exceptionally stoic bunch.

After Lt. Strac—"Strac" being a term from the 1950s and 60s meaning A No. 1, per regulation, meeting the highest standards—and his boys left, we proceeded to the area of abandoned and largely dismantled huts that we had laagered at the previous night. The women and children made themselves at home, too much at home to suit me. I was anxious to have them out of there. They were a burden, a distraction, and would be a real hindrance if we ran into any of their armed brethren. Consequently, I spent the afternoon bugging Alpha Six about their presence. Finally, toward evening, a chopper picked them up. Given the nonchalant, knowledgeable way they scrambled into the Huey, even the youngest walker, I suspected this was not their first encounter with the dreaded Americans. Hell, in a month or so they might even be back in their hedgerow.

We spent an uneventful evening. The next day I sent Sgt. Baum's squad on a patrol to the vicinity of our pig-rice, fired-up-VC laager site. We were definitely making ourselves at home in the AO. After the squad left, I took the other squad leader, Sgt. Winters, a 19- or 20-year old black kid who had taken Sgt. Hikaey's squad leader position, on a little reconnaissance romp. Winters was a sharp guy and seemed to be quickly acquiring control of his squad. We first went east to select an ambush site for the evening. Jerome was on us again to split up at night. We found an old north-south trail, and I suggested he just dig a shallow hole in the middle of it, aim the M-60 in one direction and most of the M-16s in the other, and wait to get stumbled upon.

Winters was skeptical about plopping down squarely on the trail and about having to dig in. I told him the exact location was his choice, but I wanted him to be sure to throw up a little dirt. After reconning the ambush site, we went on a two-man patrol of our own. We circled around the laager site where Winter's squad, Sgt. Hikaey, and the platoon headquarters folks were. We were without a radio, a violation of standard operating procedure. No individual, fire team, squad, or whatever was ever suppose to go anywhere without communication. But we were young and foolish.

We checked out a fairly extended area around the laager site. Much of it consisted of overgrown fields. There was one large thicket, however, that we spent some time exploring. It was probably a good 200 meters by 200 meters, and I was convinced that it was harboring at least a few VC. We criss-crossed it several times, crawling as much as walking, but turned up nothing.

Finally, after three or so hours of playing cowboys and Indians, we returned to the laager site. Fortunately, Alpha Six hadn't been trying to contact me. Sgt. Baum and his squad came in a little bit later and presented me with another family squabble, one that contained a real element of insubordination. It seems that on the squad's patrol, PFC Randolph, the guy who didn't want to go into the leeches a few weeks previously, had decided to follow his own route. According to Baum, Randolph had walked off to the side of the squad column, varying his distance from ten to thirty meters. Baum had ordered him to get in the column but Randolph had refused.

I called Randolph over: "What's this about you not stayin' in line?"

"It was dangerous, Sir. We shoulda' been more spread out. We was walking in the open and I wanted to be near the trees."

In theory, Randolph had a point. Crossing open areas in squad column formation was not a good idea. Other formations were better for that type of vegetation and terrain. With few exceptions, however, we rarely did anything different than column formation. The easiest way was the most commonly employed, by a long shot. I had trouble imagining the situation, with the squad in column except for Randolph, who was diddle-bopping off to the side.

"Now look. Your squad leader ordered you to be at a certain place. You disobeyed a direct order. You realize that?" I didn't know whether Randolph was exceptionally smart or exceptionally dumb. He had a backwoods, southern black accent that made it easy to conclude he was dumber than dirt. In addition, he always had a stupid-looking, shit-eating grin on his face, which added to the perception one got that he was more than a bit thick. But somehow this border-line insubordination act of his made me think he might not fit the stereotype.

"I don't want this to happen again, Randolph. Your squad leader tells you something, you do it. Got that?" There was a pause. "I said, you got that soldier?"

"Yes Sir," was his eventual reply. I felt damn sorry for Baum. He was having a tough go of it. After Randolph left, I tried to buck up the young sergeant, telling him to keep at it, that he was doing a good job. He was a nice kid who should have been in college instead of in the frigging jungle. But he was a paratrooper, a volunteer, and this is where he wanted to be. I just wished he had a more compliant bunch under him.

Another night passed uneventfully. Winters' squad was on the ambush, the rest of the platoon at the abandoned dwelling site. Early the next morning we got a call from the company to conduct a search for an alleged VC hospital. The location was just over the border of Lima's AO, to the west, somewhere on a mountain. An intelligence report gave the hospital a high likelihood of being there. So we saddled up, at least most of us. I decided to make this just a day excursion. Lugging full packs somewhere on the whim of some wild-eyed intelligence officer had happened too often to this child. We would leave the packs at the laager site under the guard of a fire team and return before nightfall.

It was only a few clicks to the mountain. If we had headed directly west we would have almost gone through the company laager site. For several reasons, I didn't want to do this. One was just the general aversion to being around a higher headquarters. Another was that we had been out several days and consequently had scruffy beards. Jerome liked the clean-shaven look, or at least no more than a day's growth. And finally, the headquarters and Weapons Platoon boys were getting jumpy. A sniper had put a few rounds in their direction the previous day or so, probably not so much to cause any damage as to shut up the yammering and the soul music from the songsters in Oscar. As a result of this little contact with the enemy, the headquarters group and Oscar were spread out over the company laager site in a mood of extreme trigger-happiness. I didn't want to be within their range.

So I set a course to the south, giving the company a wide berth. The route traversed a patch of woods that we had looked at only briefly thus far in our stay in the AO. The patch was just to the northwest of the pig-rice laager site. And lo and behold, damned if we didn't find a hut, with evidence of recent occupation. It might have been the residence of Fired-Up, but he wasn't home. I called it in, and we tried burning it, but the material was pretty green. We just left it with a singed look.

We proceeded and eventually arrived at the mountain. Because we were in the jungle, we couldn't actually see the thing. The rising ground was what told us we were at the destination. According to the map, the mountain was a U-shaped piece of terrain. We were at one of the ends of the U. The first thing was to get on top. The slopes and top were covered with thick vegetation. The slopes were also steep. A sort of straight-line cut in the vegetation went directly up a side. I was suspicious of such an obvious man-made gap. It could be a firing lane for an automatic weapon. The hill was too steep for someone to design a path straight up. Initially, we tried zigzagging up the slope to the right of the cut. The undergrowth was too thick for easy progress, however, so I cast caution to the wind and took the cleared area. We had to go hands over feet, pulling and clawing to keep from loosing ground. We gained the top without incident, but a well-placed RPD, a machine gun of the VC and NVA, would have about demolished the platoon.

The top was deserted, with no sign of habitation or even visitation. As we started following the ridge on its curving course, however, I thought I detected an odor of medicinal alcohol. The odor became stronger as we proceeded. I asked if anyone else smelled it and got mostly shrugs. I started sending a few troopers a little ways down the hillside. A cave entrance might lead to an underground hospital. But we found nothing. We followed the U all the way to the other side and returned, making frequent forays down the slopes. No hospital, no recent signs of Victor Charlies, but for me, plenty of medicine odor. Eventually, it was time to head back to the laager site. I told Alpha Six that we hadn't found anything, but that the mountain had a strong medicinal odor. I gave my expert opinion that a hospital was indeed in the area. Alpha Six seemed uninterested.

Our return trip to the platoon laager was quiet. The fire team left behind had seen no VC, probably because the troopers had spent most of the day sleeping. To reiterate, sleep was a precious commodity to a grunt, something to be embraced whenever possible.

One incident during our stay in the AO exemplified the importance of small things to the infantryman. Sgt. Brown was pretty good at keeping track of the small things. I hadn't acquired his knack by the time he departed, and the relationship between myself and Sgt. Hikaey was such that I wasn't ready to rely on him to the same extent as I had on Sgt. Brown.

The squads had been following the procedure of alternating responsibilities for particular types of missions. For example, if the first squad had an ambush patrol, the next ambush patrol would be handled by the second squad. This system had worked fairly well until we began the bushwacker operations. Then the many squad-size operations—daytime patrols, nighttime ambushes—began to cause some problems. A squad on daytime patrol might also have the nighttime ambush.

So I rather arbitrarily changed the procedure to alternate squads without regard to the mission. That is, instead of alternating squads per particular type of mission, I tried alternating for each succeeding mission. For example, if the first squad had a daytime patrol, the next mission, say a nighttime ambush, would be by the second squad. The theory was to keep a squad from having to do consecutive missions while the other squad sat on its duff.

Well, good theory does not necessarily equal good action. Maybe the idea would have worked out better if I had taken the time to explain it to the squad leaders—Baum and Winters—and Sgt. Hikaey. But I just began following the new method without much of an explanation. It wasn't many days before I detected some grumbling. Sgt. Hikaey approached me one afternoon: "Sir, the men are confused by the way you're assigning patrols and ambushes."

"How's that, Sarge?"

"Well, they think you should be alternating patrols. But sometimes the same squad has two patrols in a row."

So I tried to explain my system and my reasoning. I even took out my little notebook and showed him the record I kept of which squad did what. But he was skeptical. And I had to admit to myself that sometimes the new way of doing things was no less burdensome on a squad than the old way. A squad might catch a long patrol, the next squad might have an easy ambush, and the first squad might catch another long patrol. Still, I saw some advantages to my way of doing things. And the fact that Sgt. Hikaey was questioning it just dug in my heels. The matter was left a bit up in the air, with me not retreating in appearance but in fact being a little more attentive to who did what.

The platoon stayed together the night after we returned from the wild goose chase to find a hospital. The laager site was astride a trail, so there was a slight chance we might have some action. I had begun enforcing a policy of limited air mattress use. A full or even partially full mattress was a noisy sonuvabitch. Each twist and turn of the body produced a loud movement of air among the mattress' chambers. I was convinced the noise could be heard 100 or more meters away. Thus the normal nighttime tossing and turning could be revealing our position. In addition, we had several snorers who could wake the dead. To reduce our noise signature, I had ordered that while on these bushwacker operations only a minimum of air be blown into the mattresses. No tight squeaky mattresses, and no partially full mattresses acting as bellows. The troopers weren't too happy with the policy. It and my propensity for digging probably made me not the most popular platoon leader around.

On this particular night, I came down with an hellacious case of diarrhea. I don't know what brought it on, but it was severe. I spent most of the night at the edge of the platoon headquarters' shallow trench, bent over clutching my gut. When I had to go, which was frequently, I walked about ten meters out into the field, squatted, let the liquid flow, wiped the rawness, and struggled back.

Keeping me company for a good while was Eugene Washington, spec. 4, the platoon sergeant's RTO. This night he was in a talkative mood, which was a good thing because I wasn't. He was a Vietnam old-timer, having been in country for close to nine months. Thus he was getting short. As I sat on the edge of the hole enduring the periodic gut-grabbing pains, Washington rambled. He had been through Junction City, seen a fair amount of action, gotten shot at. He talked about A Company's activities during that operation, about the casualties that the unit had taken. He also talked about his mother back in the states. He evidently had a close relationship with her and missed her.

My end of the conversation was mostly "uhs" and "uh-huhs," punctuated by frequent trips to the field to relieve myself. I didn't pay a whole lot of attention until he began talking about how short he was and about how he was going to make it. "I got through Junction City, Sir. They're not going to get me now."

This kind of talk bothered me. Practically every war movie I'd ever seen, practically every war novel I'd ever read, had a guy who swore he was going to make it home. The guy always died. Infantrymen needed to be fatalistic. The feeling of almost certain death that I'd experienced when my branch transfer came through, and again later when I'd first joined the 173rd, had subsided somewhat. Survival can make you cocky, and I had survived for a time, but I still wasn't thinking about the future. The infantryman's life was day-to-day, and that was how I was trying to take it. Washington was violating the infantryman's unspoken code—don't speak of the future. I didn't have an instant, fist-in-the-gut foreboding about Washington, but his confidence made me uneasy.

I survived the night, and the diarrhea subsided towards dawn. After a few hours sleep, I was ready for another day in Lima's own personal AO. The place was becoming our home. A few more weeks criss-crossing it and there would be few nooks and crannies we hadn't visited. But homes are meant to be left, and our time in the area, indeed in the coastal mountains of Tuy Hoa Province, was drawing to a close. To the west, on the far side of Vietnam, in one of the country's remotest corners, the 173rd Airborne Brigade's meeting with destiny, and tragedy, was about to be called to order.

We had a few more days of comparatively carefree existence. One morning we even found tiger tracks—unbelievably huge imprints that caused me to envision a prehistoric sabertooth. Then it was time for a resupply rendezvous with the rest of the company. Jerome had called for the resupply at a new site. He was apparently tired of getting harassed by marauding VC at the old place. By this time, the locals probably had the names and serial numbers of every member of the headquarters group and Oscar. So on the morning of the rendezvous, Jerome moved his boys to the west, into Mike's AO. The new company laager was to be just off the main east-west trail that crossed through the center of the AOs of each of the platoons and that went right by Lima's pig-rice, fired-up VC laager site. We passed by that old place on the way and proceeded on the trail into Mike's

AO. We were easing cautiously along—I didn't like the trail here because the undergrowth was thick and encroaching, good ambush territory—when the radio came alive. "Lima, this is Alpha Six!"

Jerome was not his usual laconic self. I responded: "Six, this is Lima."

"This is Six! Return immediately to the old company laager! We are to be picked up there!"

"This is Lima. Understand that we are to go to the old laager site? That we are leaving?"

"This is Alpha Six! Get a move on! We are to be extracted pronto!"

Nothing like a cryptic instruction given in an excited voice to get one's blood pumping. I turned the platoon around and began retracing our steps. It wasn't long before we were approaching the old company laager site. And all hell was breaking loose.

Several Hueys, one of them the battalion commander's, were buzzing the treetops. Lima was the first platoon to return. Alpha Six was trying to talk to me on the radio, but I couldn't hear much because of the noise of the choppers. I did get the impression that the battalion commander had seen several VC checking out the laager site and was trying to chase them down from the air. And he was relaying instructions to me through Alpha Six. I yelled into the mike, "Six, this is Lima! I can't hear what you're saying! The choppers need to back off!"

Jerome probably couldn't hear me either, however, because the chopper noise was likely all that was going out from my transmissions. As best I could, I made the platoon aware that VC stragglers were probably checking out the laager site. We spread out and swept over the area as I kept pleading with Jerome to get the choppers away. They were preventing us from hearing the radio, noises in the woods, and each other. The scene was pretty damn close to chaos. The headquarters group, Oscar, and the other two rifle platoons appeared shortly. It was a wonder we didn't blow each other away, the battalion CO didn't start firing into our midst, or some irritated trooper didn't put a few rounds in the choppers' direction. The interest in the VC didn't last, however. This struck me as unusual. A live VC was such a rare commodity that much effort was usually expended in chasing one down. But bigger matters were on the agenda.

A second unusual thing was that we were picked up by a Chinook, the big two-bladed choppers that could carry thirty or so troopers at a time. Chinooks were not commonly used to insert or extract troopers from unsecured or semi-secured areas. These jobs were left to the Hueys. But here was this big ol' Chinook plopping down in a field adjacent to which Victor Charlies had just been galavantin'. Moreover, the other side of the field was hostile territory—unsecured, in other words. The whole damn company was clustered in one little corner with instructions to pile on anything flying. Haste had taken total precedence over normal security procedures.

The Chinooks shortly had the company on the way to the Tuy Hoa airfield. The VC were left to forage through the company laager site at their leisure. The Americans were leaving the area for another hunting ground.

Dak To, And A New Job

At the Tuy Hoa airfield, Jerome gave us a quick briefing. The North Vietnamese were charging over the border near a place called Dak To, a small dot on the map close to the point where South Vietnam, Laos, and Cambodia came together. The terrain was remote, mountainous, and jungle-covered with practically no roads. The brigade had operated there during the summer, in the rainy season. It had been a miserable time that I had heard much about. The unceasing wetness had made the mountain trails a nightmare. Two steps forward were followed by a step-and-a-half slide to the rear. The brigade's summer sojourn at Dak To had also resulted in one of the largest massacres of U.S. troops in the whole Vietnam War. Almost 80 paratroopers, more than two platoons' worth, died one June day. Surprisingly, however, except for this one incident, contact had been light, just weeks and months of humping the steep muddy trails.

Jerome said that the 173rd's 4th Battalion, which had remained in the Dak To area when the 1st and 2nd Battalions came to Tuy Hoa in September, had made heavy contact with a sizeable North Vietnamese force. Reinforcements—the 1st and 2nd Battalions—were being rushed in. We would fly by C-130 across Vietnam to Kontum, a distance of about 125 miles. From Kontum it was about a 35-mile chopper ride to Dak To.

The news and mission had barely registered when Jerome made another announcement, one that concerned me particularly. He was bringing Lt. Wayman, the company executive officer, to the field. Wayman had been the XO for almost six months and was extremely anxious to get his bush time. And another lieutenant, Kane, was joining the company. He was to take November, the 3rd Platoon. Lt. Kline, he of the endless enthusiasm, Ft. Benning procedures, and by-the-book equipment wear, was to go to the rear as the XO. Wayman was to have Lima, my platoon. I was to go to Oscar, the Weapons Platoon, which had been without a platoon leader for the several weeks since Lt. Monroe had gone to the battalion staff.

One consequence of the moves was that the company would have a full complement of officers for the coming encounter with the North Vietnamese Army. It was a shame, however, that Lt. Kline was going to the rear. He was the most competent and conscientious platoon leader of the lot of us. He had been shepherding November for six months with hardly a hostile encounter. And now he was about to miss one of the most substantial encounters of the entire war. Ah, the fickle finger of fate. On the other hand, as conscientious as he was, he might have gotten his butt killed performing some chore that a lesser platoon leader would have let slide or delegated to others. Over the next few weeks, a number of conscientious competent company grade officers of the 173rd ran out of time and luck.

At the conclusion of Jerome's briefing, I walked with my new platoon sergeant, Sergeant First Class, E-7, Thurmond, over to the Weapons Platoon. I wasn't particularly upset about leaving Lima. I was still in the field, and that's what counted. My taste of the hardships and dangers of the grunt's life hadn't yet persuaded me that I should be elsewhere. Nevertheless, I was a little apprehensive about being the Weapons Platoon leader. My knowledge of what was required as the leader of a rifle platoon had been abysmal when I had taken over Lima, but at least I had played a lot of cowboys and Indians as a kid. I had never played anything that prepared me for the technical aspects of the mortar, however.

Fortunately, Alpha Company's Weapons Platoon needed little from its platoon leader, or its platoon sergeant for that matter. I was to discover that the platoon essentially ran itself. It had barely 15 members—and only one mortar—but those 15 were the most self-motivated group of soldiers that I encountered during my two and a half years in Vietnam. They weren't perfect, and they were to make a few mistakes in the days ahead, but they had a unique capacity to analyze their own actions and discern where improvements could be made, and they never ceased striving to make those improvements.

But on this day about all I knew of the platoon was that it and the company headquarters contingent seemed to have about zero noise discipline. While the rifle platoons had been sneaking around on the bushwacker operations, Oscar and the headquarters people had been sitting in one place, screeching away at each other. Early on, someone in the Weapons Platoon even had a cassette deck, but after one-too-many sniper rounds, Jerome had banned it.

When Sgt. Thurmond and I got to the platoon, he announced the changes and turned it over to me. I summarized what we were about, stated that I was a babe in the woods as far as the mortar was concerned, and in general tried to convey the impression that it was to be business as usual, except I would like for them to lower the decibel level a little. Because I had been in the company for awhile, I was somewhat of a known quality to them. Not having screwed up too badly or been openly incompetent, I was probably viewed as acceptable.

Dak To, And A New Job 135

My first indication about the character of the group came while we were still at the Tuy Hoa airfield waiting for the C-130s to take us to Kontum. We were given a resupply of C-rations. As per standard procedure, we unpacked what we wanted and left the cardboard boxes and outer containers in a disorderly pile on the concrete. We were lounging around on the concrete and on heaps of cargo when Lt. Monroe, the former platoon leader and now S-3 Air of the battalion, delivered a message from the battalion executive officer, a hard bitten old major. He wanted the mess policed up and thrown in some nearby large trash receptacle. I said something like, "Yeah, sure," and continued with my lounging. I wasn't about to jump out of my ass for Monroe's benefit.

Well, a short time later, above the continuous sounds of aircraft of all sorts taking off and landing, came a roar of extraordinary force: "HOLLAND, YOU WERE TOLD TO GET THE GODDAMN TRASH CLEANED UP!"

I immediately sprang up from my semi-nap—the state of the resting grunt—and searched for the source of the attack on my well-being. The major was standing beside a jeep a good 50 meters away. Lt. Monroe was near him, not looking any too happy. Monroe's life probably took a turn for the worse when he left the dangers of the field for the major's tender presence. Before I had a chance to get my heart out of my throat, Harold Campton, Sergeant E-5, said, "Let's go mortars. Let's get this mess cleaned up." And the entire Weapons Platoon was shortly scrambling around, making the area airborne presentable.

Thus I was introduced to Oscar. The initiative displayed on the concrete that afternoon was unusual. The normal group of troopers would have waited for me to regain my composure and give an order. But these guys were way ahead of the action. They had little need for detailed supervision.

The small platoon of 15 had five primary leaders, although most of the 15 were leaders of sorts. Sgt. Thurmond, a black, was the platoon sergeant. Like me, he was largely superfluous. His good point was that he realized it and let the platoon operate pretty much as it desired. His bad point was that he was one of those lifers who'd had enough of these games in the woods. He had been a young soldier in Korea, had remained in the Army, in the airborne, but had acquired that deflator of a combat attitude, a family. Back home in Fayetteville, North Carolina, the location of Ft. Bragg and the 82nd Airborne, he had a wife and several kids. The fact that his profession could lead to his death caused him much greater concern now than it had in his youth.

Next on the platoon totem pole was an E-6, Staff Sergeant Berkley. Like Sgt. Thurmond, Sgt. Berkley was an old timer and black. Sgt. Berkley was not a bit shaky about his profession and situation, however. Indeed, he seemed to revel in them. In theory, he was the section chief of the team that actually fired the weapon. In practice, he left the gun to the younger troopers, limiting himself to general guidance. If not the strongest soldier in A Company, Sgt. Berkley was damn close to it. He had a balding head but a massively muscled body. Back in the world, he did some heavy duty lifting. He carried the largest, heaviest rucksack in the company. In his luggage was even an extra set of jungle fatigues. No one else I knew of carried extra clothes. He probably also had his gas mask, making him and Lt. Kline the only two members of the company ready for chemical warfare. Topping the load off were the two mortar rounds that most members of the platoon carried. Each round was about ten pounds of dead weight. The platoon's basic load was about sixty rounds. The platoon itself carried about half the load, with each trooper carrying two, except for the platoon sergeant and platoon leader. When I joined the platoon, the practice was for the platoon sergeant and platoon leader to carry one round each. The remaining mortar rounds were spread over the two rifle platoons not on point for the day.

The active leadership of the platoon came from three young troopers, two of whom were sergeant E-5s, and one of whom was a spec. 4. Harold Campton, the initiator of the airfield cleanup, was one of the E-5s. His official position was second in command of the gun crew, but in fact he was pretty close to being the real leader of the platoon. A black, he had a couple of years at a black college in the east. He was apparently a superb athlete and had been a quarterback on the football team. Outgoing, quick-witted, highly intelligent, a natural leader, Harold Campton was in sum an extraordinary individual.

Sergeant Jeff Williams was a young white guy. He was the chief of the support section. In truth, the difference between the support section and the gun crew was not all that clear. The platoon only had one mortar, a considerable shortfall from the standard of, I believe, three. Most of the platoon members could perform all of the duties associated with firing the mortar, with the exception of operating the fire direction center. Williams kept track of administrative and logistical matters. He also personally lugged the mortar base plate, probably the heaviest piece of the gun.

The final member of the platoon leadership was Spec. 4 James Truman, a white guy from Georgia. Truman was the operator of the fire direction center. In a full-fledged artillery unit, the fire direction was a big time operation, with a number of individuals making various calculations. In an 81mm mortar platoon, however, the fire direction center was simply a large, unwieldy plastic-covered circular board, about three feet in diameter. It had a movable arm that could rotate 360 degrees. By using various tables and the board, the operator could transform the location of the gun and the location of the target into elevation and azimuth settings for the gun and into powder bag numbers for the ammunition. The board was carried in a large canvas bag. Truman was an outgoing guy, second only to Harold Campton in sharpness, although he himself probably would never concede first place. He and Camp engaged in a perpetual competitive but friendly banter, each striving to be the verbal king of the castle. As the platoon fire direction center, Truman controlled information, which is power.

Other platoon notables included "Pinhead" Clemons, the Rican, Gene Timmons, Doc, and Will. Clemons was a black guy, a primary member of the gun crew, and like Truman, from Georgia. Back in the World, they were from different worlds. In Vietnam, they were each an important cog in the small, closed environment of Alpha Company's Weapons Platoon. The Rican was from Spanish Harlem, with the fast mouth of the street-wise New Yorker. Timmons was another southern white guy. He often served as my RTO, although the position was rotated occasionally. Doc, the platoon medic, was a southern black guy. He was about five feet six inches but built like a fireplug. He had big stubby fingers that you wouldn't suspect could do the delicate work that medics were often required to do. He could probe, stitch, and bandage with a touch of an artist, however. Will was another southern black guy. He was on the gun crew but also served as the platoon sergeant's RTO.

Of the platoon's 15 or so members, only four—myself, Sgt. Williams, Truman, and Timmons—were white. One idiosyncrasy was that most of the platoon members wore their helmets backwards. This originated from the difficulty of peering in the mortar sight with the helmet in the normal position. The platoon had apparently adopted the backwards helmet as its signature.

The gun was the platoon's reason for being. It was an 81mm mortar, a high trajectory weapon that in effect lobbed shells. It consisted of a base plate, an outer ring in which the base plate sat and could pivot, the gun tube, and a bipod on which the upper end of the gun tube rested. The bipod was attached to the gun tube by a ring that screwed onto the tube, which had screw threads on its outer side for its entire length. Each of the four gun parts was a heavy, bulky, awkward-to-carry piece of equipment. With the exception of the base plate, which was usually carried by Williams, the gun pieces were rotated among the platoon members for carrying.

Three other components of the gun system were the aiming stakes, the sight, and the fire direction center board. Four aiming stakes, each about five feet in height and painted in red and white bands, were used in pairs. Two would be placed on an azimuth—a compass reading—from the gun. This known reading provided the starting point to aim the gun on any azimuth. The aiming was accomplished by calculating the difference between the desired azimuth and the azimuth to the aiming stakes, setting the adjustable sight for this difference, or deflection, and then lining up the two aiming stakes with the vertical hair in the sight. To prevent blind spots, two pairs of aiming stakes were used. If the gun tube prevented one pair of aiming stakes from being seen through the sight, the deflection could be calculated for the other pair of stakes.

The sight was attached to the bipod near where the latter was in turn attached to the gun tube. For a given target, elevation and deflection readings were calculated on the fire direction board and set on the sight. When the hair in the sight was lined up with the aiming stacks, the gun was allegedly zeroed on the target. Lining up the sight and aiming stakes, however, was no mean task. The effort began with the bipod. Once it was attached to the gun tube, the bipod could be picked up and moved around, rotating the tube on its base for a full 360 degrees. The bipod could also be moved closer to the tube, thus increasing the tube's elevation.

Once the tube was roughly in position, further changes in elevation and deflection could be made by turning two handles on the bipod. A single trooper turned the handles simultaneously, attempting to keep the sight hair lined up with the aiming stakes as he did so. Levels on the sight also had to be kept plum. Setting elevation and deflection readings on the sight, lining the gun up, and making the final adjustments constituted a process requiring at least a modicum of dexterity and considerable practice.

And as if the process was not already complicated enough, there was the ammunition. Each of the two-feet, ten-pound rounds had small powder bags around stabilizing fins at the round's rear. The bags resembled tea bags. The more bags, the greater the explosive force expelling the round from the tube. If the target was close in, only one or two bags would be used, depending on the gun's elevation. Excess bags were easily torn off. When he gave his instructions for a particular target, the fire direction board operator gave three variables: elevation, azimuth, and number of powder bags.

The mortar was actually fired by dropping a round down the tube, fin-first of course. The base of the round, containing a primer, hit a nail-like firing pin at the bottom of the tube. The exploding primer almost simultaneously ignited the powder bags, and the round was on its way, too fast for the naked eye to catch anything more than brief blur. A safety in the head of the round allegedly kept the round from arming until it had gone a certain distance from the mortar, but rightly or wrongly the troopers put no great faith in the device.

As with most things military, the firing of the mortar was supposed to be done according to a standard procedure. The location of the target was given to the fire direction operator. The location could come from a number of sources, including a rifle platoon leader, sergeant, or trooper, the company commander, the artillery forward observer, or the mortar platoon leader or platoon sergeant. In theory, Oscar was supposed to have enough people for several forward observer teams of its own, but theory had been abandoned long before my arrival. As noted, Alpha Company barely had sufficient troopers to man one measly gun.

When he had made his calculations, the fire direction operator called out the settings to the gun crew. The leader of the gun crew repeated the settings. The gunner in turn repeated the settings as he was making them on the weapon. When the gunner had made the settings and aligned the gun on the aiming stakes, he called, "Gun Up." The gun crew leader was then supposed to verify the settings and the alignment of the gun with the aiming stakes. This verification step was frequently skipped. As the gunner was attending to the settings and the sight alignment, an assistant gunner was removing the appropriate number of powder bags. He then handed the round to the actual firer, who verified the number of bags. At this point, the gun crew leader gave a command such as "Round in the Tube." The gunner placed the base, or fin end, of the round in the top of the tube. The gun crew leader then gave the command, "Fire." The gunner let go of the round, and gravity took over. When the round was fired, the gunner and others in the firing area averted their faces. This certainly wouldn't have done much to prevent major damage in the event of a premature explosion, but it might preclude minor facial damage by some bit of metal flung loose in the firing process.

A number of things can go wrong with toys that go bang. Probably the most feared thing regarding the mortar—other than an explosion by the round in the tube or just as it was exiting, an event no use worrying about because those in the immediate vicinity would have no chance of surviving it—was a "hang fire." This was a round that didn't leave the tube. It either did not fall down the tube to hit the firing pin, or it did hit the firing pin but the primer failed to detonate. When a hang fire occurred, the first procedure was for the gunner to face away from the tube and give it a backward kick with the bottom of his foot. This was designed to dislodge a round that had become stuck on the way down, allowing it to fall to the firing pin and, it was hoped, exit the tube under its own power.

If the kick didn't work, things got dicey. The mortar was allowed to sit for a few moments. The round might have struck the firing pin but be undergoing some sort of delayed reaction. Conceivably it could "cook off" and come booming out of the tube on its merry way. Assuming there was no cook off, however, the gun crew began gingerly disconnecting the tube from the base plate. One trooper then joined his thumbs and forefingers over the mouth of the tube, not over the center but around the edges. The base of the tube was raised upward, causing the mouth to pivot downward, the pivot point being the bipod, which was still attached to the tube. If all went well, the round slid toward the mouth of the tube, being stopped by the trooper's thumbs and forefingers. He caught the round before it could protrude from the tube enough to release the safety device. Assuming no explosion thus far, the round, with safety device locked in the safety position by the trooper, was allowed to slide all the way out of the tube. The trooper then cradled it in his arms and carried it well away from the area.

Regarding setting up, the mortar was practically always positioned within the company perimeter, usually near the center. It needed an open area with no tree branches to deflect the rounds or cause them to prematurely detonate. Oftentimes, trees had to be cut to get the proper clearance. Standard procedure was to dig a hole for the mortar. The hole was a circular affair about two feet deep and about eight feet in diameter. This was a lot of dirt to move, requiring considerable pick and shovel work. Incidentally, the major digging implements of the company were not the standard Army entrenching tools but full size picks and D-handle shovels. Each platoon had several shovels and at least one pick. There were plenty of entrenching tools, but the heavy work was done with the D-handles and picks.

On that hot November day on the concrete of the Tuy Hoa airfield, the various personalities of Oscar and the procedures of the mortar's operation were largely unknown to me. They were things I was to learn in the days and weeks ahead. Shortly after the trash incident, a C-130 pulled up. We boarded, a scruffy bunch of grunts, the flesh and blood tip of the American military's high tech spear. We sprawled around the interior of the plane, laying back on our packs. The hot glare of the airfield disappeared as the rear ramp rose. The C-130's engines powered up. Soon we were roaring down the runway, the plane lurching and bouncing before becoming airborne. The date was November 7, 1967, and the 1st Battalion (Airborne), 503rd Infantry, 173rd Airborne Brigade (Separate), was on the way to Dak To, Republic of Vietnam.

The flight was short, less than a hour. The approach to many airfields in Vietnam was not a gradual descent. Instead, the plane stayed as high as it could for as long as it could, and then dove. The idea was to avoid flying low over enemy or contested terrain. Airfields in the Central Highlands were the locations for especially aggressive practices of this tactic. Many of the fields were in valleys surrounded by extensive mountain ridges. The prudent course was to stay as far above these mountains as possible. Hence flying into a Central Highlands airfield was a stomach-in-your-throat experience. We were alerted to our imminent arrival by a gut-churning plunge of several thousand feet.

Kontum was a dusty mountain village, the capital of Kontum province. The airfield was much more rudimentary than Tuy Hoa's. The field was paved, but the acres of concrete that existed at more developed locations weren't present. Much of the apron area was PCP—large steel sheets with many regularly spaced holes. The buildings were minimal. The field did not handle jet fighter-bombers, which cut down considerably on the required infrastructure.

Trucks were waiting for us. They shuttled the company, and the other companies and units of the 1st Battalion, to a laager site about a quarter-mile from the airfield. The site was an area of pathetic bushes and scraggly grass. The rainy season was long over, and a fine film of red dust covered almost everything. Since rain wasn't expected, no one put up hooches. Jerome held a short meeting, announcing that choppers would be taking us to Dak To, about 35 miles to the north, in the morning. After a few other administrative matters, he implied that we were free for the evening. Or at least he didn't say we weren't.

As the night unfolded, Jerome undoubtedly came to regret this state of uncertainty. Except for the two-night standdown some weeks earlier in Tuy Hoa, this evening was the company's first period out of the field in some time. And unlike the Tuy Hoa standdown, this evening in Kontum was unstructured—no hooches in a line, no orders to clean weapons and gear, no showers, not even a hot meal. Without really being aware of it, I was primed for a bout with debauchery. The many weeks with practically no alcohol meant a drunken spree was overdue. And the change of platoons left me with an attitude of no responsibility. I had felt that Lima needed constant supervision, and if I had still been with Lima, what came to pass that night might not have. Even though I had been the leader of the Weapons Platoon for only hours, I had already developed the impression that they needed little supervision. So when Harold Campton and the boys started heading to the nearby main road and Sgt. Thurmond said "Let's go grab a beer, Sir," I was on the way.

The road was a semi-paved, rutted affair. The village of Kontum began about a quarter of a mile away. Before the buildings began, however, we came upon several road-side stands selling beer, Ba-Moui-Ba, the Vietnamese variety. The bottles were in dark-looking water in rusty metal tubs. Tired blocks of ice cooled the brew somewhat. Despite the suggestion of dirt and disease and the lack of decor, it was close to the best damn beer I have ever had, before or since. I downed about three in the quarter of a mile to town.

Kontum resembled nothing so much as a wild-west cow town. The place was fortunate in that Alpha Company's Weapons Platoon seemed to be the only group of field soldiers on the streets. The remainder of the 1st Battalion either hadn't been given the freedom to wander or weren't taking advantage of it. No large U.S. base was in the area and consequently there were no hoards of bar-hopping rear-echelon Americans. The local U.S. contingent consisted mostly of provincial advisers and airfield personnel. The town was also fortunate in that we had left our weapons back at the laager site.

Naturally, the first building on the street into town was a bar. We stopped and had a few more beers. By this time, I was drunker than nine dogs, fourteen cows, and a chicken, to use a popular, at least with me, expression. The weeks of C-rations, the dropped pounds, left me with little tolerance for alcohol. I was on my butt. It was an aggressive, looking-for-trouble drunk.

The next stop was a barber shop. Haircuts in the field were an occasional thing. A barber shop was adjacent to the bar, and it seemed like a good idea to get a little trim. Sgt. Thurmond had close-cropped hair, almost, but not quite, shaved. In my drunkenness, I thought it would be nice to go all the way, to get a shave. I convinced the barber that this was what I wanted, pointing to Thurmond and saying "same-same". So he clipped it all off, and then went for the heavy artillery. My whole scalp got the straight razor treatment. And Charlie was good—there wasn't one nick.

A few more bars followed. By this time, the group had broken up. Sgt. Thurmond and I were still together, but the others had gone their own way. My way was to find some local talent to satisfy the lust created by weeks in the field and beaucoup beers. My memory of the rest of the evening is blurred. I believe I succeeded in the mission, but couldn't swear to it. I have a vague recollection of Sgt. Thurmond trying at one point to persuade me to return to the company, but I was having none of it. The fires of youth were raging.

My first firm recollection was of an old Vietnamese man shaking me awake. It was grey outside, the pre-dawn shadowiness. I was lying on a cot in a solidly built masonry room. My belt was missing, but I seemed to have most of the rest of my possessions. The old guy eventually got me up and led me out into a corridor. After turning a couple of corners, I was through a door and into the street, without the vaguest idea of how to find the company. I turned back to the building, and the old guy jabbered some Vietnamese and pointed down the street. Getting drunken soldiers out of the whorehouse and on their way in the morning must have been his official function. He probably had been doing it when the French were marauding around the Highlands.

It turned out that I wasn't far from the laager site, no more than half a mile. I staggered in just as the Company was beginning to move out to the airfield. One of Jerome's RTOs said, "There's Lieutenant Holland now, Sir." Jerome and others turned and stared. There I was alright, a shiny knob for a head, swaying slightly, eyes hideously criss-crossed with red streaks. My appearance was such that activity in the vicinity came to a complete halt as one and all contemplated the work of Demon Rum. Finally, Jerome said, "Better get with your platoon, Lieutenant. We're on the way to the airfield."

I made my way over to Oscar and my gear. Sgt. Thurmond didn't look any too good either, but at least he hadn't called attention to his activities by a last minute arrival. He said, "You made it, Sir. I didn't know if you would. The captain was really giving me a hard time."

Incapable of a coherent thought, much less the expression of it, I just grunted. I was still drunk as a skunk. The first thing I did was to put on my helmet, which I had left behind the night before. The helmet hid my bald head. I then rigged a replacement for the lost belt from an extra strap on the rucksack. We walked the quarter-mile to the airfield; no trucks this morning. The walk with the pack started my sobering up process. Along the way, I drank a canteen of water, trying to ease the thirst that follows a night of alcohol. The water helped, but it also had the usual effect of recirculating the beer in my system, keeping me in an alcoholic fog.

Chinooks were waiting for us. About 25 troopers boarded each chopper. The 35-mile flight to Dak To took about twenty minutes. I dozed against my pack, the noise and vibrations of the chopper off-setting somewhat the growing pounding in my head. We didn't fly to Dak To itself. In fact, most of us never saw the village and its adjacent airfield, which could accommodate C-130 aircraft. The Chinooks took us directly to a fire support base on a hill in a large, broad valley. Off to the east stretched low rolling jungle-covered foothills. On the other side, perhaps three miles away, toward Cambodia and Laos, the valley ended against the abrupt rise of brooding, formidable-looking mountains.

The hill on which the fire support base sat had been denuded of vegetation. What remained was a dusty pale-red clay. At least two artillery units were on the hill, a 105-mm battery and an 8-inch battery. The battalion's four-deuce mortars were also temporarily setting up there. The fire support base contained considerably more than a standard battalion-sized operation. Various engineer and other units were also located in the perimeter. Alpha Company was given responsibility for about a third of that perimeter. Normally, one company could man the entire circumference of a battalion fire support base.

On the side of the fire support base facing the mountains, the perimeter swung down to the valley floor. Several large webtocs—tents with wooden frame and floors—were at the bottom of the hill and inside the barbed wire that encircled the perimeter. On the other side of the hill, the perimeter stopped about half-way down the slope. On that side, the jungle started about 50 meters beyond the wire. Also on that side were 55-gallon drums about every 30 meters. The drums lay on their sides with one end facing down the slope. The up-slope end of the drum was partly buried in the hill and covered with a mound of dirt. The drums contained phu-gas, a napalm-like substance that could be released and ignited if Charlie started coming through the wire. The phu-gas began to bring home to me that we were about to play a different game than the one we had been playing in Tuy Hoa. The phu-gas contraptions seemed designed for countering something more than armed farmers.

Amid all the fire power on the hill, Oscar's little 81mm mortar seemed a bit unnecessary, even pathetic. Nevertheless, Jerome had us set it up. Several large living-sized bunkers were in the vicinity of the gun's location, and we commandeered those for sleeping quarters. They had been constructed by bulldozers scooping out part of the hillside and grunts making walls and roofs of sandbags and PCP. I plopped my gear in a corner of one of the bunkers. We were to be in the fire support base all that day and overnight, and there being nothing else to do, I proceeded to get some sack time. The best thing for my gawdawful state was sleep.

A kick awoke me a little after noon. "Who th' hell is this?" a black-accented voice growled. In response I heard Harold Campton, "Hey muthafucka, that's our new platoon leader. Watch what th' hell you doin'."

I groggily sat up. Harold Campton said, "Sorry Sir. This is one of 'em misfits from th' Four-Deuce Platoon. He don't got good sense."

Misfit chimed in, "Yeah, sorry Lieutenant. I ain't used ta officers sleeping with th' EMs."

"That's alright," I said. My mouth felt like it was stuffed with cotton, but at least my head was feeling better. I staggered out into the glare of the midday sun, leaving Harold Campton, his four-deuce buddy, and other members of the platoon to their privacy. The company CP was just down the hill from the bunker. I could see some of the headquarters people sitting around perusing the *Stars and*

Stripes and decided to risk Jerome's ire for a little reading material. If I kept my helmet on, maybe he wouldn't be reminded of my recent waywardness.

The *Stars and Stripes* was, and still is, a semi-military paper. It had a largely civilian staff but military overseers. By-and-large, its coverage was fair and objective. And it was the soldier's main contact with the world. In fact, for the field grunt *Stars and Stripes* was often the only source of news. It was the only paper, and few troopers had commercial radios in the boonies to provide access to Armed Forces Radio. The resupply and mail choppers usually had a handful of *Stars and Stripes*, and they were avidly passed around. So when I saw that a new batch was available, I headed down.

Jerome, apparently having decided to let my conduct slide, greeted me with some unexpected news. According to an article in the paper, the Army was speeding up the promotions of first lieutenants to captains. From something like 30 months, the time-in-grade requirement had been dropped to something close to 15 months. The demands of the Vietnam conflict were creating a great need for company grade officers. The result was that I would be promoted in a little less than three months, at the beginning of February 1968.

This was disturbing news. I hadn't planned on being a captain, had no desire to be one. Being a platoon leader was responsibility enough and was the extent of my military ambitions. Moreover, being promoted meant that I would have to leave Alpha Company after only about five months. I had assumed a much longer stay in the field, indeed had applied for my latest Vietnam extension on the belief that I would be a platoon leader for a long time. Given my lack of formal infantry training and the fact that new captains rarely got commands, an infantry company was not a real possibility for me.

So my future was significantly altered, assuming I was destined to survive my time in the field. And the thought of survival led to another thought. It occurred to me that the shortened prospective period as a line doggie could be detrimental to my mental well-being. When getting out of the field is only a distant, remote prospect, adopting a fatalistic attitude may not be easy, but it is possible. But when removal from danger becomes imminent, fatalism for most individuals becomes extremely difficult. And a healthy degree of fatalism was a good thing for an infantryman to have.

Concern about loosing my fatalism was soon put to rest, however. Alpha Company, and all the other occupants of the fire support base, were about to get a distinct visual reminder of what we were about and of what out destinies could be.

I scrounged a copy of *Star and Stripes* and retreated to Oscar's area to digest the details of the change in promotional policy. As I was sitting on the top of the bunker, I noticed a chopper, barely a dot in the sky, coming our way from across the valley. We had been told that the 4th Battalion was on the other side of the valley and had been in several tough firefights over the previous few days. A particularly vicious one was supposed to have occurred the preceding day and evening. As the chopper came closer, its appearance became more distinct, and the unique whump-whump that identified it as a Huey became noticeable. Also becoming noticeable was a dark dot beneath the chopper.

As the chopper approached the fire support base, the dot took on the shape of a human, and a straight line, a rope, connecting the human to the machine about 20 feet above became visible. The human was obviously dead. He was held in a loop at the end of the rope, the loop going around his chest and under his arms. He hung at about a 75-degree angle with the ground, his feet jutting downward and back, his head lolling forward with his chin on his chest, his hair over his forehead and separated a little bit from it by the breeze and gravity. By the time the chopper was near the collection of webtocs at the base of the hill, all eyes were fixed on the sight. The chopper hovered lower, allowing the body to touch the ground. Several individuals removed the robe, and the chopper rose, turned, and headed back across the valley.

Simultaneously, a number of troopers began running toward the bottom of the hill. Conspicuous among them were several of the medics, who seemed to take a clinical, professional interest in the dead. The individuals who had removed the rope placed the body on a stretcher and carried it into one of the webtocs. It dawned on me that the webtocs belonged to a mortuary unit. Jeez, this looked like it could be serious stuff. The Army was preparing for the worst, and us line doggies would be the main additions to that "worst."

The chopper flights with the dangling dead continued intermittently for several hours. The mood among the watchers on the hill, particularly among those of us who suspected we would shortly be going to where those bodies were coming from, was somber. The word circulated that the bodies were making their journey in this macabre fashion because a landing zone had not yet been cut on the hill where yesterday's firefight had occurred. The unit involved was indeed a company of the 4th Battalion.

Toward evening, Jerome called a briefing. In the morning, we would be going across the valley, to the hill—a mountain really—where the bodies had been coming from. The 4th Bat company had fought off a sizeable assault by a North Vietnamese Army regiment. The number of American dead was in double figures. The hill was supposedly strewn with NVA bodies. We would be going into an LZ on the hill's slope. Assuming the landing went satisfactory, the company would set course along a series of ridge lines toward the Cambodian border. Jerome emphasized that we could be going into some heavy shit. He reiterated his standard operating procedure in the event contact was made: fall back into a horseshoe perimeter and let air and artillery soften things up.

Jerome also said that the company was to carry more mortar rounds. Fifteen additional rounds were to be distributed among the headquarters group and the rifle platoons. Oscar was to find a way to hump another five. Back at the platoon, I laid out the new ammunition requirement and said that I would take an additional round. I had been feeling bad about the prospect of carrying only one round while most of the rest of the platoon carried two in addition to various pieces of equipment. The increased load gave me an excuse to move up to two rounds without directly reversing Sgt Thurmond's and Lt. Monroe's practice of only carrying one. I might not know much about the gun, but I could hump a load. Sgt. Thurmond took the hint and said he would carry two rounds also.

That night, we had a ringside-seat view of the war. We were in a large amphitheater, miles in dimension. The sky was exceptionally clear. Multitudes of stars sparkled against the blackness. Portions of the valley and the mountains beyond were lit periodically by flares from artillery and aircraft. The mountain that was the scene of the 4th Battalion's battle and that was our destination for the morrow received particular attention from the illuminators. Another mountain about 70 degrees off to the left and beyond the first line of ridges was also lit up. In addition, it was receiving tender loving care from Puff the Magic Dragon, the Air Force plane armed with gatling guns. The distance was too far to hear the guns, but the arching red streaks of descending bullets were clearly visible.

The hill that was the subject of Puff's attention was occupied by a company from the 4th Infantry Division. Somehow we found the company's frequency on the radio, and as we gazed out across the valley, we listened to the unit's transmissions with its parent. The company was taking incoming small arms and mortar fire, not a lot but enough to be called a fire fight. Laconically, the company commander reported the occurrences of fire and adjusted Puff and the artillery support. He was talking in such a low-keyed manner that it was easy to forget death and destruction were the business at hand.

Indeed, the whole scene had a seductive and dangerous beauty. We sat on top of the bunker, mesmerized by the stars, the dim dark profiles of the far mountains, the occasional flares, Puff's arching blood-red expectorations, and the 4th Division company commander's calm soothing voice. Also very real, almost palatable, were memories of the dangling death we had seen that afternoon and visions of what we would face tomorrow. The usual line doggie banter was absent. Each trooper was occupied with his own thoughts. Sleep was a long time coming.

Into The Maelstrom

Alpha Company was ready to go bright and early the next morning. Most were anxious to get the show on the road. The war wasn't yet ready for us, however. We had packed up and moved down the hill to just outside the perimeter for the pick-up, but although a number of choppers were flying about the valley, none came our way. Alpha Company was just a small part of the effort to mash this audacious invasion by the NVA.

Finally, a little after noon, the other priorities were taken care of, and Alpha was number one on the runway. The first lift consisted of a rifle platoon and the headquarters contingent—about six choppers' worth. The Weapons Platoon and one of the remaining rifle platoons would be in the second lift. We waited for the returning choppers, but there was a delay. From what could be gathered from the fragmented and broken radio transmissions, the first lift had taken .50 caliber fire on the way in. How intense the fire was and whether any casualties had resulted were unclear. We waited on the pick-up zone, leaderless and uninformed.

Eventually, the word came down that the fire had been just a few isolated rounds and that the insertion was resuming. The choppers reappeared. We scrambled on, anxious to get the flight over with and our butts back on the ground. The nakedness and vulnerability one feels sitting on the hard metal floor of a Huey going into a possible hot LZ pushes the activity pretty damn high on the I-want-this-over-with meter. My constant expectation was to see a bullet hole appear in the floor between my legs. A combat assault would send my scrotum heading for refuge inside my groin, and this combat assault produced an even more pronouncement effect than usual.

But we made the trip without incident. I heard no fire as we came in, but given the surrounding mountains it was easy to understand the potential. We landed just outside the perimeter of the 4th Battalion's company. In one sense, I was disappointed. I had expected to see mounds of NVA bodies. None were in sight, however. Jerome was on the edge of the clearing, and I said, "Damn Sir, I thought there'd be a whole passel of bodies up here. Where are they?"

He laughed and said maybe they had cleaned them up or thrown them down the hill. Or maybe they had exaggerated, I thought to myself. This matter of body counts was to crop up again in the days ahead.

A bit later the third lift arrived, and the company set off down the mountain side. The terrain was much steeper than that of the Tuy Hoa area, and more rugged. The vegetation also differed. Although the underbrush was about the same thickness, the trees were taller. The open areas were significantly fewer. And there was bamboo, not little finger-size shoots but massive six-inch in diameter, 20-foot tall trees that grew in clumps and groves ten to twenty feet across. The hearts of these clumps and groves were essentially impenetrable. By the time we commenced our move, it was past 1500. Consequently, we didn't go far, maybe a kilometer down the mountain's massive slope. An adequate but not great laager site was found, and we set up for the night.

The next day was one long hellacious hump along the side of the mountain. Walking on the steepness would have been bad enough, but the gullies and stream beds meant much scrambling up and down, often hand-over-hand. And the bamboo groves and other clumps of underbrush made maintaining a straight course impossible. This was my first hump with mortar rounds. They added whole new dimensions to the struggle with the rucksack. In addition to considerably increasing the weight of the load, they made you a wider, more awkward jungle traveler. The canisters in which the rounds were kept were about two and a half feet long, which resulted in the ends sticking out on each side of one's body. If a bamboo tree, a wait-a-minute vine, or a bush was in the vicinity, the protruding rounds were going to catch it.

Walking in this environment was best done with a turning, swaying, rolling motion. Progress was easier if, instead of brute-forcing the way forward, you first pivoted one hip to the front, then the other. Bamboo, wait-a-minute vines, and other hindrances would tend to slide off the canisters and other parts of the ruck. "Tend" is the crucial word because a considerable number of recalcitrant hindrances still existed that weren't about to yield their grip without a struggle. Fortunately, we were moving pretty slow, taking the time to investigate thoroughly the route. The point fire team would go out the usual 100 to 150 meters, check the area, and call back for the main body. The procedure was the standard one we had been following when we moved as a company, but everyone was being extra cautious.

The mountain was a massive piece of terrain, and we spent the entire day making our way around its slopes. Eventually, in late afternoon, we came to a ridge stretching away to the west, toward more mountains and ridges. Like practically all of the area, the ridge was heavily forested. It was relatively wide and flat on top, however, and a trail with evidence of much recent use ran along its top. Jerome decided to laager there. The mortar crew found a spot with a little opening to the sky, and we dug in the gun.

The next morning, the lead platoon, Mike, set out to follow the trail. The platoon had barely cleared the laager site when an automatic weapon let go with a prolonged burst. Other small arms joined in. The cacophony of noise was punctuated by a few whumps of exploding grenades. Most of the stuff sounded like it was outgoing. Jerome and the headquarters group rushed forward. The other two rifle platoons and Oscar hesitantly remained where we were. We were packed up and sort of half way formed for departing the laager site, but we had no room to move.

The radio traffic consisted of fragmented transmissions among Mike's point, Mike, and Alpha Six. For a long time, no one called Lima, November, or Oscar, so we just sat. We spread out a little in a sloppy defensive perimeter, but because we expected to be called forward at any time, the effort at defense wasn't much. A concerted attack up one of the sides of the ridge would have caught us in bad shape.

What was happening was that artillery, lots of it, was starting to come in. Jerome and Mike were putting the steel in about 200 or so meters to our front. The explosions shook the ground and seemed to make the air vibrate. The shaking and vibrations were nothing, however, compared to what an occasional air strike was producing. This was my first experience with up close air support, and it was damn scary. The roar of the incoming planes and the subsequent concussions of the 500- and 750-pound bombs were things I felt physically. Sometimes the concussions were replaced with a sort of whoosh—napalm.

From what could be discerned over the radio, Mike's point had initially seen NVA in a machine gun position just off the trail. Mike's people fired first, and then backed up. The first artillery barrage came next. After that, probes by Mike alternated with artillery barrages and air strikes. Each time the point encountered fire, Jerome backed it off for the heavy stuff. Moreover, the point was discovering a large bunker system, big things capable of holding six to ten people and with five and more feet of overhead cover. Each bunker had to be checked before it could be passed. And on top of everything else, Jerome was apparently getting considerable pressure to get through the bunker system and move along the ridge complex. Although the rest of us didn't know it until the evening, Charlie and

Delta Companies about five kilometers away were fighting for their lives and begging for reinforcement. Battalion wanted Alpha Company to get the lead out.

After several hours of cringing through the artillery barrages and air strikes, we in the rear guard finally began doing a little something. Jerome gave orders to cut an LZ, and the two rifle platoons commenced to whacking away. As for Oscar, at some point we put the gun back up and let Jerome know we were ready to fire. During a lull in the big stuff, we received orders to put out a few rounds. Then occurred an incident that I should have taken more seriously and personally but because I felt like an observer with, rather than the leader of, the Mortar Platoon, I didn't think much of it.

In response to the fire mission, Truman made his calculations and relayed them to the gun crew. The gun was aimed, the round prepared, and all was ready. When the round was dropped in the tube, however, nothing happened. I called Jerome over the radio: "Alpha Six, we've got a hang fire."

I was about 20 feet from the mortar and suddenly feeling extremely vulnerable. Harold Campton and the boys immediately went into the hang fire drill. After a kick to the tube produced no result, the gun crew began the ticklish business of partially dismantling the gun and pivoting the tube-bottom upwards. One of the troopers stretched his fingers over the end of the tube and caught the descending round. He carried it off to the side. I watched the proceedings, restraining myself with a massive effort from moving considerably farther away. It wouldn't do for the troops to see their platoon leader high-tailing for safer ground, even if he didn't have anything to do.

The cause of the failure to fire was quickly determined. A cleaning rag had been left in the tube, preventing the round from striking the firing pin. Given the general excitement and the haste with which the gun had been reassembled after being dismantled for the move, the error was somewhat understandable. Still, errors in combat were not something one liked to see a lot of. Fortunately for the Weapons Platoon and its leader, Jerome was preoccupied with the prodding from battalion and with Mike's efforts to get into the bunker complex. He didn't, then or later, make an issue of the hang fire. After clearing the tube, the platoon managed to get off a few rounds before having to stop for the next air strike.

A bit earlier, during an artillery session, a piece of wayward shrapnel—friendly fire—had found the chest of one of Mike's point men. He died instantly, and his body, wrapped in a poncho, was brought back to the laager site. For the several hours that he was there, he was visited by a steady stream of morbidly interested troopers. They wanted to see the killing wound. The medics especially, as I've noted before, had a fascination with the dead. I stayed away, not understanding the desire to gaze on our own killed. I suppose the troopers' interest had something to do with getting a handle on their own mortality, but I don't really know.

As the afternoon wore on, Mike finally began making some progress into the bunker system. The pace was slow, however, and it was obvious that Alpha Company wouldn't be going much further. The plan came to be that Alpha would laager in the bunker complex. When Jerome instructed us to be prepared to come forward, I said: "Don't forget the KIA back here. Is someone gonna pick him up?"

"Roger, Oscar. Someone'll be back for 'im."

As time went on, however, and we awaited the order to move, the dead guy weighed more and more heavily on me. It seemed that he was being forgotten. I called Alpha Six several times to remind Jerome. With each call, he became more and more irritated. Obviously, I could have taken the initiative and had the body carried forward when we went. But for some reason, I wanted this decision made at a higher level. Eventually, we were ordered forward. I noted one more time the need to retrieve the body and got an exasperated "It's being taken care of" from Jerome.

We made the trip to the bunker complex in short order. A huge area, about the size of a football field, had been cleared of trees and underbrush by the air strikes and artillery; not only cleared of vegetation but rearranged. Three overlapping craters about 15-feet deep and 20-feet across told of the destructive power that Charlie had to put up with. Any bunkers, and occupants thereof, that had been where the craters now sat, were no more. But a considerable number of bunkers had survived. They were formidable structures, attesting to the ability and seriousness of the North Vietnamese Army.

By this time, it was late afternoon. A chopper came in to evacuate the KIA. The company set up its perimeter, which encompassed the cleared area. Most of us were a little subdued. We had laagered the night before less than a click from this battalion-size enemy complex, and we had avoided blundering into it only because our point saw them before they saw us.

As evening fell, we began getting the story of Charlie's and Delta's day. Jerome briefed us on what he knew, on what battalion had been telling him, and on what he had been hearing over the battalion net. The story, as was fleshed out over the next few days, provided a marked contrast to Alpha's experience. Delta was an ad hoc company that had been put together just before the battalion left for Dak To. It was made up of the battalion Recon Platoon and some other odds and ends, including levies on the other three line companies. Its Weapons Platoon—one

81mm mortar like Alpha's Weapons Platoon—was culled in part from the battalion Four-Deuce Platoon. One of the members was Sgt. Cooper, who had shared a shallow hole with me the night of one of Lima's ambushes back in Tuy Hoa. The Delta Company commander was a big black captain who seemed to be on the battalion commander's—Shafter's—shit list. Of course, everyone seemed to be on Shafter's shit list.

The Charlie Company commander was Captain Thomas McNevers. He was a loud outspoken southerner, aggressive and quick to offer his opinion. His platoon leaders were a cocky, our-shit-don't-stink lot. There was Cedric, who I had run into in Tuy Hoa, Charlie Jones, who was always referred to by both names, and Storch, an odd character who for some reason preferred regular Army fatigues to jungle fatigues.

Two days before when Alpha had been inserted on the mountain side, Charlie and Delta, operating together, had been inserted on the other side of the mountain and somewhat further to the west. The previous day they had advanced to another mountain top about five kilometers to the west of Alpha's position. In the morning, the point, like Alpha's point, had barely gotten out of the laager site when it encountered NVA. Unlike Alpha's point, however, Charlie's point had given chase, running down the ridge to catch them Commies. The rest of the lead platoon was not far behind. After a few hundred meters, the troopers met a classic U-shaped ambush. The enemy force stretched across the ridge and along each side. The lead platoon was smack dab in the middle of the U.

McNevers got the remainder of Charlie and most of Delta on the way to extract the lead platoon. A few elements, mainly the mortar people, were left on the hill. Instead of extracting the lead platoon, the would-be rescuers from Charlie and Delta also became pinned down. And an enemy force soon swept over the hill, killing all those who had been left behind, including Sgt. Cooper. He wouldn't be making it back to the wife and child in Fayetteville, North Carolina.

Charlie and Delta fought desperately. They were subject to hours of intensive automatic weapons, rocket, and mortar fire. The fighting allegedly became hand-to-hand at times, with a few NVA even being killed with entrenching tools. The survival of the units was in doubt, and the battalion commander, a man of violent temper, was apparently beside himself with rage. The officer who reportedly kept his head and made the decisions that led to the relief of Charlie and Delta was the battalion S-3, Major Sills.

The first rescue option was Alpha Company. We were blocked by the bunker system, however, and Jerome, to his great credit, was not going to be stampeded into a reckless charge into another possible ambush. When it became apparent that rescue by Alpha was out, battalion requested help from the brigade. A company of the 4th Battalion was inserted in the vicinity of Charlie's and Delta's original LZ. The company set off on a fast-paced movement to the hill-top laager site. It surprised the NVA rear-guard occupiers and drove them off. To get to Charlie and Delta, the 4th Bat company commander put his men on line, told McNevers to have his troopers keep their heads down, and started the company moving forward, sending a heavy stream of shoulder-height lead screaming over the heads of the trapped troopers. The procedure worked, and the 4th Bat company swept through Charlie's and Delta's position.

With the NVA temporarily thrown off balance, the three units were able to pull back to the hill top. The movement was somewhat frantic, and several dead were left behind. All told, Charlie and Delta had approximately 25 dead or missing, a figure that included the ten or so troopers who had remained on the hill. The wounded numbered in the dozens.

When Jerome related the day's events to us, he hinted that there was some unhappiness at battalion about Alpha's inability to provide reinforcement. He defended his conservatism in probing the bunker system, however, and indicated no regrets. That night, we monitored some of the radio traffic from Charlie's and Delta's hill top. Artillery was being adjusted. The voice on the radio contained an element of fear, almost panic. He seemed to want the protective umbrella of the artillery but was deathly afraid of rounds falling on his own position. He was giving frantic instructions to move the impacts hither and yon. If his voice was any indication, Charlie and Delta had indeed had a bad day.

Alpha's mission for the next day was to move to Charlie and Delta's hill. Those two units were to stay in place, and try to retrieve their dead. We set off a little after daybreak. The tree-covered ridge we were following had much evidence of an NVA presence: freshly made trails with steps cut on any significant inclines, communications wire, and various bunkers and holes.

We had gone several clicks when automatic weapons fire broke out. The company immediately went into Jerome's U-shaped drill, only not everyone was on the same script. While Oscar proceeded to set up the mortar where we were, the two trailing rifle platoons rushed forward to find their positions on the legs of the U. I shortly realized that our little band of 15 was quite alone. The U was being formed elsewhere. I scanned the jungle, expecting to be the subject of a charge at any moment. The sound of heavy firing was still coming from some distance forward.

156   Vietnam, A Memoir

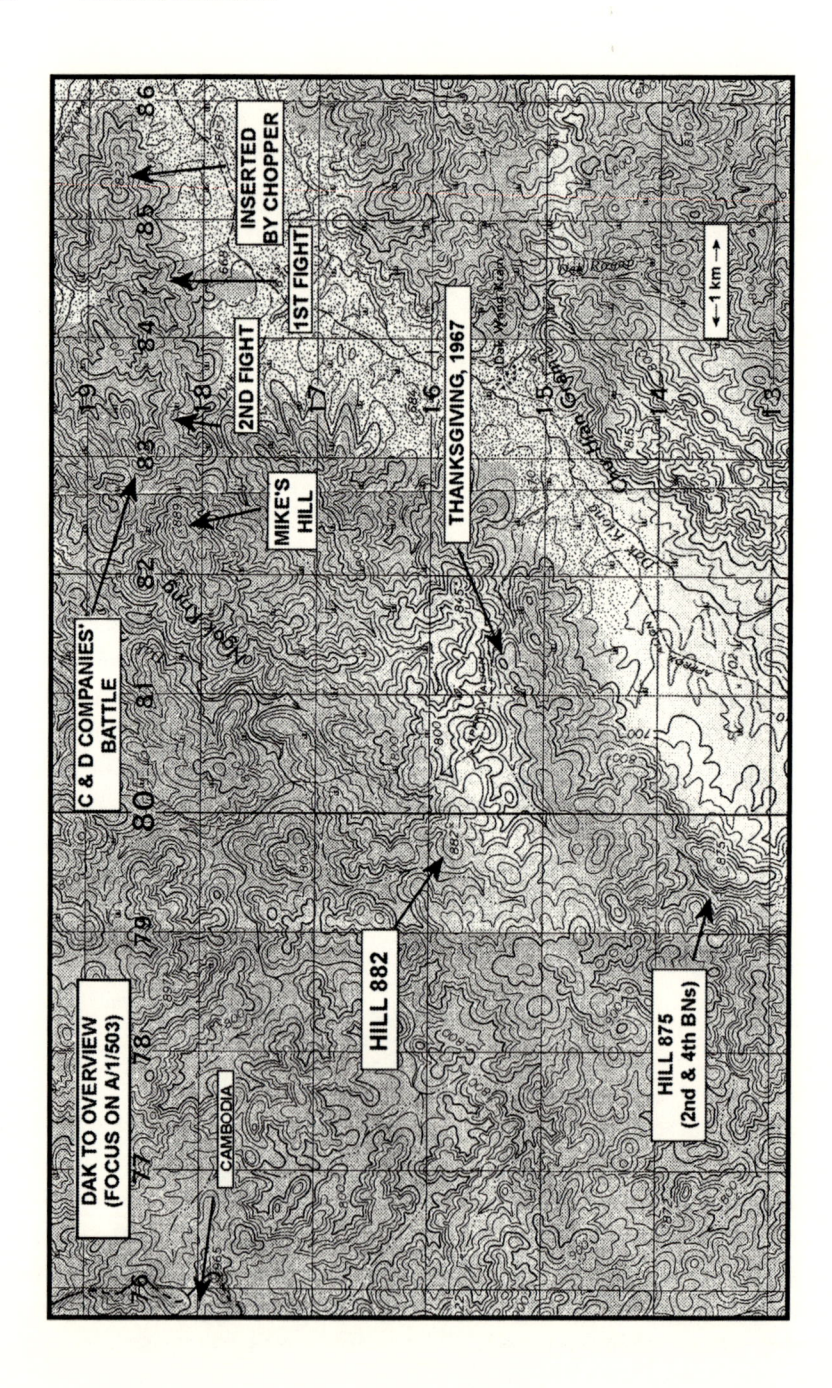

I ordered the gun dismantled. We set out to rejoin the company. Its location wasn't as easy to find as might be expected, however. We were at least 50 meters behind the rear portion of the forming perimeter. The vegetation was thick, the ridge-top was wide, and the route taken by the three rifle platoons and the headquarters element was not readily apparent. We made our way gingerly forward, guided as much by the firing as by anything else. I had this deep fear of bypassing the company and putting ourselves between it and whatever was being shot at. We eventually stumbled safely into the left flank of the company, however. Near the middle of the perimeter was a small clearing, and Harold Campton and the boys set up the mortar. November was the lead platoon. It was maneuvering against what appeared to be a small blocking position. The incoming fire was sporadic. Most of the action was out-going. November's troopers were firing their M-16s, M-79 grenade launchers, and M-60s with great gusto. Artillery and air strikes were also playing a part, being called in about a kilometer from our position to catch any retreating NVA or to hinder reinforcement.

During a lull in the air strikes, Jerome instructed Oscar to put out a few rounds. Once again things didn't go right. The first round did not fall down the tube but slowly descended with a sort of whine. It did not fire, and for the second time in two days the gun crew went through the hang-fire procedure. This time we were in full view of the headquarters group, including Jerome who cast some disapproving looks my way. The crew got the gun back up. The barrel was given a swabbing with the swapping rod, and another attempt at firing was commenced. This time the gunner, instead of just dropping the round down the tube, flung it down with considerable force. The round fired, but the procedure prompted a tongue-lashing from First Sgt. Duckett, who had just come back from November's forward position: "Goddamnit, that's not the way to fire that weapon. You people know better than that."

Well, I didn't but I suppose the gun crew did. At least no one overtly contradicted the first sergeant. I did notice, however, that the other three or four rounds fired were also started down the tube with more than a drop. The gunner just disguised his effort a bit better.

Harold Campton's later explanation was that moisture—condensation—in the tube had prevented the round from dropping properly. The tube should have been swabbed before the firing was attempted. Once again, at the time I wasn't disturbed. I still thought of the Weapons Platoon as extremely competent and myself as somewhat of an observer. In hindsight, however, I should have felt ultimately responsible for the misfirings of the two days and should have determined, or at least discussed, corrective actions with the appropriate members of the platoon. Before the reader concludes I was completely shirking my duties, however, I should note that I was carrying and wading through a manual on mortars that Sgt. Thurmond had lent me. Each time the company paused in its daily hump, I plopped back against my pack and read mortars.

By this time, November and the artillery seemed to have cleared the blocking position, but not without casualties. The one in the worst shape was November's medic, Pasquez. He was brought back to the small clearing where the mortar was. The wound was in his chest, which was wrapped in gauze bandages stretching entirely around his body from his armpits to the bottom of his rib cage. Blood was seeping through. He was conscious but very pale and generally not looking too good. He was being attended to primarily by the two November RTOs, Ricky Hays and Jackson. The latter had cross-trained as a medic during a stint with Special Forces at Ft. Bragg.

Pasquez had to be medevaced, but an LZ was lacking. The decision was made to lift him out in a basket, an enclosed wire stretcher-like contraption that was lowered from a chopper. As we waited for the medevac, sporadic firing continued to come from the point's direction. Although the NVA position had allegedly been eliminated, some doubt evidently existed. After about 15 minutes, the dust off arrived overhead. "Dust off" was the common term for a medevac chopper. The wire stretcher was lowered through the trees. The scene in the small clearing was controlled chaos. Leaves, bark, and other debris were swirling around in the wind created by the chopper blades. The chopper's noise prevented communication at anything less than a shout. The dropping stretcher swung and spun in dizzying patterns. Finally, it reached the ground. Pasquez was strapped in. He then began his ascent, the stretcher undergoing the same wild erratic gyrations as it had coming down.

Supervising the operation had been First Sgt. Duckett. As we proceeded deeper and deeper into the maelstrom of Dak To, he was becoming more and more of a presence. When November encountered the NVA position, the first sergeant had gone forward to assess for himself the situation. He had maneuvered with the fire team that was attempting to flank the position. When the action seemed largely over, he had supervised the bringing of Pasquez back to the clearing, and then his evacuation. Unlike some other first sergeants in infantry companies, First Sgt. Duckett spent all of his time in the field. More than a few first sergeants used the excuse of paperwork and logistical responsibilities to spend considerable time in the rear. For an old-time senior NCO likely on his second war, convincing a young captain company commander that the first sergeant's place was not necessarily in the field was hardly a challenge. First Sergeant Duckett, however, was a true hardcore field paratrooper, a fact that was to become ever more apparent in the days ahead.

With Pasquez evacuated, the several other casualties determined to be minor and capable of continuing until we arrived at a proper LZ, and the small NVA blocking force eliminated, Alpha Company prepared to resume the move toward Charlie and Delta. As we formed up, some unease and discontent became apparent in November, which now was to become the rear guard. As the headquarters element and Oscar passed through November, I overheard Lt. Kane, the platoon leader, loudly complaining to Jerome of the difficulty he allegedly had in getting some of his troopers to do what he wanted: "They just wouldn't get moving. I couldn't get them from behind the goddamn tree trunks."

For their part, a few troopers were shooting him looks that would melt granite. Obviously, different viewpoints existed about how the platoon had conducted the action. One fact was undeniable, however. The blocking position had been cleared, and three or four NVA were freshly dead in a small trench to prove it. They appeared to have been killed with small arms fire, so someone in November had done something correctly.

The remainder of the hump to Charlie and Delta was without incident. As we got close to their hill top, however, the scenery was much changed. Trees were blown down. Many of those standing were stripped bare of their vegetation. The freshly fallen leaves, already beginning to turn brown, and giving off a sweetish odor, littered the jungle floor. We were on a well-defined, newly made trail, but the fallen trees slowed our rate of march substantially.

When the link-up with Charlie and Delta was accomplished, Alpha Company received considerable razzing, and not much of it good-natured. Many troopers of the two companies, and of the 4th Battalion company that was still on the scene, obviously felt that Alpha had not done all it could have done the previous day to reach the threatened units. We followed the trail to the hill top, pushing past the scene of the major portion of the battle. The trail was lined with Charlie, Delta, and 4th Bat troopers, a sort of gauntlet.

"Where the fuck you assholes been?"

"Bout time you got yo' asses here."

"Look, this four-eyed one must be a platoon leader."

This last comment was directed at me by a hard-looking, mean black guy. I was taken back by the border-line insubordination and trying to determine how to respond when Harold Campton came to my rescue. "Yeah, that's our platoon leader, goddamn it. And he's carrying two mortar rounds like the rest of us. So back the fuck off."

Fortunately, the open hostility did not last much beyond the initial meeting. It undoubtedly was due to the previous day's frustration and anxiety. I could imagine Charlie and Delta hugging the ground, bullets snapping overhead, B-40 rockets whooshing in, mortars and grenades thudding away, the number of dead mounting, the wounded in pain, some vocally, and everyone wondering, "Where the hell's A Company?"

We took over the 4th Bat company's portion of the perimeter on the hill. Choppers picked up that unit shortly after we arrived, and the depleted 1st Battalion was all by its lonesome. The mission for the remainder of the afternoon was to search the battlefield for several bodies that had not yet been recovered. One of them was the big black captain, the Delta Company commander. He, and the others missing, were known to be dead, but their bodies had been left behind in the frantic withdrawal up the hill. The Airborne supposedly had a tradition of never leaving dead comrades behind, so the recovery of the bodies was a matter of honor. Actually, no unit—Airborne, straight-leg infantry, Marine, or whatever—wanted to lose its dead, although I had difficulty understanding the depth of the feeling. It seemed to me that if risking more casualties was the price for recovering your dead, it wasn't worth it. But that was just me.

While parts of Alpha, Charlie, and Delta manned the perimeter, the remainders of the three companies searched the saddle where the battle had centered. I first looked at the hill top position where the mortar crew, including Sgt. Cooper, had died. The gun had been in a deep bomb crater. The NVA had apparently caught the group with everyone's attention focused on the saddle. Death by bursts from automatic weapons had probably been quick.

I then went down the hill to the saddle and joined the search. The place was a tangle of fallen trees, broken and splintered underbrush, discarded U.S. and NVA clothing and personal equipment, bloody bandages, and shell casings—M-16, M-60, AK-47, RPD. As I wandered around, the thought suddenly hit me: "This is a goddamn battlefield, a real bona fide battlefield." Since my earliest reading days, I had devoured tales of battles and battlefields, and here I was standing in the middle of a day-old battlefield. It might not sound like a big deal, but at the time it struck me pretty forcibly.

A part of the search effort was being performed systematically, with troops being formed in lines that swept over the saddle. Others of us were just wandering around, poking here and there. Several of the Delta Company members had come from Lima in A Company, my old platoon. One, a small gregarious Hispanic guy, had died in the saddle, and another former Lima trooper showed me where it occurred. The two had been lying on the ground firing their M-16s when a bullet caught the Hispanic guy in the forehead. Alive and providing running commentary on the battle one moment, stone dead the next.

The black captain's body was found late in the afternoon. The NVA had apparently dragged it a considerable distance down the hill. The body was placed in one of the thick rubber body bags choppers had brought in. With Jerome in charge, six of us, including Jerome, grabbed the handholds and began trudging up the hill with the heavy load. Nobody said much, certainly not the obscene irreverent banter that usually sufficed for conversation in the field.

We stayed on the hill for two nights. All of the bodies were recovered by the following afternoon. The surviving troopers of Charlie and Delta gave many renditions of their day of horror. A number of the survivors had almost a festive air about them, an attitude of belligerent, arrogant cockiness, not at all what one is led by war movies and books to expect. The somber world-weariness of the stereotyped battle survivor fit only a few of these kids. Undoubtedly, in the months and years ahead the deaths of friends and comrades and the memories of violence and terror would weigh much heavier. Now, however, many of the troopers reminded me of high school athletes who had just won an important game.

Several of the officers were as gregarious about their experiences as the troops. Lt. Cedric and Charlie Jones gave Jerome hour-by-hour descriptions of the action. The word was that Cedric, the leader of the point platoon, had been a particularly heroic figure, even participating with a few of his men in almost hand-to-hand combat with the attackers. He related incidents of NVA unlucky enough to make it inside the perimeter being killed by blows to the head with D-handle shovels. For his actions on that November day, Cedric was awarded the Distinguished Service Cross, the nation's second highest award for valor, exceeded only by the Medal of Honor. The DSC made him the highest decorated member of his West Point Class.

The action did have one immediate noticeable effect on Cedric. From being the closest adherent to regulations regarding the wearing of equipment, he went for a short time to the other end of the spectrum. At one point during Alpha's second day on the hill, Cedric came waltzing into the company area carrying a captured AK-47 and wearing the NVA's chest magazine carrier. He proclaimed that the AK-47 was superior to the M-16 and henceforth he would carry the former. Fortunately for Cedric's concerns regarding the inadequacies of the U.S. Army's standard issue weapon, he was within a few days largely out of harm's way. He went to the rear to be Charlie Company's XO.

Alpha Company bore Charlie's and Delta's war stories, crowing, and criticisms of its failure to come to the rescue—those criticisms being mostly implied rather than explicit after the first day—largely in silence. Among ourselves, however, we considered the possibility that the two companies' ordeal owed something to their own excessive aggressiveness. As we understood the sequence of events, the point saw a few NVA and immediately charged down the trail after them. The point platoon followed, then most of the remainder of the two companies. Whether the lead elements had become trapped and the movement off the hill was mostly for the purpose of extracting them, or whether it was simply a case of "there's some gooks, let's get'em," was unclear. What was clear was that a natural defensive position, a hill top, had been hastily abandoned for a charge into an ambush. Even if the purpose had been to rescue a trapped lead element, the suspicion existed that there was a better way of doing it than putting two entire companies in jeopardy.

Contributing to our feeling that Charlie's and Delta's predicament had not been entirely unavoidable was a general faith in Jerome's standard operating procedure of pulling back into a defensive position on contact with the enemy. In the few days we had been at Dak To, Alpha Company had engaged the NVA twice. Both times the company had been moving and thus in danger of stumbling into an untenable situation. But both times the point had spotted the NVA first, and both times the subsequent liberal use of firepower and cautious maneuverings had resulted in few U.S. casualties. Consequently, the leadership and troopers of Alpha Company were for the most part not unduly upset by the implied criticisms from Charlie and Delta.

On the other hand, I was personally troubled by an unease. Thus far, I had been mostly an observer. The Weapons Platoon pretty much ran itself. Unlike the rifle platoon leaders, I had little occasion to make decisions. My platoon wasn't walking point. I was not faced with what to do if my troopers came into direct contact with the enemy. We were never the front of the company column, and the difficulties of maneuvering against a dug-in opponent were left to others. As a result, I felt I was missing a test of my character, of my courage, of my ability to function under fire. Never mind that the mortar's position could be within a few meters of the company perimeter. I was uncertain about how I would react when the shit really hit the fan.

The second evening on the hill top I received a lesson in leadership. The teacher was Harold Campton. It was past nightfall, and Sgt. Thurmond, Sgt. Berkley, and I were relaxing on a log before turning in. Harold Campton joined us and said to me: "Sir, the platoon had a meeting. We talked over the mistakes of the last couple'a days. We screwed up. We've made dumb mistakes. The mortar should have been ready to fire both times without that horse crap we went through. We let everybody know that they have to be thinking all the time. That stuff won't happen again."

"Well, that's good. I'm glad to see that initiative. Way ta' go." My inanities weren't much of a response, but they were the best that I could do at the moment. In truth, I was nonplused. I instantly realized that Harold Campton was providing leadership that ultimately should have been coming from me. It also finally dawned on me that ultimate responsibility for the platoon's faux poxes of the last few days rested with the platoon leader—me. After he left, I said to Sergeant's Thurmond and Berkley, "Damn, that guy is good." Sgt. Thurmond mumbled agreement, perhaps realizing that Harold Campton's initiative was an indirect criticism of him also. Sgt. Berkley was silent, but in the dim light I thought I detected a sly smile on his face. It occurred to me that maybe he had a little more involvement in this bit of training for both the men and their leader than appeared on the surface.

As we settled in for the night, a discussion of increasing heat arose from Lima's sector of the perimeter, which was only a few meters from the mortar's position. Lt. Wayman and my old buddy, the medic with the fear-of-the-night problem, were having a philosophical go-round, a college dormitory-type argument about the meaning of life, or some-such. It was definitely not your run-of-the-mill line doggie conversation. The rantings became loud enough to entertain the NVA on the next mountain over. Finally Jerome, down the hill about 20 meters or so, bellowed: "Goddamnit. Knock that fuckin' bull-shit off." The two discussants quieted, but I sensed they were unfulfilled.

The advance in search of the enemy resumed the next day. The three companies, Alpha, Charlie, and Delta, were to move together—a battalion-size operation. Bravo Company was guarding the battalion fire support base, now located on the hill that had been the scene of the 4th Battalion's battle prior to our arrival and on whose slope we had been inserted several days before. A captain from the battalion staff took over Delta Company. Captain McNevers remained the company commander of Charlie Company. Because of the decimated, undermanned status of Charlie and Delta, Alpha would be the point company of the battalion column for the foreseeable future.

Mike led the way out of the laager site. The first goal was the next mountain. A newly constructed NVA trail took a sharp descent to a stream, and then a sharp climb to the mountain and the ridge-line that stretched from it. The trail had footholds on the steepest portions. The area around the stream crossing showed evidence of a recent large enemy encampment.

The next mountain was a dual top affair. Mike made the first piece of high ground with no trouble. The lead elements of the main column closed on Mike, who set out for the next peak, about 150 meters away. It wasn't long before automatic weapons fire split the air. "Shit, here we go again," I thought. The main column scrambled to gain the relative security of the first peak. Jerome directed Alpha into the SOP defensive horseshoe. Charlie and Delta closed the rear of the shoe. We found a site for the mortar in a large bomb crater on the edge of the perimeter. Artillery began crashing to our front, and we settled in for what was to come.

What was to come was slow in developing. According to the radio traffic, Mike was to probe the hill after the initial bombardment. The sound of small arms fire, some of it whistling overhead, and the thumb of grenades indicated the probing was underway. Mike reported that he was up against a well-fortified position and that the platoon wasn't making much progress. Jerome pulled the platoon back and called in more artillery and some air strikes. The ground shook and the air thundered. Surely enough steel had been deposited on the hill to annihilate any living thing and to rearrange whatever inanimate things might be present. But Mike's resumed probe was again greeted with grenades and automatic weapons.

The morning and early afternoon settled into a series of unsuccessful probes followed by unsuccessful artillery barrages and air strikes. Both high explosive bombs and napalm were used. For lunch in Oscar's bomb crater, I had my favorite C-ration, canned apricots. I was developing a fatalist's notion that saving the best foods was not the course to follow when your tomorrow, or even your next hours, were in doubt. At one point I went up to the company CP. First Sergeant Duckett was just back from the "front," about 25 meters up the trail. He said that the NVA had an extensive trench system and formidable bunkers. The most direct route into the position led across a large bomb crater. Grenades had been coming out of the trench system toward Mike's forward elements on our side of the crater. Duckett said that he could see a hand lobbing some of the grenades and had spent some time trying to hit it. He had the spot zeroed but couldn't get the timing right. He recommended that entering the position from the flank should be investigated. Going across the bomb crater would require a charge that could be costly.

More artillery and air, both Air Force fighter-bombers and Army helicopter gunships firing rockets, were to be tried before the first sergeant's recommendation was pursued, however. The battalion commander even got into the act. His chopper made several runs over the hill. The chopper would start its charge at tree top level down in the valley, come racing up the slope of the mountain, and zip over the top, the door gunners blazing away with their M-60s and the battalion CO popping away with his CAR-15. The chopper was over the hill for all of two seconds. A more ineffective effort is difficult to imagine, but battalion COs received Silver Stars for less.

Oscar's bomb crater was close to Charlie Company's CP, and at one point during the afternoon I overheard McNevers giving his views on how the operation should be conducted. "I don't know what the hell Jerome is so afraid of. I'd just charge the goddamn bunkers. You got to be willing to fight in a goddamn war."

Yeah, right, McNevers. You know about charging, alright. You charged right into a frigging ambush.

Eventually the first sergeant's recommendation was tried. One of Mike's squads, with a machine gun, made its way down the side of the mountain and along the slope. Then it slowly made its way up toward the fortified hill top. For the last 30 meters or so, the squad leader had the M-60 fire close to a continuous burst, and the squad advanced at a brisk walk, the troopers blazing away with their M-16s. The hill top was achieved without any friendly casualties, but without any dead NVA either. There were some enemy weapons, however. One of them was a Chinese or Russian .50 caliber machine gun, a big motha.

Once Mike had possession of the hill, the rest of the battalion moved up. The hill top was a mass of downed trees and stripped and burned vegetation. The NVA trench and bunker system was largely intact, however. The trenches were deep, six feet or more, with regularly spaced firing steps to enable the NVA troopers to fire over the piled up dirt ramparts to the front. The bunkers had huge quantities of packed dirt as overhead cover. The amount of dirt ranged from six to ten feet. Only a direct hit by a 500- or 750-pound bomb would take one out. The NVA could sit out the air strikes and artillery barrages in the bunkers, each of which could hold up to ten small soldiers, and then scoot down the trenches to repel any ground attack.

The hill top provided excellent views in several directions. Indeed, in one direction the hill that was the location of the battalion fire support base and was the site of our initial landing could be seen. The .50 caliber might have been the one that greeted the lead choppers of Alpha's assault some days before.

By the time the three companies had closed on the hill, it was late afternoon. The decision was made to laager. The battalion commander flew in for a personal inspection, a hot meal appeared, and an extra supply of mortar rounds was delivered. Jerome wanted Oscar to fire some H&I fires that night. Also in the resupply were a few gentlemen from the press. We must be in something big if the grave-followers were afoot. They were going to travel with us for a few days. They wandered about, interviewing and taking pictures. The cutups in the Weapons Platoon reveled in the attention.

This was to be my first experience as platoon leader with H&I fires. Following the death of the trooper back in Tuy Hoa, Jerome had ordered that the platoon leader or platoon sergeant supervise any H&I firing—check the sight setting and gun alignment and verify the number of explosive packets. According to the platoon members, however, including Sgt. Thurmond, they hadn't been following the procedure. They viewed the requirement as unnecessary. Moreover, firing the mortar all by oneself in the middle of the night was something that many of the platoon members looked forward to. Graduating to the responsibility was considered a significant accomplish. Taking away the opportunity to fire the weapon alone would be a real morale downer.

So I was faced with a small dilemma: orders versus trusting the troops. I chose the most appealing course, equivocation. I said that either Sgt. Thurmond or myself would have to be awake for each firing but would not necessarily check each step in detail. Sgt. Thurmond and myself divided up responsibility for the four firing times. I had no expectation that he would be awake for his shifts, but a platoon sergeant had to be given some leeway. My fear was a repeat of the Tuy Hoa incident with me asleep. A firing foul-up occurs, men die, and the platoon leader is catching Zs. When my turns came, I sat up on my air mattress—we had been sleeping in the open because it was the dry season—and watched the gunner move the gun, check the sights, count the powder bags, and drop the round in the tube. The firings occurred without incident.

The mission for the next day was to follow the ridgeline toward the southwest, toward Laos and Cambodia. Oscar was fourth in the company column, behind November, the headquarters group, and Lima. The last trooper in Lima, and consequently the trooper directly in front of me, was Reilly, the midwesterner who had given Sgt. Brown grief on the bushwacker back in Tuy Hoa when we had stopped at the stream to clean up before rejoining the company. Thus far, I had been aware of no overt hostility toward the members of the media who were with us. Just as the column was clearing the laager site, however, a couple of late-starting clean-fatigued paunchy news guys brushed past us to get closer to the head of the column. Reilly let go with a stream of invective.

"Goddamn fuckin' death-smellin' pieces of shit. They just wanna see us die. They outta all be shot."

Several troopers in front of him seconded the opinions. The news guys overheard, and one of them even attempted a response: "We're just doing our job. We're trying to tell your story."

"That's a fuckin' crock'a shit. I hav'ta be here. You don't."

That seemed the crux of the matter for Reilly. The media types could come and go as they pleased. Reilly didn't have any options or choice. The news guys didn't appear surprised by the outburst. Apparently they had encountered the attitude before. They continued past us. Reilly continued his rantings. It was a long time before he calmed down, eventually retreating into an angry silence.

The day was just a long slow hump along the ridge-line, which averaged about 75 meters wide and was covered with trees and underbrush. We followed the NVA's newly constructed trail but encountered no enemy. I began to suspect that the NVA, knowing the Americans preferred the high ground, were congregating in the valleys. Regiments could be at the bottoms of the slopes on either side of us, and we wouldn't know it. Late in the day, we crossed a large open area, about 100 meters across and extending for several hundred meters down each side of the ridge. The area seemed much too extensive to have been just an old landing zone. Perhaps it had been the site of a fire support base. The column stopped for the night on the far side of the open space.

A chopper took out several of the media types, disappointed that they had not seen any bang-bang. But the loss was more than compensated for by the delivery of something extraordinary—a female. She was a free-lance journalist, extremely attractive, black hair, dark eyes, tailored jungle fatigues, and an Eastern European name. The headquarters group, including Jerome and especially Corky Blake, the artillery forward observer, were ga-ga over her. A number of the other troops were uneasy, even resentful. Some felt that round-eyed females had no place in the 'Nam, particularly in the field. Others didn't like the way the headquarters group monopolized her. Jerome introduced the platoon leaders to her at our evening briefing. We had more comments and questions than usual, each trying to give the impression that he was the most knowledgeable military strategist since MacArthur.

The chopper also brought in a chaplain for a brief visit. I happened to overhear a conservation he had with a member of November, a machine gunner. The kid was a serious type, and one who seemed to see the world in black and white terms. There was no nebulousness, no nuance, no shades of grey. He was deeply bothered by certain actions of the platoon leadership during November's tangle with the NVA blocking position several days before. I couldn't ascertain exactly what the problem was, but the kid certainly seemed to believe that poor decisions and judgments were made. The chaplain wasn't offering a lot of solace. He was mostly just listening. The kid had plenty to get off his chest and expounded for some time. The conversation caused me to focus again on my own feelings of uncertainty and what I considered my lack of testing.

Sgt. Thurmond provided an interesting ending to the evening. He had befriended one of the remaining press guys, one who just happened to have a bottle. Sgt. Thurmond got snockered. As the battalion was drifting off to its watchful slumber, a loud voice began booming from the vicinity of Oscar's mortar. "Hey Lieutenant, you think the captain is warm tonight? Damn, I wish I had me a blanket like that. Didja see the tits on that babe? Arrrrhooooo."

I tried to respond in a quiet voice, hopping that Thurmond would get the hint and tone down the decibels. It was a considerable time before he drifted off to sleep, however. Meanwhile, a good portion of the battalion lay sniggering about the embarrassment that was undoubtedly being felt in Alpha's CP area.

Hill 882

The next day, November 18, 1967, Douglas Baum and Eugene Washington died, Lima was decimated, Reilly was loaded on a chopper with a massive head wound, a sergeant in the headquarters group lost both legs and screamed in pain for part of the afternoon, and Lt. Kane's chest was fragmented. Also, I answered a few questions about myself to myself, but only temporarily because some of us, despite what we may have done or gone through, never really stop wondering what we are made of.

Lima was the point platoon. The route of march continued to follow the ridgeline, which gradually curved to the right. The first goal of the day was a hill, Hill 882. We should probably reach it about noon. The media types, probably six in number, including Sgt. Thurmond's female and a couple of troopers from the brigade's public affairs section, were either with Lima or the headquarters group.

Oscar was directly behind the headquarters group. During the breaks as the main body waited for Lima to go another 150 or so meters, Jerome and the first sergeant discussed various administrative business. One matter was awards, and as he looked at me, Jerome said, "Yeah, let's give Lt. Holland a Bronze Star too. His platoon did some good stuff with those ambushes in Tuy Hoa." While I was appreciative of the compliment, the statement did indicate the casualness of a good portion of the awards business. Bronze Stars were standard awards for junior officers and senior NCOs in a combat zone. The fact that I had been in Vietnam for almost 16 months and had departed the 716th without one was probably as much a commentary on my situation and abilities as was Jerome's offhand compliment.

So the morning passed with the standard accordion-like movement: send out the point platoon, link up, repeat the process. Despite the presence of the media, the level of anticipation was probably lower than it had been since we arrived at Dak To. After all, there had been no contact during the previous day's move. Maybe we were getting back to the routine of humping all day in search of an elusive enemy.

The ridgeline approach to Hill 882 sharpened its right-ward turn and dipped into a small saddle just before rising to the rounded, jungle-covered crest. Lima reached the peak just a little after noon. The radio crackled: "Six, this is Lima. There's fresh commo wire and trails up here."

"This is Six. Be careful, we're on the way."

"Six, Lima. There's movement at the bottom of an old LZ."

"This is Six. Get yourself into a perimeter, pronto!"

As these transmissions were taking place, Jerome, close to the head of the column, was getting us moving. He radioed: "Mike, November, Oscar. We're going straight to the hill and not around by the ridge. Lima's got something and we need to get there fast. Move your people."

Just then Lima's point, Sgt. Baum, called Lima: "Lima Six, we've got NVA coming up the side of the clearing."

By this time, the main body was scrambling down the side of the ridge and before long was climbing the other side, the slope of Hill 882. This route was shorter but more difficult than the ridgeline route that Lima had followed. Initially, Lima's radio transmissions hadn't aroused the sense of concern and immediacy in me that they did in Jerome, but his haste was catching. As I stumbled and slid down the slope, grabbing trees and shrubs to break my descent, fighting for balance against the momentum of the two mortar rounds and rucksack on my back, an emptiness rose in my stomach, and a bit of sour-tasting bile caught in my throat. The adrenalin was pumping so freely by the time I hit the bottom and headed upwards that I hardly noticed what normally would have been a lung-searing, thigh-aching climb. Adding to the rising tension level were fragmentary radio transmissions between Sgt. Baum and Lt. Wayman regarding more NVA sightings.

Automatic weapons fire, punctuated by various explosions, cut loose just as we gained the crest of the hill. The fire was heavy. The distinctive snap of incoming bullets caused most to get as close to the ground as possible. Movement continued, but at a crawl or a crouch. To the front, Lima was pinned down. The hill top didn't fall away in that direction but seemed to be flat for a considerable distance. Mike moved to the left flank, trying to tie in to Lima. November was also assuming a position on the left, picking up where Mike left off and stretching to the rear. Charlie and Delta were on the back part of the hill.

An old LZ, a fairly large one, was on the right flank of the hill. It started just at the edge of the hill and stretched down the slope for about 100 meters. It was about 30 meters wide and overgrown with bushes, many well over head high. Visibility over the top of the bushes to the trees and valley below and the mountains beyond was unrestricted but the view down the LZ was limited to a few feet. The one place where the vegetation was sparse was at the very top of the clearing. There, about seven or eight meters of openness separated the trees on the hill top and the thick bushes of the old LZ.

I learned later that Alpha Company had actually laagered on Hill 882 several months earlier when the 1st Battalion was humping the mountains of Dak To. A number of holes from that and perhaps other visitations by U.S. troops offered protection from the increasingly heavy incoming fire. In Lima's vicinity, however, the NVA also seemed to be making use of the old bunkers.

Initially, we started setting up the mortar in the trees on the top of the hill. Firing from there, however, would have been limited by the overhead obstacles. So we went to the open space at the top of the LZ. Harold Campton and the boys got the gun up quickly. It must have been within the vision of some of the NVA because the snapping bullets around and over our heads increased. Lima's line, such as it was, was about 20 meters to our left front. No friendlies were to our right front or our right, meaning Oscar was now part of the perimeter. Because of the increased fire our activity was attracting and because we had been given no instructions to shoot, we crawled to cover once the gun was set up. Several large logs lay in the area, and they provided us some protection and concealment.

I yelled to keep an eye on the LZ: "Watch the bushes! There's no one down in front of us!" The LZ really had me worried because the vegetation was so thick that NVA could get within a few feet of us before we would see them. "Be ready! They could be right on top of us!"

By this time, Corky Blake was beginning to adjust the artillery. The periodic crashing of shells drowned out the small arms and the thudding of grenades. Then the first of many air strikes started in. Someone from the headquarters group yelled: "Air strikes coming! There're gonna be close! Take cover!" The roar of a jet approached. We tried to get even closer to the ground. My hands and arms went up to my helmet, pulling it tight to my head. A huge explosion tore the air, the concussion tangible. Before we had a chance to catch a deep breath, the roar of the second jet—they usually worked in pairs—could be heard inbound. Again, a tremendous detonation had us cringing. The impacts were probably no more than 150 meters away. They would get closer.

The artillery and air strikes had no effect on the volume of incoming fire. Despite the fallen logs, the open area at the top of the clearing seemed a particularly vulnerable place. The Mortar Platoon began scattering for more cover. Timmons—one of the RTOs—the Rican, and I crawled a few meters down the right side of the old LZ. This gave us a better view into the undergrowth in the cleared area. We also found an old fighting position that the three of us could squeeze in. It was narrow but deep, maybe five feet. We squatted in the bottom for a time, feeling comparatively safe.

Crampness, restlessness, and a little guilt, however, eventually overcame my desire to be as far below the steel flying through the air as possible. There must be something I should be doing. Besides, down at the bottom of the hole we weren't even watching for NVA coming through the thick vegetation of the LZ. I poked my head up and saw that a few troopers had occupied a hole about ten meters below and to the right of us. They must be the edge of the Delta-Charlie portion of the make-shift perimeter that was still being formed. I crawled down to them. "Hey, we're the end of Alpha's position. The line curves back up across the top of the clearin'. There's no good guys in the clearin' or down below. Keep a sharp eye 'cuz there're liable to be coming up the sides or in the bushes."

"Roger that," said one of them. They seemed alert and calm. In truth, the fire seemed a little less threatening these few meters down the slope than it did nearer the crest. I moved in a crouch back to the edge of the hole where Timmons and the Rican were. They had spread out into the space I had occupied and seemed contented. Climbing back into the cramped space didn't appeal to me, so I said, "I'm going up the hill to see what's happenin'. We need to be collectin' the mortar rounds from the other platoons also."

As I started toward the mortar, I heard a concussion-like popping from beyond Lima. It was just discernable above the continuing bursts of small arms fire, the exploding of grenades, and the artillery. It took an instant before I realized that the NVA were firing mortars. I suddenly felt extremely vulnerable. At that very moment, seven or eight high explosive 82mm mortar shells were on their steep arching path toward our position, maybe toward me personally. I had this vivid vision of a round landing directly in the small of my back, leaving me as only a head and legs. The ten or so seconds until impact were an eternity. I lay on the ground as flat as I could, trying to restrain the urge to curl into a fetal position. The explosions finally occurred toward November's position. I expelled my held breath, but this was to be the first of a number of NVA mortar barrages over the next several hours.

I resumed my journey up the hill. I was carrying my M-16 and had my bag of ammunition slung over my shoulder. Several members of the Weapons Platoon—Harold Campton, Williams, Truman—were still behind the logs in the cleared area. They seemed relatively composed amid the rounds snapping through the air and the various explosions, almost as if they were waiting out a summer thunderstorm back in the World. Williams was peering over the log toward Lima's position, seemingly in a deeply concentrated search for NVA. Truman had his plotting board out and was making preliminary calculations in anticipation of an order to fire. I said to Harold Campton, "I'm goin' to see what's happening at the CP. We need to be getting the mortar rounds together. You get them from the platoon, I'll check the other platoons."

"Watch out, Sir," Harold Campton responded. "They say the bastards are in the trees. We're ready to fire at any time."

I glanced up at the trees. No NVA were visible, and it was hard to imagine anybody sitting on a branch 30 or 40 feet above the ground with all that lead flying around. On the other hand, as I made my way over the logs and up the 15 meters or so to the top of the hill, I noted that other members of the Weapons Platoon and various headquarters people were intensely scrutinizing the trees and all but ignoring Lima's direction or the potential avenue of approach up the old LZ.

Controlled chaos ruled on the crest of the hill. Several wounded Lima troopers had been dragged back from the "front," approximately 20 meters away. One, it appeared to be Reilly, had his head heavily bandaged, was unconscious, and had an IV tube in his arm. The main medic seemed to be a trooper named Meehan, who had been assigned to the company a week or so before when the incipient California hippie had departed.

Because of the gentle slope of the hill in Lima's direction, the first meter or so of air above the flat crest was not in the direct line of fire for AK-47 and RPD machine gun rounds. Standing up put one in the lethal zone, however. Moreover, incoming mortars and other explosive stuff were not deterred by a little fold in the terrain. As I took in the vision of the wounded, several whooshes went by just overhead. "The sons of bitches are firing rockets!" someone yelled. The rockets and the dreaded RPGs—or maybe they were the same thing, my knowledge of enemy weapons being rudimentary at best—were making their appearance. Just then, another voice sounded: "Air strike! It's gonna be close!" As I tried to become one with the earth, I saw Jerome, Corky Blake, and their RTOs several meters away. Jerome and Blake were engrossed in their radios, Blake adjusting artillery, Jerome trying to satisfy battalion's unquenchable thirst for information, control the company, and handle the air strikes. First Sergeant Duckett was a few meters beyond Jerome and Blake, peering in Lima's direction.

The air strike rolled in, very close. Shrapnel from the exploding bombs whistled overhead. Shortly after the planes finished, the artillery resumed. It also was being brought in closer and closer. Dust and very small bits of shredded vegetation from the nearby explosions were drifting over the position, adding a layer of haze and obscurity to the scene.

A level of adrenalin-induced exhilaration had overtaken the gut-wrenching fear that dominated me during the first minutes of the action. Except during the NVA's mortar barrages and especially close air strikes, I felt very little personal threat. At one level, it was as if I was watching the battle on a movie screen. At another level, I seemed to be in a particularly challenging and exciting sports contest to which I was more and more enthusiastically devoting my energies. Despite the evidence of man's mortality that was accumulating around me, my sense of immediate vulnerability was receding.

Our female media accompaniment was in the thick of the activity. She was helping with the wounded and displaying absolutely no fear. I was to learn later that when the fight had first started and a horizontal curtain of steel was passing overhead, she had asked Jerome, "When do we charge?" She and maybe McNevers were the only Americans on the hill who could conceive of a charge into that torrent of fire.

I policed up a few mortar rounds that the headquarters group had been carrying and headed back towards the mortar. The gun was sitting unattended in the open. The unrelenting snapping and popping of incoming bullets was keeping the Weapons Platoon members behind the logs and in the holes. I skittered over the log and dropped the rounds. "Lima's taking a beating. There's beaucoup wounded up on the hill."

"They need help anywhere?" Harold Campton asked.

"I don't know. We just need to be ready to fire the gun when they ask. I'm goin' back down to the flank and see what's happening."

"We're ready to fire anytime. I'll go hunt up some more rounds." Harold Campton hopped over the log and headed up the hill. Truman had propped himself up and was continuing with his calculations. Williams was looking over the log, scanning the woods in Lima's direction. I crouched and scurried down the hill towards the hole where I had left Timmons and the Rican. I looked in the hole. The Rican wasn't there. Timmons grinned up at me. He held out a piece of metal. "Look what you missed, Sir."

I reached down and took a rocket fin from his hand. Timmons said, "It hit just over the edge of the hole right after ya left. Right where ya were lyin' before ya took off. You would'a bought the farm."

"Where's the Rican?" I asked as I looked over my near-miss. It should have scared the wee-wee out of me, and in other circumstances might have, but I was operating on pure adrenalin now. The only things scaring me were the air strikes and the mortar barrages—Holy Shit! Here came another! I slide down on top of Timmons to get the small of my back out of the open. We hunched at opposite ends of the hole, waiting for the impact of the shells. After agonizing seconds, they crashed to earth somewhere toward the back of the hill. I expelled my breath and asked again, "Where's the Rican?"

"He went back up the hill."

I remained in the hole for awhile, listening to the alternating artillery barrages and air strikes, the intermittent NVA mortar attacks, the small arms fire, the exploding grenades, and the occasional whooshing of the incoming rockets. Eventually, however, restlessness prevailed, and I began wandering again. I first crawled down to the Delta troopers in the position just below us. They appeared to be keeping adequate watch down the slope and out into the overgrown LZ. They were no more than 30 meters below the crest of the hill, and maybe 50 meters from Lima, but the destruction and chaos taking place only a short distance away seemed remote.

Satisfying myself that the flank was reasonably secure, I started back up the slope. As I came abreast of the hole where Timmons was residing, a particularly intense and prolonged burst of incoming small arms fire tore over the summit. Troopers cringed and hugged the ground even closer. I saw one trooper just on the other side of the small clearing where the mortar was. He was lying flat on the ground, on his stomach, but rapidly turning his head from side-to-side as if to prevent angry wasps from landing. His eyes were wide with fear, the whites noticeably showing. Harold Campton, on the other hand, back from his round-gathering foray, was calmly propped against a log, holding a conservation with Williams, who was still intently peering in the direction of Lima and the NVA. Truman was actually sitting up a few meters behind the log, twirling his calculation board and writing in grease pencil.

The fire let up a little after a few minutes, and I continued my journey up the hill. I hopped over the log and started a leap over an old hole. In mid-leap, I glanced down, saw Sgt. Thurmond lying on his back at the bottom aiming his M-16 straight up at my passing crotch, and commenced a series of mid-air contortions that left me in a heap on the far side of the hole. I crawled to the edge and said down to my platoon sergeant, "Holy Christ, what the hell's goin' on!?"

Sgt. Thurmond fired a burst that screamed about a foot past my face. As I cringed away from the hole's edge, he yelled, "There're in the trees! There're in the fuckin' trees!"

"Okay, but watch what you're shootin' at!"

I noticed that others were also firing up into the trees. Reverberating around the hill were cries of, "In the trees, there're in the trees!" I looked up but couldn't see anything except dust and descending bits of leaves and bark. Just then Jerome, who was about ten meters away, yelled, "Make sure you're shooting at something in the trees! It might be nothing!"

Looking up, I thought there might be something to Jerome's skepticism. If someone actually was up in that turbulent ocean of steel, it was difficult to believe he was anything but a mass of quivering flesh, hugging a tree trunk or a branch for all he was worth. On the other hand, as I made my way over the top of the hill, someone said, "Hey, didja hear, Lieutenant? One of 'em came down outta a tree by Mike. He just grinned and walked outta the perimeter. He was higher'n kite. Drugged up something fierce."

"Shit! Why the fuck didn't someone shoot 'im? I got to see that to believe it."

"Well, that's what Mike's people are saying. Just shinnied down a tree and waltzed away."

I made my way over the hill to retrieve mortar rounds from November and Mike. A short time before, a sergeant of the headquarters group had been hit in the legs by a rocket. The wounds were bad. What was left of his legs was a bloody mess. He was lying on a poncho with several people working over him, applying IVs, tourniquets, bandages, and morphine. And he was screaming, an ear-piercing howl that seemed to come from the soul. The screaming was to continue for a good while.

November was located on the back side of the hill. Its portion of the perimeter was relatively small, and the troopers were bunched together on a small line. The platoon sergeant, SFC Hernandez, was nearby. I asked him to get his mortar rounds together and bring them to the gun. He said he would. I then moved to the right and forward to reach Mike. I came across Lt. Roberts crouched in the bottom of an abandoned hole. He had a radio receiver in his hand. The cord ran to the radio on the pack of his RTO, who seemed content to lie on the ground outside the hole. Roberts had been in the field for over seven months, had been through a tough time just a couple of days before, and had struck me in recent days as a guy who had seen all he wanted to see.

"Hey, I'm collectin' mortar rounds," I said.

"You're welcome to 'em, although you might have trouble finding 'em! The NVA are all over! One of 'em came down a tree and stepped right over the hole! Just grinned at me and walked out of the perimeter! Guy had to be on drugs."

"Why didn't ya shoot him?"

"Didn't have a chance. It just surprised me so much I didn't get my gun up 'til he was gone."

I glanced at the RTO. He was gazing upwards into the trees, apparently waiting for the next visitor from above. I turned back to Roberts: "How about our mortar rounds?"

"You're welcome to whatever you find. I don't even know where the goddamn line is. We're spread out all over the hillside."

I set off in the direction of what should be Mike's portion of the perimeter. I angled toward the right, where Mike was supposedly tied into Lima. Like most of the hill top, the area was tree-covered, with some underbrush. The haze from the dust and bits of leaves and bark hung heavy in the air. Explosions and small arms fire continued to provide background noise. After ten or so meters of semi-crawling, I came to several Mike troopers behind logs and bamboo clumps. They were peering intently to the front. "Hey, I'm collecting mortar rounds. You guys got any?"

"There's some on our packs out there, but we can't get 'em."

I looked over the log. Three or four rucksacks were about five meters to the front. They evidently had been quickly dropped. "What's the problem?" I asked. No shots were being fired in the immediate vicinity, although Lima's position was just to the right.

"NVA are out there, Sir. Keep your head down."

I peered to the front. Visibility was about 15 meters through the trees and underbrush. No NVA were in sight. "I don't see nobody."

"There're out there. Better watch out, Sir." I was obviously making the troopers nervous, but I did not feel there would be any problem getting to the packs.

"We need those rounds. Keep a look out." I crawled and crouched around a bamboo clump and got to the packs. It wasn't an act of bravery because for some reason I did not think there was any danger that the packs were still under NVA surveillance. I dragged each one back to the troopers' position and unstrapped the mortar rounds. I also took a LAW, a rocket-like weapon that we might find some use for on the old LZ. Struggling with three mortar rounds, the LAW, and my rifle, I started back over the hill top to Oscar's position. On the flat crest, rounds were still snapping just overhead and chaos still reigned. Wounded, most from Lima, cluttered the area. Jerome and his two RTOs were prone on the ground toward the front of the group, feverishly engrossed in their communications. I stumbled through the turmoil, finally reached the open area where the mortar stood, dropped the rounds and the LAW, and fell down behind the log to catch my breath.

178 Vietnam, A Memoir

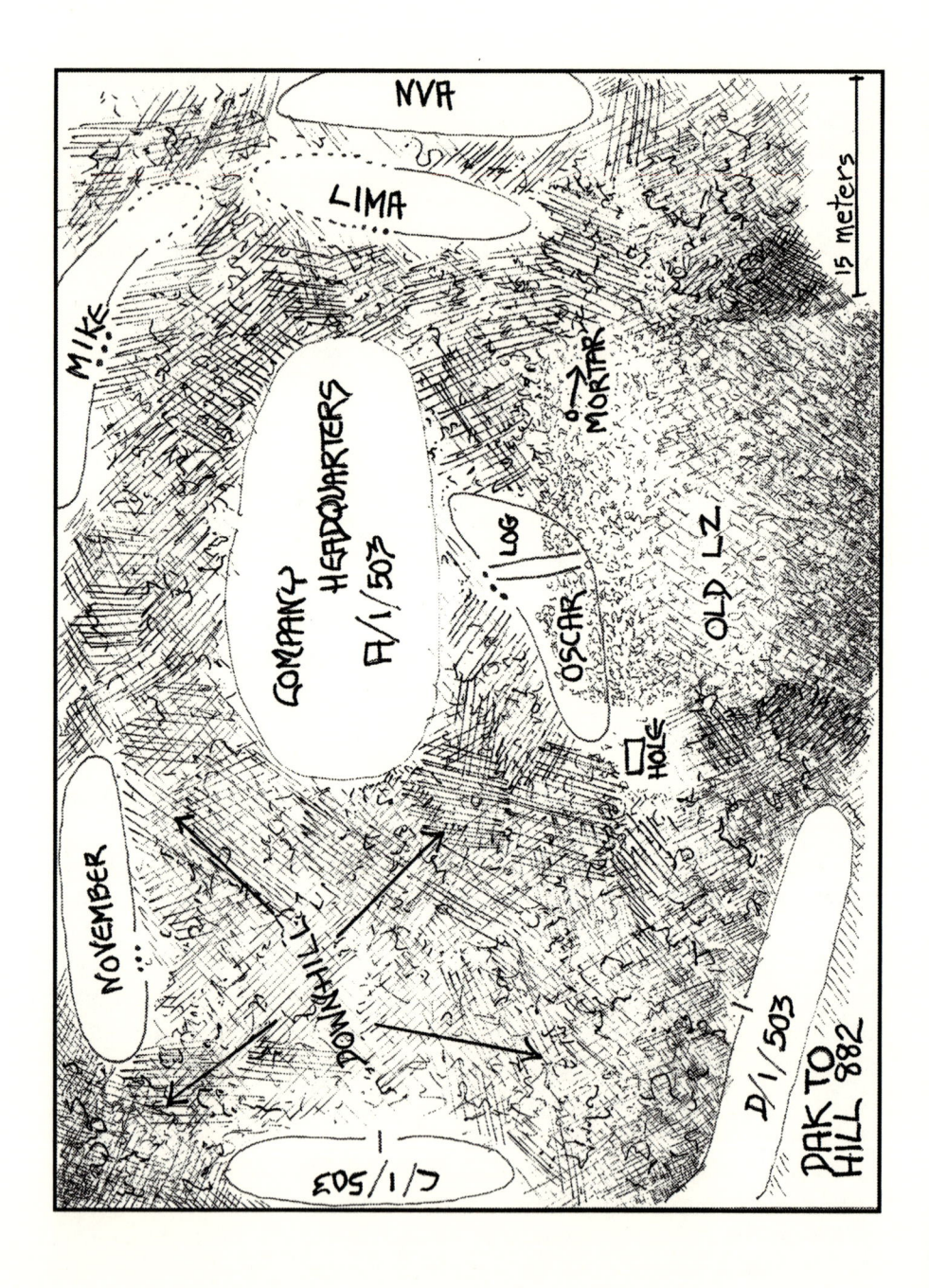

After a moment, I became aware that Sgt Williams, about two meters from me, was firing away with his M-16 toward the far side of the LZ, in Lima's general direction. "What're ya shootin' at?", I asked.

He had a quizzical frown on his face. "I see them up there," he said uncertainly.

"Are you sure? That's where Lima is. You sure you ain't firin' Lima up?" He didn't say anything but he did stop firing. I peered over the log. Lima's right flank ended just before the LZ so no friendly troops were between us and the far side of the LZ. Still, I found it difficult to believe that NVA were actually in sight. Probably more important, I had my usual fear of shooting friendly troops. "Just make damn sure you're not shooting Lima."

At about that time, the firing picked up significantly. Williams, myself, and several others crouched further down behind the log. Prolonged bursts of automatic weapons fire screamed overhead. A few rockets whooshed by, exploding back toward November and Charlie and Delta Companies. Another air strike came rolling in, causing the earth to tremble and sending shrapnel through the branches above us. Amid all the flying steel, Truman, sitting nonchalantly by a bamboo clump, calmly continued making his fire direction calculations.

I felt a little vulnerable behind the log because it wasn't completely on the ground in my vicinity. It rested on several mounds of earth near its ends, creating a three to six inch space underneath much of its middle. I kept expecting a bullet to find its way to the gap and slam into my skull. In a firefight, some felt the greatest vulnerability in their groin. I felt the greatest vulnerability for my head, envisioning it splitting like a raw egg from the impact of a high velocity AK-47 round.

Despite my concern about the gap and my skull's vulnerability, I stayed behind the log for awhile, absorbing the sounds of the battle and waiting for Jerome to tell us to start firing. Eventually, however, restlessness prevailed, and I commenced another journey up the hill. On the crest, at least one wounded soldier was loudly reacting to the pain. One of my troopers was sitting on the ground having his side attended to. "I got hit, Sir! I damn well got hit!" He exclaimed. It appeared to be a fairly small shrapnel nick. The trooper was obviously ecstatic, although his excitement had a tinge of panic to it.

I continued on toward November to see what was holding up the mortar rounds Sgt. Hernandez had promised me. What was holding them up was that the platoon leader, Lt. Kane, had been hit. He was stripped to the waist, extremely pale, propped up against a tree, engulfed in a full chest bandage, and babbling semi-coherently. November's medic and RTOs and Sgt. Hernandez seemed to have their hands full trying to control him. He kept trying to get up and seemed to be making an effort to give commands. Nothing understandable was emerging from his mouth, however. I picked up a few mortar rounds, and Sgt. Hernandez said he would get the others to the gun shortly. Kane's picture had been taken by one of the media types, and a few months later he would be on the cover of a national newsmagazine.

After making the return journey and depositing the rounds, I went back to the crest. Jerome and First Sergeant Duckett were lying on the ground, in conference. I joined them, saying "We're ready to fire whenever you want, Sir."

The statement did not seem to register. "Baum and Washington are dead. Lima's gettin' hit bad. Lt. Wayman's wounded. D'ya wanna go up there?"

"Up there" was only 10 to 15 meters away, but 10 to15 meters when you are lying flat on the ground can be a long journey. I was somewhat perplexed by the question. I had the impression that Wayman was functioning well enough and knew that few commanders liked to have someone horn in. So I asked, "How's he doin'? Does he need help?"

The answers weren't very enlightening. I don't think I was reluctant to go forward if I was needed, but I couldn't tell if I was needed. I said, "I'll be glad to go if he needs help. But I don't wanna be in the way. You sure he needs help?"

Again, the answer was inconclusive, and the matter was dropped. I've thought about the incident occasionally in the years since and have concluded that maybe what was really happening was that I was being offered a Silver Star. If I had gone forward, a Silver Star write-up would have been easy. So maybe I missed my chance for a big-time medal. On the other hand, I still feel that horning in on Wayman would not have been appropriate. In any case, it was one of those incidents in one's life that becomes permanently engraved in the "what if" file.

But I didn't have time to dwell on the matter at the moment. Jerome was now discussing another problem. "They want us to get the reporters out, particularly the woman. The first choppers that come in are for the reporters." I looked at him incredulously. The thought of choppers landing in the midst of this firefight was absurd. From a few feet in the air upwards, steel from many different sources ruled. Any chopper attempting to land would be riddled. Moreover, if and when choppers finally got in, the seriously wounded should be the first to leave.

"You've got to be kiddin'," I said.

"No, General Sweitzer himself wants the woman out." General Sweitzer was the brigade commander. Talk about misplaced priorities. Here we were in a fight for survival, and the bone-headed higher headquarters' first thought was for the media's safety, particularly the female media. The news people shouldn't be blamed for the sins of Army brass, but if they left they would certainly be the subject of the grunts' hostility.

I glanced around. The female media person was heavily engrossed in the task of caring for the wounded. "She doesn't look like she needs evacuatin'," I said.

"No," said Jerome. "When the shit first hit the fan, she even asked when we were gonna charge. Some of those other guys, though, seem to want outta here." He was referring to two middled-aged, overweight types huddled behind a nearby clump of bamboo. Fear seem to be rising visibly from their quivering bodies.

Changing the subject, I said, "Well, we're ready to fire the mortar whenever ya want." Just then one of Jerome's radios crackled with the news of another incoming air strike. I scurried back to the cover of Oscar's log. The air strikes were getting closer and closer. From the view out on the clearing, the planes could be seen making their approach parallel to our front, and even releasing their ordnance. I peered over the log as the latest charge was being made. I didn't know much about aircraft identification, but I thought the planes were F-4 Phantoms. The first one dropped two tumbling canisters—napalm. The flaming gas aroused less fear in me than did hard stuff—500- and 750-pound bombs. The dense jungle canopy could absorb much of the napalm. Even a direct hit was survivable. The hard stuff, on the other hand, left no room for error.

After the strike passed, I lingered for a bit, and then went back to the crest. Jerome was reinforcing Lima with one of November's machine guns. It went in an old hole at the corner of the LZ, in front of the mortar's location. Finally Oscar had a small buffer between it and the enemy. Jerome's batman, the Texan Holmes, was getting into the action and took over as gunner. I went over the crest to see if Mike had any more rounds. As I was returning with several, I saw Holmes fire a long burst on the M-60. As a machine gunner, he had a lot to learn. He was firing the thing John Wayne-style, standing in the thigh-deep hole, holding the gun off the ground at his waist, and bearing down on the trigger. The effect was predictable—the first few rounds were parallel to the ground, the rest went into the air as the recoil forced the barrel upward. I yelled, "Holmes!" When he turned toward me, I motioned with my hand downwards, indicating he should keep the gun down. It was an obvious correction, and he didn't let me forget afterwards that I had a knack for the obvious.

Over the next hour or so, I retraced the circuit several times—Oscar's position on the open LZ, Delta company's hold on the LZ's flank, the crest with its crowd of wounded, media types, and headquarters groupies, November's too-close together line, Mike's erratic perimeter. Nothing was more than 30 meters from a center point on the crest, but a round trip was akin to an intercontinental journey. The automatic weapons fire, the rockets, the mortars, the air strikes, the artillery, all continued. The intensity of the different items varied from time-to-time, but there was no interruption of the general crescendo of violence.

Finally, late in the afternoon after one particularly prolonged and heavy bout of incoming small arms fire, Jerome screamed, "Oscar, when are ya gonna fire the goddamn mortar?" It was no time to note that we had expressed readiness to fire on several occasions. I yelled, "Alright, let's get to it!"

Harold Campton and several others immediately ran crouching to the exposed mortar. The gun was ready, the aiming stakes had long since been put out, and Truman had made more calculations than an MIT mathematics professor on a roll. "Fire'em close as hell!" Jerome yelled from the crest.

"Where ya want'em?", Truman asked.

"No more than 50 meters out. And walk'em up and down the front!" I replied.

Truman took only a few seconds to sound off with settings for the gun. The gun crew and Harold Campton repeated them as they made the adjustments. Truman said, "No charges." We were going to be firing on the primer alone, with the tube almost straight up. A gust of wind might bring a round down on the gun itself, or worse yet the small of my back.

"Gun up!", shouted the aimer.

"Gun up!" responded the crew.

"Fire!", shouted Harold Campton, and the first round was away. We waited agonizing seconds for its impact, hoping it was going to clear the perimeter. Finally, from beyond Lima, the deep "whump" came. It was where it was supposed to be. The gun crew immediately dropped three more rounds. As soon as they were away, I yelled, "Now walk it!"

Truman shouted adjustments, the gun crew made them, and three more rounds were on the way. The procedure was repeated another 12 or so times, resulting in about 45 high-explosive mortar rounds producing a steel curtain just a few meters in front of Lima's position. The jungle was too thick for us to see the explosions, but the thudding concussions reverberated through our bodies. I halted the firings at this point as we were down to about 20 rounds. We still had an evening and long night ahead of us.

Memory is a notoriously unreliable animal. My memory of the effect of Oscar's barrage, a memory I have had since November 18, 1967, is that it broke the NVA attack. Certainly, incoming fire ceased very nearly simultaneously with the barrage. After the last round was away and Harold Campton and the gun crew scrambled back to cover, little was heard from the NVA. Because of the continuance of our artillery and air strikes, however, it was awhile before the fading of the opposition became generally noticeable. Explosions from friendly sources and outgoing small arms fire made it seem as if the battle was still in progress. Whether Oscar's barrage was what finally broke the attack or whether the barrage just happened to coincide with the NVA's withdrawal or "defeat" is something unknowable.

In any case, after five or so hours of peril, A Company's survival gradually appeared, for the moment, assured. As twilight and then darkness fell, the friendly fire slowly slacked off—the air strikes because of the planes' inability to provide close air support at night, the artillery in response to the realization that we weren't getting shot at anymore. The artillery didn't cease entirely. Corky Blake just slowed it down and moved it out a little so that friendly steel wasn't rending the air directly overhead.

The feeling of a completed battle was absent. Everyone expected a renewed attack sometime during the night, so the slackening of fire was accompanied by much feverish activity on our side of the line. Troopers began sitting and kneeling in order to scoop new holes or improve old ones. A few more of Lima's wounded were moved back toward November. Oscar began digging a gun pit near the gun's location. I hung around the crest to get news and instructions from Jerome on what to do next.

Higher was still fixated on the media people, particularly the woman. When the realization gradually dawned that we were no longer taking fire, higher began discussing plans to evacuate the fourth estate, and oh yes, the wounded. I was with Jerome when the definite word came on the priority of evacuation. No one else seemed to be interested in undertaking the responsibility, so I took it upon myself to inform the female. She was still busy with the wounded. I told her what was planned, and she was aghast: "That's ridiculous. The wounded should go first. I'm not going out when there are wounded here."

"They say you have to. Brigade wants you out of here."

She grunted noncommittally and turned back to her work. I suspect the only reason I was inserting myself into the situation was that I wanted to be near the babe. But nothing was about to happen for awhile, and she evinced no desire to continue talking to me, so I returned to Jerome's location. Lt. Wayman had crawled back from Lima's position. His face was bloodied and swollen from shrapnel wounds, but he seemed otherwise okay. Indeed, he was pumped up, on an adrenalin high, talking animatedly about the afternoon's events. As I got there, he was describing how Baum and Washington died.

Baum had been caught in front of the perimeter as Lima struggled to form a line in the first minutes of the fight. He had been trying to get his squad back into position, and was severely wounded. He was conscious and lying on the ground five or six meters in front of the forming perimeter. Wayman said he made an effort to get to Baum, but Baum mouthed and whispered that an NVA position was in the underbrush just a short distance away, and not to come. Baum apparently died a little bit after that. His body was still in front of the perimeter.

Washington had been lying next to Wayman, behind a log. He raised up to go somewhere, perhaps to make an effort to get to Baum, and took a bullet in the forehead. As Wayman talked, I thought back to the night in the mountains around Tuy Hoa when Washington had kept me company as I battled diarrhea. I remembered particularly his words about having survived for nine or so months in the 'Nam and his being absolutely certain about his return to the land of the Big PX in the very near future. Well, he was going home, but not in the way he had planned.

According to Wayman, at the height of the action Lima was virtually incapable of any movement. Bursts of automatic weapons fire and grenades and rockets greeted even the smallest wiggle. The grenades were exploding just on the other side of the logs that provided cover for the platoon. About the only offense Lima could provide were grenades lobbed from an almost prone hand. Bringing a hand above the log brought an instance response, so grenades were thrown with just a flip of the wrist.

After some more talk, Wayman went back to Lima. At about the same time, a resupply chopper arrived. It was a Huey carrying a sling load of mainly ammunition, and much of that mortar rounds. Night had fallen by this time, a typical tropical night of deep darkness. Occasional flares interrupted the blackness with an eerie flickering twilight that didn't penetrate the trees but did manage to create ghostly shadows on the open LZ. The chopper did not land. Instead, it attempted to hover and drop the load at the top of the LZ, near the mortar. The theory was that the drop wouldn't be long, no more than a few feet.

One problem was that dropping the load at the top of the LZ would put the chopper's blades almost in the trees. Another problem was visibility. The chopper had a spotlight but it could only provide a hazy outline of the trees and underbrush. A third problem was pilot concern about the NVA. Incoming fire had ceased some time ago, but no one could know what sort of attention the first chopper on the scene would attract. Consequently, the sling load ended up a considerable distance away from the top of the LZ. In fact, from the perimeter, we couldn't determine where the load had been dropped.

I was still operating on a full load of adrenalin and volunteered to find the dropped load. Jerome seemed preoccupied and little concerned about the problem, so I set off. He was busy with the next task of getting the wounded and the media out. I went the few meters down the hill to Oscar's position and said I was going to find the load. Will volunteered to come with me. Before departing on our quest, I made my way to the Delta Company position on the right flank of the LZ: "Hey, we're going down the LZ to find the load the chopper dropped. Don't fire us up."

"Alright."

As I've stated before, friendly fire was always one of my main concerns, whether on the giving or receiving end. I went back to the top of the LZ, and Will and I started down. The underbrush ranged from waist to over head high, and was very thick. We pushed and maneuvered our way slowly through the growth, leading with our M-16s. I expected to come across NVA at any moment and thought we would surely find them if we located the load. We encountered no enemy, however. Finally, about two-thirds of the way down the hill, we stumbled on the cargo net and its contents. Will and I stood silent and still for a few minutes listening for movement in the area. We heard nothing. Then I left him to guard the load and went back for a crew to carry it up the hill. Volunteers were easy to find. Soon we were lugging the cases of mortar and small arms rounds up the slope, and it wasn't long before the task was done.

My next contribution to the war effort was to get the female media person on a chopper. By the time we finished the retrieval of the resupply, plans had been solidified to get a medevac in. The company had approximately 25 wounded, six or seven of them seriously. Among the latter were the headquarters sergeant, whose screaming had finally been stifled by morphine, Reilly, who had never regained consciousness, and Lt. Kane. The plan was to get one or two choppers in that night to pick up the seriously wounded and the media people, and to leave the other wounded for daylight.

I relayed the word to the female that she was to leave. She said: "That's ridiculous. There are wounded here who need to get out. I'm not going before they go."

"The brigade wants you out. They say you have to leave."

"But that doesn't make any sense. Why are they saying that?"

I couldn't answer that. Most likely, it had something to do with the 1967 view that combat was a man's job and women shouldn't be around. But even back then I certainly didn't hold this belief myself with any depth of feeling.

In any case, the eventual outcome was that several of the seriously wounded and three or four of the media people went out on the first chopper. It came in after another hour or so. The landing and take off required a superb bit of flying. Because the only spot on the old LZ free of high underbrush was at the very top of the slope, where the mortar was, the pilot had to bring the machine to the edge of the trees. And because the cleared spot was so small, he couldn't land but had to hover about two feet above the ground. Then to get out of there, he had to swing the chopper around, moving it down the slope backwards and sideways as he did so to prevent the tail from hitting the trees. Once the chopper was turned around, the pilot could head out over the valley, perhaps diving a bit down the old LZ to gain some speed.

And oh yes, all this maneuvering was being done in the dark of the tropical night.

The female got on the chopper reluctantly. The other media folks boarded with alacrity. You can say what you want about the correctness of women in combat, but on November 18, 1967, on a remote hill in a remote corner of the Republic of Vietnam, a certain attractive brunette with a convoluted Eastern European name functioned with the best of men, and displayed courage and competence that a few of them didn't.

A second chopper picked up several more seriously wounded, and we were then on our own for the rest of the night. Sporadic explosions from artillery protective fires continued throughout the night, but otherwise it was uneventful. About midnight I left the crest and went down the hill to the vicinity of the hole where Timmons, the Rican, and I had spent portions of the afternoon. I didn't have the energy or the desire to blow up my air mattress. I just unfolded it and lay on top under my poncho liner. Later I also pulled my poncho over me. A nip had developed in the Central Highlands' night, sending a chill over the living, and the dead.

Thanksgiving 1967

Everyone was up with the dawn. I went to the crest of the hill and the company CP, and then forward toward Lima. Russell, one of Lima's RTOs saw me approaching and exclaimed excitedly, "Get down, Sir. They're still out there." I didn't think he was correct, but I turned around anyway. Lima's troopers were obviously still pretty jumpy.

Several tasks pressed for the battalion's attention. The wounded had to be evacuated. The area in front of Lima had to be searched and secured. And the body count—the number of dead NVA—had to be determined. Indeed, higher headquarters had been screaming for a body count since almost the height of the battle. Securing the area and the body count were undertaken simultaneously. Jerome sent a patrol out to sweep across the front. It came across no opposition but did find two wounded NVA who were brought back. One was unconscious; the other had a nasty wound under his eye, a gash extending about three inches across his face. The edges of the gash were grotesquely swollen, and his eye was almost closed. He was forced to lie down near the mortar to await evacuation.

Based on the patrol's report and the results of several subsequent sweeps, Jerome came up with a body count of 49. Maybe, but I had been around long enough to be skeptical about body counts. They had become too much influenced by the need to satisfy the insatiable cravings of higher-ups. Jerome was basically an honest guy, but since I didn't see all 49 bodies myself, I wouldn't swear to them.

After a bit, the wounded NVA began to attract some attention. Specifically Moste, Lima's bully boy who had taken a machete to the dead VC back in Tuy Hoa, came to vent his spleen. Moste had been wounded in the face and upper body by shrapnel, but the wounds were largely superficial. He was wandering around, loudly expounding on the battle, the NVA, and whatever else crossed his mind. He spotted the wounded NVA by the LZ, and proceeded to the attack. For a few minutes, he stood over the dazed soldier, uttering imprecations in a voice that gradually rose to a scream. He worked himself into quite a froth. The fact that the NVA made no response, just lay there, only roused Moste more. Finally, he let go with two sharp kicks to the NVA's wounded face.

I had been watching the show from a few meters up the hill, in the vicinity of the company's headquarters group. No one, no officers or NCOs, made any effort to stop Moste. Not even the kicking caused anyone to intervene. Moste was a violence machine that was rapidly approaching an out-of-control state.

I'm no angel, and wasn't then. But this attack on a defenseless prisoner of war rubbed me wrong. When Moste started kicking and no one else moved to stop him, I said: "Hey goddammit! Knock that shit off!"

"He's just a fuckin' gook, Lieutenant! He was killin' us yesterday!"

"I don't give a shit! He's now a prisoner! Get the hell away from him!" Timmons was standing nearby. I said to him: "Timmons, you're now responsible for the prisoner. Take your pistol and guard him. And don't let anyone else get near him."

Moste skulked off. In truth, I think he was secretly thankful that someone had called a stop to his activities. If no one had, the only thing that stood between him and the torture or death of the prisoner was his own conscience. And I think he realized that his conscience was no match for his need to be on center stage.

I had occasion to recall this episode in a few years, when the My Lai massacre came to light, and much farther in the future, when incidents of prisoner abuse in Iraq, Afghanistan, and Guantanamo Bay became public. One job of officers and NCOs in a combat environment is to control the baser instincts of their troops, and of themselves. War brings out the worst in many. It gives the opportunity to commit acts of violence that are otherwise prohibited. Once released, that violence is difficult to control. It is hard to draw the line between permissible killing in combat and the impermissible killing of prisoners and noncombatants. Officers and NCOs are responsible for drawing that line.

The choppers finally started to come in. The first few were dust-offs—medevacs. I was standing near the crest of the hill when a group of Lima's troopers was carried to the first chopper. Southern, a machine gunner, had a bandaged forearm and hand. Grotesquely swollen purple fingers protruded from the bandage. Next was MacVey, a good buddy of, and striver-to-be-like, Moste. MacVey was on his stomach and elbows on a stretcher. He was stripped to the waist, and his back was a mass of small shrapnel wounds. He was smoking in a macho fashion, and said, "What d'ya think, Lieutenant?" He was obviously proud as hell of being wounded.

"Looks like ya got messed up pretty good. How'ya doin'?"

"I'm doin' great. We had a helluva time. You shoulda' been there."

Well, I was there, or at least enough "there" not to feel like I'd missed anything, but I let it pass. Others walked by or were carried to the chopper. They all exuded a hefty degree of stoicism. For more than a few of them, being wounded would probably be the defining event of their lives. Indeed, even for many of us who were not wounded, November 18, 1967, would be a day whose details would stay with us for the rest of our memories.

Line doggies had ambivalent feelings about being wounded. A good many, and practically all in an elite unit like the Airborne, secretly desired a minor wound that would merit a Purple Heart and produce an attractive permanent but not disfiguring scar. On the other hand, the difference between getting wounded and getting dead was often just fractions of an inch. And for many, a greater fear than death was permanent disability. Being paralyzed was not the price that anyone wanted to pay for a Purple Heart. Of course, near the top of the list of feared permanent disabilities was losing one's manhood. The possibility of returning to the Land of the Big PX as a eunuch was something that one tried not to dwell on.

Grunts who were lucky enough to get that minor Purple Heart wound weren't above lording it over the rest of us. Thus some who got on the choppers that morning did so with an air of successful graduates leaving behind those who didn't pass the test. Watching the wounded being loaded on the dust-offs, I in fact felt a little unfulfilled. With all the steel that had been flying around, I could at least have picked up a little nick. I shortly discovered just how close I had come to being one of the anointed.

After the first flights left, I sat down to get my personal gear in order. I cleaned my M-16 and then started checking the magazines in the bandoleers across my chest. I took each magazine out, pressed the rounds down to make sure the spring was working properly, and inspected for any imperfections. When I pressed the rounds in one magazine, one that had been pretty much centered on my chest, they moved only reluctantly. I turned the magazine over. The metal had a gash across it, not a large gash, but one that did go all the way through one side. I pulled the rounds out. Two of them, the two directly under the gash, were dented. I sat contemplating my own mortality for a moment. The piece of shrapnel had been small, but so had the piece that had killed the Mike trooper in our first contact at Dak To a week previously. My flesh and chest bone certainly didn't have the stopping capability of the magazine's steel. The long and the short of it was that I was one lucky SOB. And I hadn't even been aware of the impact. I still have the magazine.

The bodies of Baum and Washington lay at the top of the clearing. They were covered by ponchos. Unlike our first encounter when a rush to see the dead guy had occurred, no one seemed interested in looking at them. Death had become more commonplace. They took their last ride from the field on the next chopper.

By mid-morning the wounded and dead had been evacuated, the resupply completed, the obligatory visit by the battalion commander made, and the perimeter adjusted. The mission was for a substantial force to conduct a patrol in the direction of the departed NVA. Delta Company would provide the bulk of the force, accompanied by a platoon each from Alpha and Charlie companies. November would be Alpha's contribution. The patrol departed about noon. It proceeded along the ridge of which Hill 882 was a part. The ridge sloped gently downward for about a click, and then dropped abruptly to a stream. The patrol was out for several hours, finding much evidence, including blood trails and bloody bandages, of a hasty NVA departure. The artillery and air strikes had made the area a mass of downed trees and churned-up ground.

As the patrol was returning, it came upon some live NVA. A brief firefight ensued, and two Delta Company troopers were killed. The NVA got away. The patrol resumed the return journey, carrying the two dead troopers in ponchos. They were deposited beside the LZ to await evacuation. The Delta platoon leader, who I didn't know, helped carry in the two troopers, and stayed with them for an hour or so until the chopper came. He sat on the ground between the two bodies, not saying anything. Others avoided the group. Finally, the chopper arrived and the bodies were loaded. The platoon leader remained until the chopper disappeared over the hills. He then turned slowly and moved off toward Delta's position.

While the patrol was out, Corky Blake had been adjusting artillery around our position. He was bent on getting the stuff as close to the perimeter as possible. One of the batteries he was adjusting was an 8-inch howitzer unit. Eight-inchers were big, big guns. You knew when 8-inchers were coming in because a shell's arrival was proceeded by a prolonged roar with the decibel level of a freight train. The noise was especially frightening if the shells were passing overhead. For me, being in the vicinity of an 8-inch barrage was like being in the middle of a severe thunder and lightning storm.

Blake was determined to ring our perimeter with a curtain of steel. He walked the artillery, including the 8-inchers, up the far side of the position and then started on the LZ-side, our side. I put a thick tree between me and the LZ and hoped that there wouldn't be any stray rounds. Occasionally I peeked around the tree to see if the impacts were within view. They sure as hell sounded as if they were trying to get in my pockets.

Some troopers were taking my play-it-safe tack and were huddled behind trees or in holes. Others were being macho, trying to be nonchalant and acting as if nothing were happening. Jerome was standing near me talking to McNevers from

Charlie Company and several others. The crashing from the direction of the LZ and the roaring of the incoming shells were making conservation difficult, but Jerome and McNevers seemed to be in a contest to see who would flinch first. In one of my peeks around my tree, I saw an explosion in the crown of a tree on the lower side of the LZ. Being in the crown, the explosion was on the approximate level of the hill's crest, and only about 100 meters away. It seemed to me that the frigging explosions were much too close, but Jerome and McNevers weren't blinking. Blake was a few meters away, apparently determined to bring a round down on his own noggin.

Finally, the inevitable happened. A trooper standing a few meters away from my tree suddenly went down in a heap. Two others immediately ran to his side. He sat up. At least he was alive. His nose and mouth, however, were a bloody mess. A chuck of metal had slammed into the space between his upper lip and his nose. This provided sufficient incentive for Jerome and McNevers to end their game of chicken. Jerome turned to Blake and said, "I think that's close enough. Just register that location and call it quits." A medevac shortly arrived to take out the poor guy with the bloody lower face.

We expected to move on the next day, but a battle was getting underway a few ridgelines to the south that would be the main event of the 173rd's November at Dak To. It would last until Thanksgiving Day, November 23, and would result in the decimation of the brigade's 2nd Battalion. The 4th Battalion would eventually have to rescue the 2nd. The action took place on Hill 875.

But the pummeling that the 173rd would take on Hill 875 was unforeseen on November 19, the day after A Company's moment of truth on Hill 882. For each of the next four days, we expected to move on. And for each of the next four days, we held in place. Daytime platoon- and company-size patrols were sent out. Several more contacts with small bands of NVA occurred, and at least one more trooper was killed. There was even a tentative plan to send a small group of only two or three all the way to the next hill to the west, but it didn't materialize. Holmes, Jerome's batman, got extremely enthused over the possibility when it was suggested. I was with Jerome when it was first discussed and was caught off guard when Holmes said, "Hey Sir, Lt. Holland and I'll do it. It'll be great. We can sneak all the way to Cambodia with no problem. Can't we, Lieutenant Holland?"

What could I say but, "Well, yeah. We can do that. When do we leave?" Cooler heads prevailed, however.

Oscar's location in the little clearing at the top of the old LZ gave us a ringside seat to the comings and goings over those four days on Hill 882. Brigadier

General Sweitzer, the brigade commander, even put in an appearance before he got caught up in the battle for Hill 875. He toured our cramped hilltop and spoke briefly with Jerome.

By far the most frequent visitor was the battalion commander, LTC Shafter. His visits, particularly one of them, gave me a chance to see first-hand why he was not a popular individual. During the visit I remember most vividly, he gave Capt. McNevers a public tongue-lashing of exceptional ferociousness. McNevers to his credit fought back, but Shafter was apparently well-practiced in the art of berating people. The incident occurred near Alpha's CP on the crest of the hill. When I became aware of the discussion, Shafter was loudly questioning McNevers's courage, referring particularly to Charlie's and Delta's battle for survival on November 11. McNevers was vigorously defending himself: "Goddamit, Sir. You've got no reason to accuse me of cowardice. You can ask anyone who was there. I was in charge the whole time. I constantly stood up in the line of fire to do my job."

Shafter cut him off and continued with the harangue. I found out later that the central matter of dispute was McNevers's recommendation for a Congressional Medal of Honor for one of Charlie's dead troopers. The individual had died when he threw himself on an incoming grenade. Shafter's position was that people who commit suicide don't deserve the Medal of Honor. The fact that more than a few recipients of the nation's highest award for valor had received the medal for sacrificing themselves to protect fellow soldiers from the blasts of incoming grenades seemed to have escaped Shafter. The recommendation did eventually go forward, but only after Shafter had left the battalion. And the trooper was posthumously awarded the medal.

The Shafter-McNevers show continued for a good twenty minutes. Everyone discretely evacuated the immediate vicinity, but Shafter's screaming could be heard over much of the hill. McNevers had an ego the size of Montana and could take it, but no subordinate should be subjected to the type of public humiliation that he received from Shafter that day. Shafter had a screw loose somewhere. His only saving grace as far as I was concerned was that he had given a certain MP lieutenant with little formal infantry training a chance at being an airborne infantry platoon leader. Jerome was apparently one of the few people reporting directly to Shafter who were not routinely subjected to his tirades. Whether this was due primarily to Jerome's generally superior competence or for some other reason, I don't know.

One other incident from those four days on Hill 882 stands out in my mind. It was not an incident of any consequence, and why it stayed with me over the years is difficult to say. It involved Jerome's way of teaching, and maybe the burden his method put on the student is the reason for my recollection. On the typographical map, Hill 882 was not an easily identified feature. The map merely showed a ridge stretching for at least a kilometer. The high point, the pinnacle, was not sufficiently higher than the rest of the ridge to be indicated. On the second or third day, I went up to Jerome and said, "I can't quite figure out where we are on the ridgeline on the map, Sir. Can you show me?"

The response of nine people out of ten would have been to point out the location on the map, or at least discuss the matter. Jerome's response was a curt, "That's your job, Lieutenant. You figure it out. What if you had to call in artillery or air strikes?"

We weren't getting much detail about the battle on Hill 875, but we were hearing enough to know that a real shellacking was occurring. The 2nd Battalion had been ambushed on the slopes of the large mountain. It had pulled back into a tight perimeter, putting its many wounded in the center. A wayward 750-pound bomb had found the center, and 40 paratroopers were dead, victims of friendly fire. The 4th Battalion had been inserted at the base of the hill. It eventually reached the 2nd Battalion's position, but as of the day before Thanksgiving, the hill still hadn't been taken.

On that day before Thanksgiving, the 1st Battalion finally received orders to move. The next day, Thanksgiving, we were to head southeast to a fire support base. There, we would be given a Thanksgiving dinner. So on Thanksgiving Day, 1967, the 1st Battalion left Hill 882.

A massive explosion marked the start of the trip. The approximately 150 mortar rounds that had been dropped the night of the battle and that Will and I had searched for in the dark had been sitting in their packing crates between the company CP and the mortar for the preceding four days. A lucky or well-placed shot from the NVA might have done to us what the U.S. Air Force did to the 2nd Battalion. Fortunately, such a shot hadn't materialized. One hundred fifty rounds, however, were at least twice as many as we could hump out, so Jerome decided to blow the remainder in place. Two members of the headquarters contingent were combat engineers knowledgeable about making things go boom. They rigged the boxed rounds with plastic explosives. After the three companies were clear of the perimeter, they blew up the ammunition resupply that some courageous chopper pilot had risked his butt bringing to us in our hour of need.

The move to the fire support base was uneventful, but difficult. Once we left the ridge that contained Hill 882, we crossed several extremely steep ridge-valley combinations. On one down-slope, we skirted a massive bomb crater, one of the largest I had ever seen. It was at least 20 feet deep and more than 30 meters wide. The final climb to the fire support base was almost a hand-over-hand effort.

We arrived in late afternoon. The base was on a largely barren hilltop. The barrenness appeared due to substantial bulldozer work. It certainly wasn't natural for a hill in the Central Highlands to be devoid of vegetation. The artillery consisted of a 105-mm battery. We occupied a portion of the perimeter and awaited the holiday meal. Choppers returned several of our lesser wounded, including Lt. Wayman and Oscar's own casualty. Both were bubbling over with enthusiasm and anxious to tell of their hospital stays. Wayman made sure we all knew the doctors had wanted to keep him and he had checked himself out of the hospital against their advice.

General Westmoreland or some other bigwig had been quoted in *Stars and Stripes* as saying that all troops in Vietnam, including line doggies and especially the paratroopers of the 173rd Airborne engaged in the heavy fighting around Dak To, would get a Thanksgiving dinner. Well, we got one, but I can't say it was memorable. It was the standard mermac-can dinner prepared in the rear and flown out on choppers. Turkey, potatoes, and dressing were fairly common ingredients of Army meals anyway. What would have made the day special would have been beer, but that was not to be.

We heard that the 4th and 2nd Battalions, or what was left of the latter, had also received Thanksgiving dinners. That morning, they had finally taken Hill 875. The last assault was largely unopposed, the NVA having departed the denuded knob. Very few enemy bodies were found, and there has little crowing about a body count.

Thanksgiving in Vietnam was a day earlier than in the states. The holiday period was undoubtedly much harder on the families of 173rd troopers than on the surviving soldiers. A number of families received the dreaded visit from the death team—the officers or NCOs bringing notification of the death of a son or husband. Those families that didn't but that paid even cursory attention to the news were aware that their loved ones' unit was involved in one hellacious fight. Reports of the battle began with the 4th Battalion's first contacts near the beginning of the month and continued, growing in detail as the media flocked in and as the casualties mounted. The culminating action—the taking of Hill 875—made headlines in the Thanksgiving day papers back in the World.

Much later, I was given a description of Thanksgiving at my home in Williamsburg, Virginia. As usual, my mother spent the morning and early afternoon in the kitchen preparing a meal for an amorphous group whose members would be wandering in and out throughout the day. At the core were my father, my sister, and her husband-to-be. Appearing at various times in the afternoon would be my father's two daughters by his first marriage, and their families. My father's two brothers and their families also sometimes dropped by. The headline in the local paper, *The Richmond Times-Dispatch*, was large and grim. The accompanying article described how the paratroopers of the 173rd Airborne Brigade had finally, after heavy casualties, taken Hill 875. The family kept the paper out of my mother's sight for most of the day, but after the hordes had left and the dishes were stacked, she read. The uncertainty and anguish she felt were shared in many other households across the nation. A little less than two months had passed since I had broken the news of going to the infantry. Now, for all she knew, she was reading of the death of her only son.

We didn't know it as we ate our Army-issue Thanksgiving dinner on that barren hill, but the Battle of Dak To was over. Indeed, for me personally, I had experienced my last firefight as an infantry platoon leader. I was to be in the field for two more months, but the only adversaries I was to encounter were bugs, heat, mountains, the rucksack, and a new company commander. There was much learning in the weeks ahead, but my encounters with the immediate possibility of death were, for the time being, over.

To Christmas

The fire support base where we had our Thanksgiving Day meal was only a one night stand for A Company. The next day we returned to Hill 882, but by a different route. The fire support base was on its own ridge, and we followed this ridge for a bit before cutting across the narrow steep valley to the ridge that culminated in 882. The route took us through an area that had been the site of heavy fighting several weeks before, probably involving elements of the 4th Battalion. The area was populated with dead NVA. Some of them were above ground, others were buried. The above-grounders were in a desiccated state. The flesh had largely decomposed, and the skin was stretched taut over the bones. Wide open mouths, protruding teeth, empty eye sockets, and bony fingers greeted us as we made our way through the napalm-burnt area.

Although spooky looking, the above-grounders were not as disgusting as their comrades just below the surface. The below-grounders had been hastily placed in shallow graves, apparently by NVA burial teams. The earth had slowed their decomposition so that they were still pretty ripe—"wet" to use a term I once read that folks in the mortuary business use. Only a few inches of earth covered the ripeness. The sickly sweet smell of decaying human bodies hung over the area. During one pause, I plopped down with my pack against a log. I slowly became aware that the decayed death smell was much stronger. Looking around, I noticed that I was sitting on freshly turned earth. Moreover, something very grayish was protruding from the ground beside me, actually touching my left buttock. I was up like a flash, jerking the heavy pack with me as if it were a pillow.

"What's wrong, Lieutenant?"

"Goddamn dead mothafuckers! The goddamn dead sonuvabitch got on me!" Those in the immediate vicinity displayed general merriment, although more than a few also discretely checked to be sure they weren't unknowingly embracing Nguyen Stiff. I didn't sit down again until we had passed through the area.

When it arrived at Hill 882, the point encountered a NVA scavenging party searching for all the goodies that U.S. soldiers habitually left behind. A few shots were fired, but no casualties were suffered on either side. We assumed our old positions and spent an uneventful night.

The next day, we finally made it to the next hill, the one that several days previously Holmes had volunteered he and I for. A very well-defined trail climbed from the stream in the valley between the two hills. Footholds were cut in the steep portions. The hill top itself had received a tremendous plummeting from air strikes, and downed trees made maneuvering difficult. It was early in the afternoon when we arrived. Shortly after we established a perimeter, a chopper brought in a big load of letters and packages. Mail had been backing up for much of the Dak To battle. Resupply and evacuation of the dead and wounded had higher priorities. But the logistics pipeline was finally beginning to flow properly again.

One of the packages was for me, a care package from home. It contained items that made the grunt's life just a little more bearable: pre-sweetened ice tea mix that could significantly improve a canteen of water, hot sauce for the C-rations, hard candies for the sweet tooth. My mother had also sent kool aid, which I tried for the first and last time. One envelope was unsweetened raspberry. I emptied the package into a canteen, shook it, and took a long swig. Almost immediately a diarrhea attack of tremendous force commenced. There wasn't time to get to a bit of privacy outside the perimeter. I frantically dropped my pants and set my butt over a log. What spewed forth was pure liquid. I left the rest of the kool aid for the NVA scavenging parties.

The next day, the battalion split up into company-sized elements, a sign that someone believed the NVA had melted back into Cambodia and Laos. Indeed, the night before the sky over Cambodia, about five miles to the west, was lit up, and we heard distant faint noises of grinding gears and straining motors. The North Vietnamese Army was resupplying and reorganizing and could come charging back to renew the battle, but for the moment it appeared to be licking its wounds.

Beaucoup NVA stragglers and small patrols remained on the South Vietnam side of the border, however, and we had a strange encounter with one such group, or perhaps only an individual, shortly after we left the laager site the morning after my bout with diarrhea. Oscar was fourth place in the column, behind the point platoon, the headquarters group, and a second rifle platoon. I was in front of Oscar, following the rear trooper of the second rifle platoon. The company was moving in the standard stop and go fashion—send the point out, bring the main body up, send the point out.

On one of the link-ups, we came to a fork in the well-worn trail we were following. The three troopers directly in front of me went to the left. I paused, noticing that what appeared to be a U.S. rucksack was disappearing up the right-hand fork. In a loud whisper, I called after the troopers on the left-hand fork: "Hey, you guys goin' in the right direction?" The last trooper looked back, then said something to the two in front of him. The three stopped, conferred briefly, and quickly retreated to the trail fork. The trooper who had been in the lead was pale, grinning, and excited, all at once.

"Shit, Sir," he said, "I musta been following NVA. There were guys in front of me in khaki."

"You sure?" I asked somewhat incredulously. "They were NVA?"

"Well, I didn't get a real good look, but I was sure following something."

"He's right, Sir," chimed in the trooper who was second in line. "We were following somebody. I saw 'em."

We started moving on the right-hand trail and shortly caught up with the rucksack I had seen. It indeed belonged to one of our guys, who was with Alpha Company's main body. So whoever the trooper had fallen in behind on the left fork hadn't been part of A Company. The column was stopped, and I moved up to Jerome. "I think we had some NVA in our column for awhile. Guys in front of me followed them for a bit back at that fork in the trail." Jerome didn't appear particularly concerned. And truth be told, after the events of the recent weeks a few NVA marching with us didn't seem like anything to get excited about.

For the next week, we moved mostly north, pretty much sticking to the ridgelines. Fresh trails, deep bunkers, and fighting positions were in abundance, but we encountered no NVA. The valleys could have contained thousands, but we stayed on the high country. We moved at a leisurely pace, the point being extremely careful about checking the area prior to calling up the main body. It wasn't long, however, before we fell for the most part back into pre-Dak To mode. As soon as we linked up with the point, we plopped down and dug out paperbacks, magazines, and comic books from the large pockets in the jungle fatigue pants. The main body became one long library reading room. The days were warm and pleasant, and the nights were cool.

At one resupply, we received a few temporary replacements. They were legs—not airborne qualified. The brigade had been so decimated by the Dak To fighting that USARV—United States Army Vietnam, the overall U.S. headquarters in-country—had diverted legs to bolster our numbers until the replacement pipeline could produce sufficient airborne troopers. Although with about 85 people in the field Alpha Company was under-strength, it was better off than most units. Nevertheless, we were given a few of the leg replacements. The airborne veterans of one of the biggest battles of the war hardly acknowledged the leg

FNGs' existence, and within a few weeks they all had been transferred to proper homes.

One afternoon after we had reached our laager site for the evening, a chopper brought out one of the brigade chaplains. He was to conduct a memorial service. He arranged his paraphernalia near the company CP. The Weapons Platoon was located close by. At some point during the preceding few weeks the ridge where the laager site was located had been the target of numerous air strikes, and the area was a maze of blown-downed trees.

Religious services in the field were usually voluntary affairs, and being pretty much of an agnostic, or at best a deist, I generally avoided them. Indeed, I was feeling particularly anti-religious at the moment. Some people find God in the foxhole. My thinking at the time was that if there was a loving, caring God, how could there be so much nastiness and death? So I was just loitering by the mortar, not intending to participate in the activities. Gradually I became aware, however, that the service was not getting underway. A large group had gathered, and they were just standing there. Jerome was alternately looking toward Oscar's location and toward the group. A few other Weapons Platoon members had not gone to the service. After a couple more minutes, Harold Campton passed me on his way to the group. "You goin' to the service, Sir?"

I was pissed that I was being pressured into attending a religious service I didn't particularly want to attend. It was a memorial service, however. I could see several pairs of boots on a log. The boots represented our Dak To dead, including Douglas Baum and Eugene Washington. Finally, with some purposely overt indications of irritation, I slammed my steel pot on my head, grabbed my M-16, and noisily climbed over the fallen trees to the service. I took up a position in the rear. As I did so, Jerome made a motion to the chaplain, who commenced. It was a short service. I concentrated on the boots, wondering if Baum, Washington, or God gave two hoots about this grubby little group of grunts on a desolate hilltop in the middle of nowhere.

After several more days, the company reached a broad valley. At one time a major road—at least by the standards of northwestern Vietnam—Highway 4 it might have been, had followed the valley into Laos. It was now only an overgrown little-used cart trail. We laagered in a large perimeter. That evening, a mail chopper came in, and I received the first letter from home since Hill 882. I had written and asked for any news articles about the fighting. My mother sent a bunch. Her covering letter said that she hadn't thought I would want to see them. I detected a subtle note of rebuke. And it was probably deserved. I realized I was treating the death and destruction like a sports contest. Maybe that's why there are wars. Too many young men view the action as extensions of adolescent athletics.

The next morning we were extracted by chopper. Our destination was a clearing about a quarter of a mile from a fire support base. Charlie and Delta joined us there. A dirt road that began some miles away at the village of Dak To itself passed by the fire support base. Somewhere along the road between us and the village of Dak To was the hilltop fire support base at which we had disembarked after the flight from Kontum eons ago, at the beginning of November.

We stayed at the clearing for two nights. A combination memorial and award ceremony was held on the second day. The three companies stood in a U-shaped formation. Empty boots representing the fallen were placed in front of each company. Before the ceremony, Jerome told me one of the awards, a Bronze Star, was going to Harold Campton for his actions on Hill 882. I was a little surprised. Harold Campton had certainly performed admirably, and I didn't begrudge him a medal. But others had performed well also. Truman came particularly to mind. The vision of him calmly sitting amid the chaos, working with his plotting board, rounds buzzing about his ears, explosions reverberating over the hillside, was compelling.

The medal business, I was gradually coming to realize, was not a straight-forward award-for-performance deal. A few people received medals they didn't deserve. A lot more deserved medals and didn't get them. For some members of the military community, any firefight, no matter how insignificant, was looked on as a medal opportunity. The career officer corps was the most guilty of this attitude. Platoon leaders, company commanders, and battalion commanders were not above politicking for a little chest spaghetti. A chest-full of ribbons could be a significant career-enhancer. A few battalion commanders—being old-timers and knowledgeable about what medals could mean—were especially egregious violators of a humble approach toward acquiring medals. On occasion, these few all but ordered subordinates to recommend them for awards.

But as I said, I didn't begrudge Harold Campton a Bronze Star. A few others got medals also. One was the company medic, Meehan, who pulled a number of Lima's wounded from the line. It was too soon for the biggies—the Silver Stars and Distinguish Service Crosses—to be approved, but eventually some members of Alpha Company were recipients of the nation's third and second highest awards for valor. Perhaps not surprisingly, Jerome and First Sergeant Duckett received Silver Stars, and Lima, Lt. Wayman, received the DSC.

During the company's short time at the clearing, a small incident occurred that let me know something of the events back in the World. Lima's medic, the grubby Doc, had been on R&R during the battle for Hill 882. He had since rejoined the company. During one of the afternoons, I saw him wandering near the company CP. He had acquired an earring while on R&R. Jerome happened to see the small gold ring at about the same time I did, and exploded. In a loud voice, he yelled, "Get that thing outta your ear. This isn't the place for that goddamn hippie mess."

Earrings? On paratroopers? What was happening? Actually, the earring itself didn't bother me that much. My detached observer approach to the human condition enabled me to be pretty accepting about such things. But I was surprised at Jerome's vehemence. After all, he had been extremely tolerant of the numerous beaded necklaces, several with attached feathers, that had adorned the previous company medic. Perhaps the antagonisms that were beginning to polarize the home front were finding their way to the battlefield.

After two nights outside the fire support base, we resumed our humping. The route was a circuit to the west and back that took about a week. We didn't get as far as the sites of the battles of the previous month. We just searched the inner ranges of hills to the west. The hills weren't as high as those closer to the Cambodian and Laotian borders, but they were at least as steep. Moreover, the vegetation was thicker, requiring much more machete work to make progress. The journey was demanding, but uneventful. The company struggled up the hillsides, sometimes going to all fours, and pushed through the bamboo and wait-a-minute vines.

No matter how thick the jungle, we had to cut a landing zone each night. The rationale was to be able to evacuate wounded. One result was that secrecy and surreptitiousness were sacrificed. After sneaking along all day, we would announce our presence by a lot of loud chopping. At one location, the growth was so formidable that a chain saw was lowered to facilitate the construction of the LZ. We didn't find much sign of NVA, but if any enemy soldiers had been in the area, they wouldn't have had difficulty in keeping track of our progress.

I don't know at what level of command this new standard operating procedure originated, but looking back I see it as part of the beginnings of the U.S. Army's retreat into defensiveness, and ineffectiveness, in Vietnam. Casualties were mounting, the possibility of military victory was fading, and concerns about immediate trooper welfare were beginning to dominate. Never mind that improving trooper welfare in the near term might be incompatible with victory and long term trooper welfare. As I was to realize more fully several months later, decisions about operational matters were being usurped by the politicians and armchair generals back in the World. A congressman blisters the Pentagon because of a constituent's complaint about the length of time a medevac took, and the Army responds by ordering that LZs be cut every night, resulting in the tactical principle of surprise being compromised.

The pleasures of the infantryman's life were few and simple. I have a vivid memory of one of those few and simple pleasures during this period. In one of my five canteens I had taken to carrying whiskey. The supply dated back to my visit to the Tuy Hoa PX during my finger treatment about two months before. A canteen of whiskey over a two-month period indicated a rather slow rate of consumption. But every few nights I would have a little nip. One chilly evening during this circuit through the Dak To valley, I brewed up a cup of coffee at the bottom of the platoon bunker, and flavored it with a generous two fingers of booze. Crouched on that hillside, with a view of the stars in the tropical night, I sipped the whiskey-laced coffee and enjoyed a deep feeling of peace and contentment.

With a long hump that ended at the clearing where we had laagered a week or so before, the company finished the circuit of the Dak To valley the next day. The initial portion of the hump was in the hills. Then we encountered a sizeable stream bridged by a flimsy bridge. It had several intertwined vines and ropes for a footway. Parallel to the footway and at about shoulder height were two ropes for the hand-holds. These were connected to the footway by occasional pieces of small rope and vine. The contraption was built for 130-pound Montegnard tribesmen, not U.S. paratroopers who fully loaded were 200 pounds or more. Unfortunately, the stream was too deep and swift to wade. Consequently, it was several hours before the 90 or so troopers all succeeded in floundering and cursing their way over the bridge.

Once across the bridge, we hit the dirt road that led in one direction to the village of Dak To and in the other to the fire support base. We trudged the dusty track toward the latter destination. A few Montegnard vendors with portable establishments—baskets at each end of a pole balanced over the shoulders—trailed us, selling trinkets and cokes. We passed the fire support base and made our way to the clearing that was to be the laager site for the evening. The next day we were to take over the perimeter of the fire support base for a few days. Saying that I would soon be a captain and a possible company commander, Jerome sent me to recon the perimeter. The purpose was to count the positions and recommend how they should be divided among the platoons. I did a half-assed job, not getting detailed enough regarding numbers of bunkers and platoon responsibilities, but the company eventually was able to take over the guardianship of the guns and the battalion CP.

The fire support base was the most miserable place I encountered during my time as a 173rd platoon leader. The whole area had been bulldozed of all vegetation. The ground wasn't just dirt, however. It was a fine black dust, about four inches thick. Each step kicked up a small dark cloud that joined with many other small dark clouds to put a permanent haze over the place. In addition, every time one of the howitzers fired, the vibrations would raise large dark clouds. And the howitzers included biggies: 8-inchers and 155s. The noise of these babies going off was deafening. We hadn't been in position for an hour before we were all covered with the dust. It coated our faces and clogged our noses and throats. It crept into our packs and buried our air mattresses and poncho liners.

We endured this for three days. Humping the hills, hacking through the underbrush, fighting the rucksacks, would have been much preferable to living in and breathing this hell. There was one bright spot, however. On the afternoon of the last day, Harold Campton approached me: "Sir, we got a few beers comin' in this evenin'. One of them Montegnard peddlers is sellin' 'em to us. Ya want a couple?"

"Ya know I do. How much do I owe ya?"

"Nothing. There're free."

"Ya sure? Us officers get paid too, ya know."

"No sweat. I'll bring 'em to ya this evenin'."

So about 1830, Harold Campton approached with two ba-moui-bas under his shirt. My residence was one half of an above-ground bunker that had sandbag walls and a PCP—steel plate—top. I retreated to this sanctum and started sucking down the brews. They were quickly gone, and the craving for more was overpowering. I went looking for Harold Campton. He was in back of the sandbagged tent that was the four-deuce's fire direction center. He and the troopers of the mostly black Four-Deuce Platoon were tight and spent time together on the occasions when Alpha was the palace guard. He was sitting with a group of five or six four-deucers.

"Hey, ya got any more?" I brazenly asked.

"Yeah, we might have one," he said. He was a little cool. The four-deucers glared hostilely. He handed me a bottle, and I staggered back to my sanctum. It wasn't until a few years later, after I got back to the World and began hearing about the drug problems among the troops in the 'Nam, that I realized Harold Campton and the boys were probably blowing a little pot. In the 173rd in late 1967, drugs had not yet become the problem that they were in other units, and were to become generally later. For one thing, we were so far out in the boonies that those so inclined had little opportunity to acquire illicit stuff. My free beers were most likely a payoff to overlook an evening of pot. If Harold Campton had known how naive I was, he could have saved himself the expense.

Finally, after three days of hell, we left the dust bowl. Choppers lifted us to a hilltop fire support base some distance to the north. Grass, sweet grass, covered the area. The only negative aspects were shit and cold. The shit came from the previous occupants. A small fire support base had been on the hill for the previous week or so. Our arrival coincided with the expansion of the base to accommodate another battery of artillery. Consequently, the perimeter moved outward. The area where Oscar set up was beyond the old perimeter, and was where a few of the old perimeter occupiers shat. So little piles of barely buried human defecation were all around.

The other negative aspect was cold. The hilltop was one of the highest points around, and breezy. Even in the bright sun of mid-afternoon, we were chilled. By nightfall, we were positively cold, and most of us spent a miserable first night shivering under the blankets of both ponchos and poncho liners. The next morning, Jerome asked that field jackets be sent out. And many of us decided that the way to fight the cold was to dig into the grounds like moles. Thus we spent the day constructing bunkers big enough to sleep in. The work itself helped hold off the cold. Moreover, wonder of wonders, the field jackets actually arrived on a resupply chopper before nightfall. Consequently, by the second night most of the company was equipped for the frigidness.

We played palace guard for several days. One of the companies out humping the boonies in our stead was Bravo. The illustrious Bravo had spent the three weeks of the Dak To battle guarding a fire support base. It had suffered one casualty. A ricocheting round had nicked a trooper while the company was conducting a mock assault for the benefit of media people. Thus Bravo was looked upon with some disdain by the other line companies of the battalion. The feeling was that it had some catching up to do.

One morning on the hill, I received a map-reading lesson from the Sergeant Major of the whole frigging brigade. The height of the hill and the lack of trees produced an unobstructed view across a wide valley. On the horizon, maybe three miles away, was a long high ridge. In the valley between us and the far ridge were a number of ridgelines of lesser elevations. Several had crests crowned only by grass and a few boulders. To a mortarman, the setting was an ideal target range. The wide vista of the varied terrain afforded numerous opportunities to practice judging distances, and the distant boulders provided great targets to shoot at. Jerome agreed to a little target practice, and so we were given a hefty supply of rounds to hurl out into the valley.

Truman and his plotting board, myself, and several others went to a location near the top of the hill to play forward observer. We had a radio to give instructions to the gun crew. We selected a boulder on a distance ridge to destroy, estimated the distance, gave that and the azimuth to Truman, and radioed his instructions to the gun crew. They fired off a round, and we waited expectantly for an explosion on the ridge. Instead, a muffled thud rumpled out of one of the valleys. We couldn't pinpoint its exact location.

So we made a distance adjustment and tried again. And again, we waited expectantly. And again we got only a muffled thud from an undetermined location. The boulder sat untouched.

This wasn't going right. We all agreed that the distance was about 1,500 meters and that we must be hitting just over or just on this side of the ridge, whose slopes fell steeply and sharply into valleys. Since there was general agreement on the distance, our corrections were small, a hundred meters at a time. Well, to make a long story short, we kept this up for a good 20 rounds. Not once did we discern an impact.

We were thoroughly engrossed in the mystery of why we couldn't hit the ridge when there was a clearing of throats behind us. We turned, and there was a damn general, General Sweitzer, himself, the commander of the whole darn brigade. With him were the battalion commander—the infamous LTC Shafter—and the brigade sergeant major. "Sir!" I stammered.

"What're you doin'?" the general asked, friendly like.

"We're practicin' with the mortar, Sir. We're A Company's 81mm mortar."

"What're you shootin' at?"

"That boulder on that ridge," I said pointing.

"Are you hittin' it?"

"Can't seemed to, Sir."

"What's the distance," the sergeant major interjected.

"About fifteen hundred meters," I said.

"Try twenty-five," said the sergeant major as they moved off. We looked at each other skeptically but reset the distance. Sure enough, the next explosion was on the ridgeline. A little experience goes a long way.

On our last day at the fire support base, we were treated to an awesome display of American firepower that was at the same time instructive regarding the difficulty of achieving victory in this odd war. A B-52 strike, called an arc-light, was scheduled for the slope of the high ridge on the far side of the valley. We were notified of its pending occurrence and took up seats to watch the spectacle.

We had no warning of the falling bombs—no sight or sound of the high-flying aircraft, no contrails, no black dots descending to the earth. Instead, the mountainside suddenly and silently erupted. Where a moment before was only an expanse of dark green jungle, now existed a great oblong cloud of smoke and dust. Still, as large as it was, the cloud was just a blemish on the vastness of the mountainside. America's most powerful blow had merely scarred a small portion of the landscape. Dozens of air strikes would be necessary to cover the remainder of the mountain, and the wilderness of the Central Highlands and the Cambodian-Laotian border region contained thousands of mountains, not to mention the surrounding valleys.

Our respite ended the next day. By chopper, we departed the frigid mountain top—maybe one of the few nippy places in Vietnam—for the heat and sweat of the valleys and hillsides. The LZ was near the site of the B-52 strike on the far side of the valley. We encountered no hostiles and were soon refamiliarizing ourselves with the unpleasant things the rucksack can do to the human body. About mid-morning, we rendezvoused with the always cocky Capt. McNevers and the boys of Charlie Company. The good captain had taken to wearing a captured North Vietnamese issue AK-47 chest ammunition carrier. His weapon of choice was a CAR-15, the shortened version of the M-16. The CAR magazines fit the slots in the AK-47 ammo carrier. Watching McNevers strutting around with his mixed equipment ensemble, I could understand why he might rub wrong the battalion CO, LTC Shafter.

One interesting fact came to light at the meeting with Charlie Company. Unlike Alpha Company which rotated the point among platoons and within platoons, Charlie had a full-time point group. McNevers had taken five or six volunteers, relieved them of all other responsibilities, and assigned them to be the permanent probers of the path. It was just the thing for a young trooper who wasn't getting enough action and excitement just being in an infantry company in a combat zone. And a real benefit was that the point group did not have to carry rucksacks. Their burdens were distributed among the rest of the company.

Although an argument for an elite point group could be made, I suspected such an outfit had its downsides. Most of the troopers in A Company looked forward to a stint on point. Moreover, A Company certainly hadn't been adversely affected by a rotating point. During the Dak To battles, we encountered sizeable NVA forces on four separate occasions. Each time, our point spotted them before they spotted us. So I wasn't sure that McNever's approach presented any significant advantages, or any advantages at all.

Alpha and Charlie joined forces for a day of traveling together. Only the day stretched into the evening. For some reason, battalion had given us a certain destination that we had to reach before calling it quits. So we struggled on as dusk descended. The terrain was steep and rough. We were not following a trail, just bushwhacking cross-country. As the twilight faded, the anxiety level rose. The troopers weren't used to moving in darkness in unknown terrain under full rucksacks. In the pitch blackness of the tropical night, we couldn't see the man in front of us. We were moving almost solely by sound, with occasional resort to a quick flash from a flashlight. Any flashes brought forth a roar to can the light, although the noise we were making offset any light discipline we might be maintaining.

A principal source of noise was coming from behind Oscar. November was the platoon to our rear. With the wounding of Lt. Kane on Hill 882, November had come under the command of SFC Hernandez. He appeared to be doing an admirable job, but on this evening one of his troopers was getting out of hand. Johnny Pots, an M-60 machine gunner, was expressing his displeasure with the proceedings in an ever louder manner. Cursing at close to the top of his lungs, Johnny P. questioned the intelligence of whoever was responsible for this idiotic move in complete darkness. He had a point, but he was seriously compromising our position. Any NVA within a kilometer would have been able to home in on us with ease.

I heard Sgt. Hernandez attempt to quiet Pots. Hernandez progressed from persuasion to orders, but nothing was having any effect. Pots was pretty close to berserk. Anger over banging around in the dark, falling down inclines, and getting hit in the face with branches was most likely the cause of his extreme discontent. It certainly couldn't be fear as his conduct was compounding the dangers of this night move. The column was a lurching, stumbling hunk of disorganized humanity that could become a mass of dead and wounded if Johnny P. completely lost it and resorted to his M-60 to ease his internal tensions. I considered going back and trying to aid Sgt. Hernandez in calming Pots but figured that staying as far away as possible was the more personally prudent course of action. Besides, from the sound of things, a bullet to the head would be all that could end the tirade.

Finally, after struggling up the side of a particularly horrendous gully, a cooler head prevailed, and we came to a halt. The stopping point was a thicket on a flat portion of a ridge. The two companies somehow strung together a perimeter and settled in for the night. Once we stopped, Pots piped down, but his outburst was to be the root cause of a difficult episode in a few weeks.

The next day the company made its way to the destination that we had been so bound and determined to reach the night before. What was so special about it was not evident. It was just one more ridge in the vastness of the tri-border wilderness area. We arrived before noon. Charlie Company continued on to some other jungle-covered ridge, Jerome sent out two platoons on daytime patrols, and Oscar slept. I enjoyed a restful afternoon snoozing on my air mattress in the warm sunshine of a small clearing.

A U.S. plane was almost added to Alpha Company's trophy shelve the next day. We descended and ascended several ridges. On one of the ascents, we were snaking up an open area when a small plane flew high overhead. Small, piper cub-like planes were not unusual in Vietnam. Air Force forward observers, the guys who directed air strikes, often flew piper cubs. In addition, province advisory teams usually had one, and one or more aviators on the staff to fly it. The province planes were used primarily for reconnoitering purposes. The aviators would fly around the province, looking for suspicious activity, sometimes just to report it, sometimes to call in air strikes or artillery.

But a certain adventuresome breed of province advisor flyer existed that was not content just to observe. The piper cubs carried a few rockets. The primary purpose was to serve as spotting rounds for faster moving aircraft. Some of the piper cubers, however, viewed the spotter rockets as their own personal way to fight the war. And the rockets were indeed lethal weapons, with a bursting radius considerably larger than that of a grenade.

When the piper cub made a pass high overhead, we did not think a great deal about it. Even when it made several more lower ride-bys, not a great deal of notice was taken. Suddenly, however, the plane was diving on our column moving up the mountainside. A rocket impacted about 50 meters off to the side, in the jungle. "Holy shit!" someone yelled. "The mothafucker is shootin' at us!"

Looks of panic spread over the column. Those near the top of the clearing scrambled for the cover of the jungle. Those near the bottom were torn between retreating to the comparative safety of the jungle at their rear and not wanting to give up any hard-earned hillside. Those of us in the center felt extremely naked and helpless.

The plane did a wide turn and prepared for another run. I saw Jerome near the top of the clearing frantically talking on the radio, trying to get this Bird Dog called off. The plane dove and fired another rocket. It exploded on the edge of the clearing. Again, it missed, but the pilot's aim was improving. Moreover, I was afraid that he was just marking our position for an air strike, and I had visions of a couple of Phantoms rolling in with napalm and 500 pounders. The pilot began a turn, apparently in preparation for another dive. Those of us still in the clearing were scrambling and struggling upwards for the trees. The Bird Dog leveled out, and as he did so I saw an M-60 gunner and several riflemen lay back against the hillside. The riflemen put their M-16s to their shoulders, the M-60 gunner put the gun butt against his hip, and they prepared to meet the next assault in a different way. The plane began his dive, and a burst of tracer rounds charged skyward. Just at that moment the pilot veered off, whether in response to a radio call or to the burst of gunfire it was impossible to say.

We never did hear an explanation for the attack. Presumably, the plane was one of ours that was not aware of the 173rd's presence in its area. But I've always wondered whether it could have been an NVA plane from just across the border. One odd thing about my vivid recollection of the incident is that my mind's eye has a vision of a plane with no markings—no white star, no numbers, no nothing. Maybe Alpha Company had the distinction of being the only U.S. unit that sustained a hostile air attack in Vietnam.

The laager site that night was centered on a narrow tree-covered ridge. Because of the narrowness of the ridge, the perimeter stretched down the slopes. The only clearing for the mortar was on the hillside, so the gun was on a considerable slant. The next day, the hump was a short move to another ridge. Although it was short, the route involved an extremely steep climb. We arrived at the destination about mid-afternoon, December 23. This was to be our home for the Christmas holiday, my second Christmas in Vietnam.

A Christmas cease-fire had been declared by the Allied command for December 24 and 25. It was always unclear to me if the NVA and the Viet Cong also abided by holiday cease fires, but what the heck. We got a small break. We would be encamped on the hill until the 26th.

The hilltop had a large clearing—indeed, the top of the hill was almost bald—that would be the LZ for resupply and Christmas goodies. The perimeter encompassed the LZ and woods on each side. The headquarters CP, the Weapons Platoon, and November were in proximity on one side of the perimeter. The headquarters CP was in a grove of trees just off the LZ. Oscar was below the headquarters group, scattered around an irregular clearing apparently created by an old air strike. The clearing contained a number of stumps. November's portion of the perimeter stretched from the side of the LZ, around the headquarters

CP, and into Oscar. One of the other rifle platoons picked up the perimeter on the far side of Oscar. Thus, once again Oscar occupied a portion of the perimeter.

We dug a mortar pit, a bunker, and set up house-keeping. Since we were part of the perimeter, we set out a claymore. It was about ten meters down the hill from the mortar pit, on a stump about three feet high. Shortly after dusk, several large explosions rolled up from the valley below us. Battle stations were assumed, but nothing further developed. The rest of the night passed uneventfully.

The next morning, I was having breakfast—a cup of coffee and a C-ration pound cake—when my gaze happened to focus on the stump where the claymore was. My hootch was about ten meters to the side of the mortar pit and thus about 15 meters from the claymore. The damn thing was aimed right at me! A cold knot immediately formed in my stomach. I traced the firing cord with my eyes and saw that it went into the mortar pit. No one was in the pit at the moment. Several Oscar troopers were having breakfast just behind it. One of them was Harold Campton. "Hey Camp," I called, "That fuckin' claymore's zeroed in on me!"

He, I, and several others went down to the stump. "How in the hell did that happen?" I asked.

"Don't know, Sir," said Harold Campton. Several possibilities presented themselves. The claymore had been set up carelessly in the first instance; someone had accidentally jerked the wire and turned it around; an NVA with a sense of humor had crawled up during the night and repositioned it; or the thing had been deliberately aimed into the perimeter. I dismissed the last possibility. I didn't think I had made any enemies in the platoon. In addition, "fragging," or deliberating exploding things around officers, had not yet become a threat, or even something much talked about. To the extent that "fragging" was a problem for the Army, and I don't really have a feel for whether it ever was an extensive problem, it didn't become so until late in the American involvement, after the war had gone sour.

That left inadvertence, an accident, or the NVA. Needless to say, I kept a close eye on the stump for the rest of our stay.

Sometime that day, Christmas Eve, a chopper brought out a hefty load of mail, much of it Christmas cards and packages. It also brought out several garbage cans of ice and beer, which were set aside until late afternoon. Among the packages were a number from civic groups addressed to just "A Soldier." A wide variety of groups did such things, put together small goody boxes, mostly of food. I was given a package from a Jewish Veterans organization. Its contents included a salami-like tube of meat.

Late in the afternoon, after the beer was made available, I cut into the salami. Within a short time, the combination of tropical heat, warm greasy meat, and lukewarm beer created an ominous rumbling in my stomach. As dusk fell, I retreated to my hooch, curling up on my air mattress in a fetal position. The stomach continued rumbling, and a nasty taste welled up in my throat. It was obvious I was going to be miserable for a good while.

Meanwhile, a party was getting underway at the CP bunker, about 15 meters up the hill. The headquarters group seemed to have gotten more than its share of beer, which wasn't surprising. Indeed, a few of the boys were shortly on the way to a bona fide drunk. One new addition to the headquarters group was a young black PFC radio operator. Holding his liquor was not a skill that he had yet mastered, or apparently even considered. It wasn't long before he was down at the bottom of the CP bunker, alternately howling wolf howls and yelling, "the Dai Uy, he's numbah one." "Dai Uy" was Vietnamese for Captain. Other members of the group weren't as out-of-control, but the raucousness level was definitely rising.

I lay in my misery, listening to the developing party. Before long, Christmas carols were being butchered. The singing was interrupted from time-to-time with howls and "the Dai Uy, he's numbah one" from the bottom of the bunker. The party irritated the hell out of me. Part of it was my salami-induced misery. Part of it was a general feeling that partying in the boonies was not right. We were supposed to be sneaking around killing commies, not having a beer bust. And part of it was just the cantankerousness of my own anti-social self. I half hoped Charlie would ignore the cease fire and disrupt the shindig.

Most of Oscar was also participating in the party. Several times Will, who had made the trip with me down the slope of Hill 882 to find the dropped load of ammunition, made his way to my hootch and tried to get me to join the festivities. "Lieutenant Holland, c'mon have a beer."

"No Will, I'm doing okay here." I tried to say this as nicely as possible, but my teeth were gritting. Will was probably too snockered to notice, however, and he was more snockered with each trip. Eventually, about midnight, the party began winding down. The participants had enjoyed a good Christmas. For me, I felt a strange unsettleness as I drifted off to a troubled sleep.

Christmas day was anticlimactic. The party had produced a lot of hung-over troopers who spent the hours trying to do as little as possible. An air-conditioned room is perhaps the best place to recuperate from the effects of alcohol, but no air-conditioned rooms were available. I was still tasting the warm salami. The sight of the thing brought a wave of nausea. I eventually threw it far down the hill. No offense to the Jewish War Veterans, but salami and the tropics don't quite fit.

Late in the afternoon, the traditional Christmas dinner was choppered out. Compared to the fare of the day before, it wasn't bad. There was no beer, but most of the beer drinkers had pretty much worn themselves out anyway. The battalion commander, LTC Shafter, came with the dinner. He apparently intended to make a circuit of the perimeter, saying hello to the troops and wishing them a happy holiday. He started with November, just down the slope from the headquarters CP and the mortar position. His good intentions came to an abrupt end with SSG Parker, a November squad leader.

Sgt. Parker was an outspoken black soldier. He was a lifer, but he didn't have the kowtowing, accepting attitude of many lifers. He could piss and moan with the best of the two- and three-year troopers who thought of the Army as the Green Zoo and counted their days until discharge. His outspokenness stopped short of open revolt or insubordination, but its intensity was unusual for a career NCO.

LTC Shafter evidently caught Sgt. Parker in one of the latter's more irascible moods. Shafter was no backslapper in any case. One got the impression that the farther he could distance himself from the lowly grunts, the happier he was. His effort to shake a few hands on Christmas was commendable but totally out of character, and the troopers knew it. Shafter in his spit-shined jungle boots and pressed jungle fatigues began working his way along November's position. "How ya doin' soldier?" "Have a Merry Christmas." "Everything goin' okay?"

The troopers grunted noncommittally and somewhat sheepishly, not knowing quite how to react to this obviously forced effort at camaraderie by the battalion commander. Sgt. Parker knew how to react, however. He was sitting on the sandbagged overhead cover of his bunker, eating his turkey dinner. Shafter approached: "How ya doing, Sergeant? Havin' a good Christmas?"

"Fuck no, I ain't havin' a good Christmas, Colonel. How can ya be havin' a good fuckin' Christmas in this mothafuckin' place?" The statement was loud enough to be heard at the CP bunker and in Oscar's position. Except for SSG Parker's eating, all activity stopped. Shafter stared in astonishment at the sitting and eating sergeant. Troopers in the vicinity stared at the battalion commander staring at the sitting and eating sergeant. For agonizing seconds, the tableau was frozen. Then Shafter turned abruptly on his spit-shined heels, charged past the CP bunker, angrily mumbled something to Jerome in passing, got in his chopper, and impatiently waited as the crew fired it up. He was shortly gone. And despite

Sgt. Parker's statement to the contrary, I suspect that the good sergeant had an enjoyable Christmas after all.

Kontum, And Again A New Job

On the day after Christmas, we were lifted by chopper to the vicinity of the village of Dak To. There, we were loaded on trucks, mostly tractor-trailer rigs, and driven the 35 miles or so to Kontum. The trailers were open-bedded affairs that were piled with supplies and various pieces of brigade equipment. Apparently the 173rd was moving out of Dak To lock, stock, and barrel. The troopers sprawled on top of the baggage. Although I wanted to ride in the rear, Harold Campton insisted that as the MFWIC—mothafucker what's in charge—I belonged in the cab. He and his boys probably wanted to blow a little pot. The driver of the truck was a young soldier who belonged to a transportation unit. He was in awe of chauffeuring paratroopers and particularly the 173rd, the "victors" of the Battle of Dak To. I accepted his hero worship with as much casualness as I could.

The road between Dak To and Kontum was bumpy and dusty. The jungle had been plowed back a distance of 50 to 100 meters by Rome plows, powerful machines that given enough time could do a job on even the thickest vegetation. Small outposts—some Vietnamese, some American—were situated every few miles. Some of the outposts even had a tank. A lone tank on a desolate mountain road didn't strike me as a particularly powerful bit of security, but I wasn't running the war.

Once again, we spent the night near the Kontum airfield. This time, however, there were no trips into town. Jerome had learned his lesson. He was looking directly at me when he said at the evening briefing, "And there'll be no goin' into the bars tonight. Tell your people to stay right here."

One thing was similar to our stop-over of almost two months before, however. Jerome made a platoon change, and I was the subject of the change. November had been without an officer since Lt. Kane had gotten whacked on Hill 882. Sgt. Hernandez, the platoon sergeant, had been running the platoon. He was departing for R&R and would be gone for at least a week. Jerome was not going to leave the platoon in the hands of Sgt. Parker, particularly with the Christmas day incident involving the battalion commander so fresh in mind. So without ceremony, he finished up the evening briefing with, "And oh, Lt. Holland, I'm moving you to November. Sergeant Hernandez is staying behind tomorrow for R&R, and November needs a platoon leader."

Consequently, I moved my gear over to November, and Sgt. Hernandez broke the news to the platoon CP group and to the squad leaders, Sgt. Parker and Sgt. Ricketts. Parker would also serve as platoon sergeant in Hernandez's absence. Ricketts was an Australian who somehow had found his way into the U.S. Army and the U.S. Airborne. He was a good squad leader but had a much different leadership approach than did Sgt. Parker. The latter was a lifer, a brass-disliking lifer, but still a lifer. Sgt. Ricketts, despite having four stripes, had an attitude closer to that of the short-term troopers. He was the boss of his squad, but the relationship was more of a big brother-little brother thing than a military-chain-of-command deal. The squad engaged in considerable good-natured banter with Ricketts, who gave as good as he got.

The different leadership styles contributed to a noticeable degree of tension between Parker and Ricketts. The tension never escalated to outright hostility, but it was there. And with Sgt. Parker's assumption of the position of temporary platoon sergeant, the tension acquired an extra edge. Parker was the giver of orders, and Ricketts was the receiver. Parker couldn't help adding a little extra "umph" to the giving, and Ricketts couldn't help displaying a little extra sullenness in the receiving. Fortunately, the command relationship would last for only a week, until Sgt. Hernandez returned from R&R.

No problems of tension existed in the platoon headquarters. The two RTOs were both from Virginia, making them and me fellow good ol' boys. Ricky Hays was from Virginia Beach. Nineteen and a confirmed non-lifer, his goal was to become a Virginia State Trooper. The other RTO was Wayne Jackson. He was also from southeastern of Virginia. He was a semi-lifer, maybe 24 years old. He had spent some time in Special Forces at Ft. Bragg, receiving training as a medic. Special Forces medics who received the full training were pretty close to doctors. Jackson apparently hadn't received the complete course, but he seemed to know at least as much as the regular medics. He had taken over officially as the platoon medic when Pasquez, then the medic, was wounded during the company's second contact at Dak To.

Pasquez had just returned from recuperation, so Jackson was back to humping the radio for the platoon sergeant. Pasquez, as one might deduce, was Hispanic. Ricky Hays and Jackson were white. Between one quarter and one third of the platoon's approximately 30 individuals were black. Like Harold Campton in Oscar, Ricky Hays had one of those names that are commonly uttered in full. Instead of "Hays," others addressed him as "Ricky Hays."

I took over November with a sort of caretaker attitude. I didn't have much time left as a platoon leader in A Company. With the new promotion policy, I would be a captain in little over a month, in the beginning of February. Moreover, my extension for another six months in Vietnam, which I had submitted before Dak To, had come through approved. I was going for 24 straight months in the 'Nam. Not many soldiers were that loony. But the extension meant that I had a 30-day leave coming. Finally, after almost 18 months—a year and a half—I was feeling an urge to visit the Land of the Big PX. Some of it was the awakening of a long-dormant bit of homesickness. Some of it was guilt, particularly as far as my mother was concerned. I was having all this fun in a combat zone, participating in the war that I had dreamed about since my earliest years, and my family bore the burden of waiting for that dreaded knock on the door by a somber, unsmiling Army officer.

So when the extension approval came through, I very shortly developed a strong desire to begin my 30-day leave. I didn't want to depart the field until I had to—until I made captain—but I wanted the intervening period to go quickly. Thus I took over November knowing that it was for no more than a month. I was glad for the opportunity to hone a few skills of a rifle platoon leader, particularly map reading, but I didn't approach the job with the gung-ho possessiveness that a newly-minted, first-time platoon leader would.

Most of the next day was spent beside the Kontum airstrip waiting for choppers to take us to the boonies. Finally, late in the day we loaded up and were inserted next to a battalion fire support base just being established. We made our way to a little brush covered knoll a short distance away and set up camp. The ground was extremely rocky, pretty close to impossible to dig a hole in. I was called upon to make my first command decision as the boss of November. "Lt. Holland, we can't dig in this hard shit. And how the hell we gonna make overhead cover?"

"Alright, forget the holes. Just scrap out what you can, fill the sandbags with dirt, and pile 'em in front of what you've scrapped out, as a berm." Not on the job for even a day and I was already flouting one of the 173rd's most sacred rules. It was fortunate that I was only going to be around a month.

November was on point the next day. Thus I would quickly get back in the map responsibility business. During my two months with Oscar, I had closely followed the company's route as we moved, but following and being the one doing the route selection were two entirely different things. The mission was to roughly parallel a stream down a lengthy valley and eventually take a side valley to a laager site. The problem for the morning's portion of the move was that in many places the stream banks and the sides of the valley were too steep for parallel travel. They could be climbed, but they could not be traversed sideways.

I found my way out of the laager site and down to the stream without too much trouble. The jungle was thick and required a fair amount of chopping to make a passage. We crossed the stream because the terrain appeared flatter on the other side. The path of least resistance led diagonally away from the stream and up the hillside. We proceeded along this track for awhile, until I thought we were getting too far from the stream. Then I tried paralleling the hillside but the going became damn difficult. Finally, Jerome could restrain himself no longer. "November, this is Alpha 6."

"This is November." I knew what was coming.

"November, ya think ya could find a more impassable route?"

"This is November, we'er trying to find a way." Nothing like saying the obvious.

"Well, see if ya can get on track."

"This is November, Roger."

We ended up back at the stream. The grass appeared greener on the other side—the terrain smoother, the vegetation less thick—so we waded again. Naturally, the reality did not match the appearance, so it wasn't long before there was another fording. The stream was only about calf deep and five meters wide. Consequently, the crossings weren't difficult, only annoying. We continued this zigzagging for most of the morning.

In the afternoon, the valley's vegetation changed. Trees and bushes gave way to tall thick grasses, well over head-high and extremely difficult to move in. I took the path of least resistance and started tromping down the middle of the stream. The going was easier, but stops while the point did its movement were uncomfortable. No one was anxious to plop down in the water itself, and resting places on the banks were few and far between. Alternatives weren't evident, however, and Jerome didn't complain.

As we neared where the side valley was supposed to be, I kept a sharp lookout. The closeness of the contour lines on the map indicated that the valley would be very narrow. I was determined to find it before Jerome. I particularly didn't want to go beyond the entrance and have him call me back. So I scrutinized the map and the main valley wall carefully and continuously. Sgt. Parker, serving as both squad leader and platoon sergeant, was moving with the point fire team. Late in the day as I was leading the main body up to the point in one of the link-up moves, I saw a small stream entering the main stream. Something clicked in the recesses of my brain, and I looked even more closely at the side of the valley. Sure enough, there was a narrow slot, barely noticeable. Hot damn! I had found the sucker! I called the point back and directed them up the small stream. It was one of my finer map-reading moments.

We made our way a short distance up the valley. Dusk was approaching, so Jerome called a halt before we had gone very far. The laager site was on the valley floor, with some positions at the base of the slopes. It was a lousy location, but climbing to one of the ridges above would have taken at least an hour. At the evening briefing, I couldn't refrain from reminding Jerome of my map-reading coup. He just grunted.

The next day we climbed out of the valley and followed ridge lines in a wide lazy circle back toward the fire support base we had left the day before. November was now last in the company column, so my responsibilities were minimal. The laager site that night was on high ground about five clicks from the base. The hill had in the not too distant past been cleared. It was now covered with thick second-growth young trees and shrubs. Cutting fields of fire and paths between positions and inside the perimeter took considerable effort.

We received a break of sorts the following day. The company stayed in place, and the rifle platoons conducted day patrols. November drew a difficult route down into a river valley and up a ridge. The vegetation was beaucoup thick. In fact, the climb up the ridge was done at a crawl. The growth was 10 to 20 feet high and consisted of clumps of bushes with narrow bases and spreading tops. The path of least resistance was close to the ground, and that's where we went. Once on top of the ridge, we were supposed to investigate for a couple of clicks. We might have gone a click before Jerome called us back. The issue of exactly how far we had gone would come up the next day and cause me a bit of discomfort.

In the afternoon back at the laager site, a chopper brought in a hot meal, and Sgt. Parker and the Mortar Platoon began a crap game. This was the first bit of gambling I had seen in the field. It didn't last long, but the participants were certainly enthusiastic. The meal was an occasion for the first sergeant to give me a little hell. Platoon leaders normally did not eat until their troops had eaten. The call went out for November to go through the line, and I waited near the first mermac can until I thought all the platoon members had been fed. Shortly after I had grabbed a plate and started through, however, a couple of November laggards appeared. They followed me through. I didn't think anything of it.

But First Sergeant Duckett was supervising the chow line. He let me know that he was not happy. "You're not supposed to eat until your men do, Lieutenant."

I stammered a rebuttal of sorts: "I waited Top. I thought everyone'd gone through." It was a small thing, and unlike in other instances, I didn't think my conduct was that reprehensible. Maybe the first sergeant had lost money in the crap game.

The mission for the next day was for the company to trace and go beyond the ground November covered on the patrol. We were to continue on the ridge where I had stopped, descend into a high grass-covered valley, and climb a ridge on the far side. One of the other platoons was on point. It followed November's trail, including the portion where we had crawled up the hillside. The crawl was done with packs, which was no easy task. At the top of the ridge, Jerome called on the horn, "November, what can we expect now."

Well, since we hadn't gone very far the day before, I had no real idea. "It just follows the ridge."

"Yeah, but at what point should we turn for the descent into the valley?"

Now what the hell was he grilling me for? He could head into the valley whenever he wanted. How far we had or hadn't gone the previous day was immaterial. "About another click or so," I answered.

"What's the terrain and route like?"

Damn. Was he trying to trip me up? To see if I was fibbing about how far we had gone? "About like it is now."

"That's not much help. Six, out."

Well, at least the grilling was over. Maybe I should be more careful about giving my positions when operating away from the company. Or maybe Jerome also lost money in the previous day's crap game. In any case, after a long, hot day, we were on the top of the far ridge, setting up for the evening.

At the platoon evening briefing after I had given out the next day's mission I had received at the company briefing, Sgt. Parker casually mentioned that he had submitted Pots' name in response to a requirement from First Sergeant Duckett. The requirement was for personnel to be transferred to the 3rd Battalion, which was a relatively new addition to the 173rd. The 3rd Battalion had been in-country for about six months. I noted earlier in these pages that a major problem for a new unit in Vietnam was rotations. It wouldn't be good to have the unit turn over en masse, so efforts were made shortly after a unit arrived in-country to work in soldiers with different DEROS dates. Also, some members of the new unit were transferred to other units.

This policy had a decidedly negative impact on unit cohesion and morale. After months of training together in the states, a unit came to Vietnam and promptly started to change personnel. And taking soldiers out of old units made for unhappy old units and unhappy transferred soldiers, although in some cases the old unit's unhappiness was mitigated by the opportunity to rid itself of a malcontent.

When Sgt. Parker was given the first sergeant's requirement for a name for the 3rd Battalion, he evidently didn't ponder long. Pots, the machine gunner who had screamed through the night movement several weeks before, was the candidate. When Sgt. Parker informed me of his submission of Pots' name, I thought to myself that the matter should have been cleared with me, the platoon leader. But I didn't make an issue of it. After all, I was both a care-taker and a short-timer, just trying to hold the lid on for a few weeks. Moreover, the possible transfer did not seem imminent. So I let the matter slide by.

Once again, the laager was a two-night affair. The company conducted patrols the next day. November's route took us over a ridge and into another heavily-grassed river valley. Or probably it was just the same river valley we had crossed the day before, only we were hitting it farther down-stream. The patrol was uneventful, and the next day we packed up the rucks and moved on. November was the point of the company column, but the route wasn't difficult. It was mostly following an azimuth off the ridge, through a wide thickly-vegetated valley, up another ridge, and along the high ground for a few clicks. Late in the afternoon, Jerome called real friendly like, "Ya found a laager site yet, November?"

"This is November. We could go with any place along this ridge. It's fairly wide."

"Do ya want me to come up and help ya look?" His tone was not threatening or displeased, but the question struck at what I considered my prerogative as the point platoon leader. I could find a laager site my own damn self. "Nah, I've got it under control."

"This is Six. Watch yourself, November." Now he was sounding threatening or displeased. I suppose my tone was a bit too flippant. But we were about on top of a possible laager site anyway, and the little give-and-take ended. "This is November. I think we're at a spot now."

"Six. Roger, Out."

The laager site was at an elbow on the ridge line. Having been the point, November was on the far side of the crook, stretched in a U-shape across the ridge. Lima and Mike tied in to either end of November's line and extended back around the crook. On the outside of the crook stretching down the slope was an overgrown clearing that with a little machete work became an LZ. A chopper was due in, probably with mail. It was a standard evening situation, and I was giving it little thought until First Sergeant Duckett yelled out: "Sgt. Parker, get Pots ready to leave. He's going out on this chopper."

"Roger, First Sergeant. Hey Pots. You're leaving on this chopper. Get yer gear together." Sgt. Parker's instructions were also issued at a high decibel level.

This was the first Pots and his comrades had heard about his transfer. "What the hell d'ya mean?" Pots screeched. Genius that I was, I realized a sticky situation was rapidly developing. Without warning, a family—Pots and his little group of buddies—was about to be torn asunder. Only this wasn't an ordinary family. Its members were armed to the teeth. Pots himself had his M-60 machine gun. A sour knot of fear grabbed my bowels.

"You're being sent to the 3rd Battalion. It's part of the brigade's rotation plan. Ya havta go." Sgt. Parker's explanation was not given with any evidence of sympathy. Indeed, Parker's glee in getting rid of a thorn in his side was all too apparent.

"The fuck you say! I ain't fuckin' goin'!"

"You ain't got no choice. Go talk to the first sergeant."

Pots went storming towards the company CP and the LZ, screaming that he fucking well wasn't about to leave. From the vicinity of the CP, about 30 meters away, a heated discussion ensued. In his own inimitable way, First Sergeant Duckett explained that Pots had no choice but to get his ass on the inbound chopper, and that he didn't have much time to get his gear together. Pots ranted and raved, but a degree of subservience was creeping into his voice. The first sergeant had many years experience in imposing his will on young troopers. The conservation ended with Pots storming back to the platoon. Once he left the first sergeant's immediate presence, Pots' minor bit of subservience vanished. He crashed through the bushes, yelling and cursing at the top of his voice.

Meanwhile, I took the coward's approach and attempted to make myself scarce. When Pots was confronting the first sergeant, I slipped along the edge of the perimeter and made my way toward the far side of the LZ. I didn't want to be the authority figure that Pots decided to take vengeance on. I wasn't worried so much about physical violence, although that was more than a remote possibility, as about having to answer Pots' "Why." Splitting up an infantry unit in combat is done only at a high cost to morale, and ultimately effectiveness. Splitting it up without warning is doubly detrimental. I didn't want to have to explain or justify the Army's boneheaded approach to solving the rotation problems of new units in Vietnam. Such tasks were best left to lifers like the first sergeant who had long ago accepted the Army's irrationality as a fact of existence.

Pots angrily repacked his rucksack. His thrashing and cursing were intimidating even his small group of friends. He left them without saying goodbye, stomping off to the chopper that by now was on the LZ. The first sergeant's "Get a move on, the chopper's waitin'" hurried him along.

With the chopper's departure, the entire company breathed a sigh of relief. Everyone had been within hearing of Pots' tirade, and more than a few were probably waiting for the shooting to start. After he left, I went up to his group of friends. The assistant gunner had already promoted himself to gunner, so the necessary combat functions were not suffering an interruption. I didn't know how to start the conservation other than to say, "So Pots didn't want to go, huh?" Again my talent for saying the obvious.

The troopers merely grunted, busying themselves with their tasks and avoiding my eyes. Finally, one of them made a comment about what a stinking thing Pots' transfer was. I attempted an explanation about why it had happened, even obliquely suggesting that Pots had been the one selected because he hadn't been your basic perfect trooper. The attempted explanation didn't sound very convincing even to me. The only untroubled person in November that evening was Sgt. Parker, who in his own gruff way was close to euphoric.

Pots' departure was not the only personnel change wrought by the chopper that evening. It also brought in a replacement for Mike, Lt. Roberts. The new guy had spent time at a rear echelon job at USARV. Roberts was to remain with the company for another day, showing him the ropes. Roberts was a quiet, humorless guy who had been in the field for a long time for an officer—eight months. He was tired and gave the impression that he had seen all the war he ever wanted to see. But he was uncomplaining and undoubtedly could have gone for a full twelve months.

The next day November brought up the rear. It was another extended hump that followed ridgelines, went through a long-abandoned small farming area that had a few hot pepper plants, and ended up on a tree-covered almost knife-edged ridge. A chopper that evening returned Sgt. Hernandez from R&R. He and I were to have little more than two weeks together, but it was an enjoyable two weeks. Sgt. Hernandez was one of the finest NCOs that I came across in Vietnam. He was conscientious, fair, intelligent, and respected by one and all. Our brief relationship didn't have the underlying tension that existed in my relationships with many NCOs. The tension arose from my feeling that they and I were not always on the same wave length. I was often uncertain that they understood what I wanted done—assuming I knew myself. Moreover, determining who could be relied on for a little initiative was constantly a problem, as was judging an old-timer's ability to handle young, intelligent, rebellious troopers. None of these uncertainties existed regarding Sgt. Hernandez.

One other interesting thing about Sgt. Hernandez was that prior to joining the U.S. Army some years before, he had been a lieutenant in the Mexican Army. Why he left Mexico and its Army, I never inquired.

Although November wasn't due to be the point the next day, Jerome bumped us ahead of Mike, who would be having its first day under a new platoon leader. The ridge we were on broadened and sloped gently down into a valley. Sgt. Parker's squad was on point. During one of the stops by the main body to wait for the point to go its 125 dogs (meters) and clover leaf, Sgt. Parker called: "November, this is November Two."

"This is November."

"This is November Two. We've got a snake here, a bamboo viper." A bamboo viper was a venomous green snake that could be two to three feet in length. I waited for more, but the radio was silent. Finally, I called.

"This is November. What's happening with the snake?"

"Oh, we killed it. We've gone one-two-five dogs and are waiting for you to link-up." Well, shit. Those assholes get me all worked up about a goddamn snake, and they then let the matter drop. And where was the thing? The 1-2-5 dogs until the link-up were going to be a very gingerly traversed 1-2-5 dogs. I called: "This is November. Exactly where is the snake? I don't wanna be stumblin' onto it."

"Uh, this is November Two. I don't know exactly. But it's dead."

"Didja leave it besides the trail, or didja throw it into the bushes?"

"It's in the bushes…, I think."

I suspected Sgt. Parker might be jerking me around. It wouldn't surprise me if he had the thing set in a bush about chest high, waiting to scare the living shit out of me. I picked through the 1-2-5 dogs to the link-up as if I were in a mine field. I didn't find the snake.

As the morning progressed, we worked our way down the gradual slope to the stream in the valley floor. Both on the hill-side and at the bottom, the growth was thick. The valley was narrow. At places, the only thing on the valley floor was the stream, which was about five meters wide and one to two feet deep. Once at the valley floor, we were to find a route up the far side. In searching for a route up the far side of the valley, I took the easiest path, the stream. We sloshed along it for a 100 meters or so, following a wide bend, until Jerome reminded me that our goal was not the South China Sea. I reluctantly directed the point to leave the openness of the stream bed for the effort to find a way up to the ridgeline.

The struggle out of the valley took most of the afternoon. The slope was steep, and the jungle was at its clinging worst, yielding to A Company's advance with great reluctance. We finally arrived on the ridgeline. It was about 30 meters wide. The vegetation was a little thinner than the growth on the slope, but not by a whole lot. The mission now was to move along the crest until it was time to laager for the night.

Following a ridgeline would seem to be simple enough, but that day Sgt. Parker made it an adventure. Maybe it was the heat, maybe it was the long day, maybe it was unconscious guilt over jerking me around about the snake, but Sgt. Parker could not stay on the top of the ridge. My instructions to him were: "We're just gonna follow the ridge. The azimuth looks to be about 35 degrees, but just stay on the high ground."

The 35 degrees was what stuck, however. Parker started off with his head down, staring at his compass for all he was worth. Before he was out of sight, I could see he was edging down the slope. I assumed he would look up and realize he was going downhill, but it didn't happen. When he called for us to link up, I proceeded along his trail, feeling more and more apprehensive as the ridge rose gradually to my left. I reached him just as Jerome called on the radio: "November, where the hell are you goin'? Is it so damn difficult to stay on the ridge?"

"Roger, Alpha Six. We'll get straighten' out."

I turned to Sgt. Parker. "Hey, stay on the high ground. Just follow the ridge. Now we need to head back up on top."

"What compass heading, Sir?"

"It's about 20 degrees, but don't worry about the azimuth. Just angle up to the high ground."

Sgt. Parker was having none of this inexactness, however. He planted his nose in his compass and headed off on 20 degrees. The course took him gradually up the ridge, but when we linked up he was on the other side, heading back down to the valley. Fortunately, the middle of the column where Jerome was traveling was on the top of the ridge. He was thus not aware that Sgt. Parker had once again shown great difficulty in comprehending the concept of high ground. I led Parker and his fire team the 50 meters to the crest, pointed him along that elusive high ground, and sent him on his next 1-2-5 dogs.

After 15 minutes or so he called: "November Six, this is November Two. We've gone one-two-five dogs and are waiting for you to link up."

"Roger, November Two," I responded. "Are you on the high ground?"

"This is November Two. That's affirmative, over."

"Roger. This is November Six, out."

So with hope tinged with trepidation, I set off on Sgt. Parker's trail. The hope began to vanish as his trail began a diagonal descent down the slope on the left. I stopped the column and called Jerome: "Alpha Six, this is November."

"This is Six."

"This is November. We're having trouble staying on the ridge. I'm halting and sending out another point."

Unexpectedly, Jerome didn't make any sarcastic comment. "This is Six, roger out." Perhaps he sympathized with the problem I was encountering due to Sgt. Parker's sudden case of loopiness. I called Parker: "Break, November Two, this is November Six."

"November Two, over." He sounded sullen. Since all company radios were on the same net, he had heard my call to Jerome.

"This is November. Your trail is headin' downhill again. I'm sendin' out another point along the ridge top. They'll be appearin' off to your right. Don't fire 'em up, over."

"The is November Two, roger out."

I sent off the remaining fire team in Sgt. Parker's squad. I called up Sgt. Hernandez's RTO so they would have a radio. The fire team was right behind me, and its members were thus aware of the difficulties Parker was having. "Look. See if you can stay on the high ground. I don't know what Sergeant Parker's problem is today. Be careful because he'll be off to yer left. Don't fire him up. Go out 'bout a hundred dogs."

The fire team set off. Despite my warnings on not firing each other up, I was apprehensive about the possibility of a little friendly firefight. Thus I was relieved to get a call on the radio after a few minutes. "November Six, this is November Five. We've gone one hundred dogs and are waiting for you to link up."

I led the column forward. The underbrush began thinning out, increasing visibility. A tableau of considerable absurdity came into view. On the ridge crest was the second fire team. The six troopers were arranged in a U-shape formation oriented towards the direction of advance. Below them, about 25 meters down the hill, was Sgt. Parker and the first fire team, also in a U-shape formation. Each fire team acted oblivious of the other's existence. I mentally shrugged. Sgt. Parker still seemed to have no understanding of his path-breaking problems. To him, there were no problems. Fortunately, evening was approaching, and Jerome decided the spot was appropriate for a laager site.

November brought up the rear the next day. The route was a long rambling excursion along ridgelines. As the point did its thing, I spent the frequent stops reading and waiting. The reading procedure was to pull a paperback out of one's jungle fatigue pants as soon as one plopped down. Then when it was time to link up, the book would go back in the pants, the struggle to rise under the weight of the pack would ensue, and the column would snake forward. As for the waiting, what I was waiting for was the month to go by so I could catch the Big Bird back to the World. I was anxious to go, and the anxiety was dramatically slowing down the passage of time.

The laager site for the evening was in a shallow valley. One of the other companies of the 1st Battalion had been there within the past few days. Consequently, the place was booby-trapped with little bits of human residue—barely buried piles of defecation. I had the pleasure of placing my air mattress on one of the piles. I lay down for a rest, and the smell wafted from under me. It was a good hour before I finished scraping and burying shit and scouting the area for other little surprises.

A severe case of allergies hit me the next day. The valley was filled with bamboo, and the fuzz from the stalks was probably the culprit. I started sneezing shortly after waking up, and the attack got worse as the morning wore on. We climbed out of the valley, but it didn't help. I was exploding at a steady rate of five sneezes per minute. I once read that in some physiological ways, a sneeze is similar to an orgasm. And indeed there is something pleasurable about a sneeze. But I suspect even a continuous series of orgasms would get old after awhile. Eventually Pasquez, the medic, gave me a pill. It eased the sneezing but came pretty close to making me a zombie. Sleep was all I wanted to do. Every exertion, each step, each movement of my arm, was an effort against a great weight. I fell into a deep slumber at the link-up stops and had to be prodded into action. Finally, after an eternity of a day, we stopped for the night on a hilltop. It was tree-covered, small, and steep-sloped. I managed to find a small flat area, blew up my air mattress, and immediately collapsed.

Ricky Hays got me up as darkness was falling. Jerome was about to hold the evening briefing, and my presence was requested. An additional person was at the briefing—Jerome's replacement. He had been choppered in while I slept. We had been expecting him for several days. Jerome had been in the field for six months. He still had a couple of months before DEROSing, but competition for company commander time was keen. Rarely did a captain get to spend more than six months, even if he had the desire.

Jerome's replacement was a short slender guy with a long Polish name, Wolfowitz or some such. He still had his own uniform with name tag and other paraphernalia, which included master jump wings, ranger tab, and pathfinder patch. The latter was awarded for completion of a tough course on laying out drop zones. Pathfinders were supposed to be the first guys in a parachute assault. They were looked upon as an elite of the elite. Despite these formidable credentials on his jungle fatigue shirt, however, Wolfowitz did not cut an impressive figure. It didn't have much to do with his shortness or slightness. It was more his manner, a tentativeness and uncertainty that was unexpected in an infantry leader, particularly one who had been through the training his shirt said he had been through.

Wolfowitz had spent his first six months in the 'Nam at brigade headquarters, on the S-3 planning staff. He shook hands all around and mumbled a few words about how happy he was finally to be in the field. He had this goofy semi-crew cut, with some hair standing up and some lying flat. He was a heavy smoker, and lit one cigarette from another as he stood there. I noticed that his fingernails were chewed down to practically nothing. This guy was going to have some problems. Jerome said he would be with us through the next day, which would include a chopper assault and a short cross-country move. Thus Wolfowitz would have one day to learn the ropes.

I viewed Jerome's departure with a feeling that I can best term as a form of nostalgia. He and I had not been close. Jerome's personality and mode of operations were not such as to foster togetherness. They were far removed from what was conducive to producing the type of relationship that some platoon leaders had with their company commanders. That relationship was almost one of hero-worshipping. The company commander was a father figure of sorts. Jerome was not a guy who would attract such unrestrained admiration, and in any case I was too cynical and iconoclastic to be much of a hero-worshipper with anyone. Jerome was sarcastic, devious at times, and stand-offish. But he was damn good. Many veterans of Alpha Company became veterans and not names on a wall because of Jerome's competence and professionalism.

When I first came to the field, Jerome exercised just the right amount of tolerance for my ignorance. I learned under him, and developed into an adequate—not great but adequate—platoon leader. Moreover, even though we had not been personally close, we were part of one of the closest social groupings that humans can experience—a unit in combat. To call an infantry company a "family" is to revert to a cliche, but it is a cliche with a great deal of validity. The intensity of prolonged challenge, especially the challenge of combat but also the challenge of bearing extreme physical hardship, creates an intimacy among the survivors that is found among few other gatherings of human beings. The little less than five months I served in Alpha Company remain to this day among the most remembered of my life. With Jerome's departure, they were coming to an end. My life was passing a high point, perhaps the high point, and there was a sadness.

Choppers picked us up early the next morning. Once again we went to the Kontum airfield. We lounged beside the PCP apron for several hours, and then after lunch loaded up for a combat assault. November was the lead platoon, and the first lift was to be the lead platoon and the company headquarters group. We flew for 10 or 15 minutes, then went into a sort of holding pattern. We were over a broad valley that contained both cultivated fields and patches of jungle. Several dirt roads or trails bisected the area. Along one section of one of the roads, a section that crossed a bridge and open space and that entered jungle-covered hilly terrain on each end, an air strike was going in. Two jets dropped napalm. They were followed by helicopter gunships. Tracer rounds drifted lazily into the tree lines. The gunships departed, and we turned for the approach.

The door gunners opened up, getting their licks in. The LZ didn't appear to be hot, but all the ordnance being expended by the U.S. Army and Air Force, the gut-pounding thumping of the Hueys, and the dizzying up-rush of the ground got the old adrenalin flowing. The choppers touched briefly, and we poured out. I ran with a fire-team for the bridge and the tree line on the far side. The LZ was secured without any indication of Charlies, and the entire company was soon on the ground.

After forming into the usual company column, we moved off the road, through a small patch of jungle, and up and across several low-lying, grass-covered hills. The grass ranged from knee to waist high. A laager site about a click from the LZ was settled upon. As we were digging in, a lone chopper descended from the sky. Without any ceremony other than a few handshakes with members of the headquarters group, Captain David Jerome boarded and was gone. Alpha Company was under new management.

Shortly thereafter, the new management, Captain Wolfowitz, held an evening briefing. His hesitancy and tentativeness had if anything increased. He did not inspire confidence, but I was too short to care. Exactly when I would be leaving was a little unclear, but it was only days away. The mission for the next day was for the company to remain in place and the rifle platoons to conduct day patrols. November was to explore an adjacent jungle-covered hill, swing over for a look at another hill, join the road that ran through the LZ, and return to the laager site. A VC supply cache was suspected to be in the vicinity of the second hill. The area wasn't quite a free-fire zone, but any locals we came across were to be viewed skeptically.

Except for the fact that the terrain did not lend itself to easy map-reading, the patrol was uneventful. Finding the first hill was simple enough—it was in plain sight several hundred meters across a small depression. Once there, however, we were in thick jungle and had limited visibility. I determined an azimuth to get us to the next hill. We hacked a trail down the slope, across a small valley, and part way up another slope. It was about noon, so I halted for an extended lunch break. Wolfowitz called for a sitrep. I told him that our location was near the top of the hill and that we hadn't found anything yet. He sounded disappointed. It occurred to me that he was new enough to the field to actually believe intelligence reports. In fact, he had probably been one of the headquarters flunkies who produced the damn things.

After we resumed our march, it became apparent that we were at least a kilometer from where I had told Wolfowitz we were. Rather then being near the top of the hill, we were some distance down the near slope—the slope closest to the laager site. Thus to search adequately the whole hill-mass, we would have to change direction and plan on an additional couple of hours of effort. As a shorttimer, I wasn't up to it. Instead, I set an angled course diagonally across the slope toward the road. We went upwards for a bit, but we didn't reach the top and we didn't fully search the whole area. A VC battalion could have been on the far side for all we knew.

Eventually, we intersected the road and followed it backed toward the previous day's LZ. Near the spot where the trail to the laager site began, I selected an ambush site with Sgt. Johnson, a fire team leader in Sgt. Parker's squad. Johnson's fire team would be on ambush that night. Johnson was a huge black man. He was a heavyweight fighter, apparently a very good one.

The trail to the laager site was impossible to miss. A hundred plus troopers moving in single file through high grass make quite an impression in the terrain. We tromped in, and I reported to Wolfowitz: "Not much out there, Sir. Even the road doesn't look used much."

"Didja, didja see any evidence of the VC supply cache on the hill?"

"Nary a sign, Sir."

"Didja get all around the hill?"

"Well, we did the best we could. As you can see from here, the jungle is thick. I can't swear there's nothing there, but there was nothin' where we were." I thought he might be about to ask for a detailed review of our route, but he dropped the matter. Even if he had pursued the subject, I had no doubt I could bullshit him. This guy just wasn't in charge.

I made my way to my little bit of luxury, my air mattress, and lay down for a nap. First Sergeant Duckett and the company supply guy had a hooch within earshot, on the other side of a bush. They were discussing Hill 882 and November 18th. I listened, hoping they would mention my exploits. Apparently I was the only one aware of my exploits, however. They rehashed the day in detail without once noting the contributions of the Mortar Platoon. I resisted the temptation to intrude on the conversation in order to try and get them to say something complimentary.

Toward evening, Sgt. Johnson's ambush patrol departed. After they had gone, Ricky Hays said, "Damn, we're changin' frequencies tonight and they don't have the new frequencies." As part of security procedures, radio frequencies and code words were changed about once a week.

"Shit, goddammit. How the fuck did that happen?"

"We just didn't think of it."

I got on the horn. "November Three, this is November."

After a pause, there was a response: "November, this is November Three."

"This is November. We're changing radio stuff tonight, and ya don't have the new items. You need to come back to get 'em."

There was a longer pause. "What about the perimeter?" He was thinking what I was thinking: approaching the perimeter with its claymores and armed troopers was always a little tricky. You never knew when there might be an accident, or even when some guy might go nuts. And approaching the perimeter at dusk doubled the pucker factor.

"This is November. Don't worry. I'll warn all the positions and meet you at the perimeter."

Again there was a long pause. "I don't know. I don't like comin' back there." Shit. For a heavyweight fighter, Sgt. Johnson was no dummy.

"Okay. You come back halfway, and I'll meet ya. Ya know that lone tree that's a little out of the woods?"

"Roger."

"That's where I'll meet ya, okay?"

"This is November Three, roger."

"November out."

So I was the one to risk the perimeter hazards. I called Mike, the platoon manning the portion of the perimeter that the trail exited, and warned the new platoon leader of my movement. I then went to the positions near the trail entry point. "Hey, I'm goin' out to give some information to the ambush patrol. Don't fire me up." Finally, I sucked in my gut and proceeded out into the fast approaching darkness.

The trip to the meeting place took about five minutes. Sgt. Johnson and one other member of the ambush were already there. I gave them the new frequencies. They departed, and I started back. The dusk was giving way to night. Visibility was rapidly dropping. The thought of encountering a Charlie or so crossed my mind, but the real worry was the perimeter. As I got closer, the hollowness in my stomach grew, and the pounding of my heart increased. I wondered if I would be aware of the claymore explosion before the pellets tore through me, or if I would hear the M-60 before the burst ripped my intestines. The last 50 meters were at an angle to the perimeter, so death could come from any of several positions. Finally, sweating much more than the evening warmth warranted, I entered the laager site. A trooper sitting on a perimeter bunker said, "Welcome back, Sir. Good trip?"

"Numbah fuckin' ten. That ain't my idea of fun."

We were lifted back to Kontum airfield the next day. After milling around for a few hours, we made another chopper assault, this time onto a narrow finger that sloped down to a valley floor from a ridgeline. The LZ was a small hole in the jungle that had been the result of an air strike. Indeed, from the number of fallen trees that littered the area, it appeared much of the finger had been visited by the fly boys. The LZ could handle only one chopper at a time, and it was well into the afternoon before the whole company was on the ground. The decision was made to laager in place, amid and amongst the disheveled forest.

Early the next morning, we made our way up the finger to the top of the ridge. The journey was only about a click, but the downed trees made for much scrambling and crawling. The ridge top was wide and for the most part tree-covered. We established a laager site, and the rifle platoons set out on day patrols. November's mission was to follow the ridgeline to the north for a goodly distance but also to investigate several side ridges. It was an ambitious effort that produced groans when I briefed the squad leaders. As an added point, I emphasized that the squad leaders should be sure that they had adequate smoke grenades in their squads. Since most of the platoon had long before adopted non-standard combinations of web gear, I was becoming concerned that on daytime patrols, when we weren't carrying all of our paraphernalia, some basic, necessary items might be getting left behind. Smoke grenades were imperative if we had to mark our position for a medevac or an air strike.

The first side ridge contained a large, well-developed bunker complex. It didn't appear to have been recently occupied, but we nevertheless moved gingerly and with extreme caution. Booby traps were on everyone's mind. On the slope of the ridge we found a man-made cave entrance. It was intriguing, and several troopers volunteered to investigate. Alpha Company hadn't come across many tunnels during my tenure. Holes in the ground held an allure for a certain adventuresome type, and allure that was fed by the many stories in *Stars and Stripes* about tunnel rats down in the III Corps area. A picture of some 25th Infantry Division leg squeezing into a crack in the ground could produce paroxysms of envy among otherwise haughty paratroopers.

Despite the readiness of several November troopers to scramble into the side of the hill, I opted for prudence. Tossing a grenade seemed more intelligent than tossing a soldier. After the grenade did its work, a trooper could still crawl into the darkness. But as Sgt. Parker prepared to throw a grenade, another thought struck me. What if the cave contained an ammunition cache, one with sufficient explosives to crater the hillside? So I made sure most of the platoon had some distance between themselves and the cave. My fears were not realized, however. The grenade exploded with a muffled thud. A trooper crawled in and was shortly back. The cave appeared to be just a dead-end tunnel, although we could have missed camouflaged doors leading to other passages.

After exploring the bunker complex a bit more, we proceeded on our journey. The route took us around and over a small hill and down a steep slope. We paused on the way down for a lunch break. At the bottom of the hill was a small stream, on the other side of which was another steep slope. It led to another finger from the main ridge. I sent a point fire team to the crest of the finger before following with the main body. I didn't want to risk getting the whole platoon trapped on the hand-over-foot hillside by any Charlies that might be on top. When the point called that it was on the high ground, we followed.

The struggle up the steep slope was exhausting, so I had the platoon pause for an extended break at the top. The underbrush was extremely thick, limiting visibility to only a couple of meters. I didn't bother to have the platoon form a perimeter. We were in a line, with me just behind the point. Three to five meters separated individuals, so in some cases we were out of sight of each other. I was lying on the ground getting my breath when a very pronounced rustling started to my left front. It was loud enough to conjure up images of a column of Charlies ambling by. My heart went into overdrive as I gripped the M-16. Behind me was Ricky Hays. Like me, he had a firm hold on his weapon. His eyes were wide with the combination of excitement, anticipation, and fear. I put my index finger to my lips in the standard motion for silence, and then turned to crawl forward. I crept as quietly as I could up to the rear point man. He was lying on his stomach, peering into the underbrush. I tapped his foot. He glanced backed, and I gave him a quizzical shrug that attempted to convey the question, "What the fuck's happening?"

He gave me a shrug in return that was easily translated: "Fuck if I know." We lay for at least five minutes as the noise continued. From my prone position, I kept my vision angled upward, attempting to look over the top of the underbrush. I expected to have a Charlie step on me at any moment. But the noise gradually died down. I slowly went to a crouch, and then to a standing position. I was barely breathing. The adrenalin was surging. There were no VCs, however. The rest of the platoon also gradually stood. Almost to a man, we had been gripped by an almost certainty of imminent combat. But looking at the lack of any evidence of nearby movement through the thick underbrush—no broken branches, no turned leaves—I concluded that we hadn't had a near miss with Mr. Charles, a pig maybe, but not Mr. Charles.

Amid a number of sheepish looks, we got started again. The underbrush thinned out as the platoon made its way up the finger to the high ground of the ridge. There, we found the trail and turned north, away from the company laager site. By this time, it was well toward mid-afternoon. I was reluctant to head in the opposite direction from the company for too great a distance. Compounding my concern was the fact that the trail was gradually descending. Every downward step would have to be matched with an upward effort. So after we had proceeded north for 30 minutes or so, I decided enough was enough. I called back, "Alpha Romeo, this is November Six. We're heading back." Alpha Romeo was the company RTO or whoever might be manning the radio at the moment. I didn't particularly want to talk to Wolfowitz, but he nevertheless came on:

"This is Alpha. Did you reach the objective?"

Well, probably not, but I wasn't going to say so. It was time to return home. "We're pretty close. The terrain has flatten' out so I'm not real sure if we're exactly there, but we're close."

There was a long pause. Wolfowitz obviously wanted to play by the rules. He didn't want to be reporting any uncertain information to battalion. On the other hand, he was still intimidated by his FNG status. Giving his veteran platoon leaders a direct order was something that was not going to happen anytime soon. Finally, he said, "This is Alpha. Roger your return to the laager site."

We started back. We were on the trail and moving steadily, not sending the point out and linking up. The point was about 35 meters ahead, and I was just following it with the main body. After a lengthy gradual climb, we passed the location where we had joined the trail. Just a bit further was a smaller trail branching off the left. It led toward a sizeable hut that was visible from the main trail. I decided to check it out. I left a fire team at the trail junction, and the rest of the platoon proceeded carefully to the hut. It was a substantially built, Montegnard-type structure with a raised porch in front and a wooden floor. It was also long deserted.

As most of the platoon took up security positions, a few went inside. There wasn't much to be found, but one of the troopers came up with a Montegnard knife and wooden scabbard that was held together with two strips of woven rattan cane, one at the top and one at the bottom. He brought it out and showed it to me. I and several others examined it, not exuberantly but attentively. It was interesting but not a throat-grabber, nothing to donate to the Smithsonian. I was turning away when the trooper said, "Ya want it, Lieutenant?"

"Hey, well, I wouldn't mind it. Ya sure you don't want the thing?"

"Nah, ya can have it."

"Well, okay, if ya don't want it." I put the scabbard and knife in my jungle fatigue pants and went about getting the platoon moving again. We rejoined the main trail and resumed the homeward journey. About half a click from camp we came to another trail junction. A trail about the same size as the one we were on crossed ours. We were to set out an ambush that night, and I pointed out this spot to the fire team that had the responsibility. Shortly thereafter we made the laager site. Even though we hadn't been humping rucks, it had been a long day, and I was beat.

After resting a bit, I began wandering about the platoon area. I came up behind a small group that included the trooper who had given me the knife. I heard him say, "And then the damn lieutenant took the knife away from me and kept it for himself."

Pissed? Jesus H. Christ, I was pissed! Normally, I was a non-confrontational guy, but this crap overcame my usual desire to avoid trouble. I stormed up. "Smith, that's a pile of crap, and ya know it. You offered that knife to me. I didn't ask for the fuckin' thing. I asked ya several times if you were sure you didn't want it. Do you want it back now?"

"No…no sir," he stammered. It was apparent that he was much embarrassed by the turn this thing was taking. From having an apparently legitimate gripe against the powers that be, he had been thrust into the position of being an accused liar. I began to feel uncomfortable for him, but still the sonuvabitch had in essence accused me of stealing under the guise of rank. I refrained from saying anything more, mainly because I didn't know what else to say. I turned and walked away. Maybe the moral of the story for a young officer is, be damn careful of what you accept from your troops.

That night, I took a turn on the radio. We had an ambush patrol out, and I didn't trust the normal procedure whereby Ricky Hays, Pasquez, and Jackson slept with the headset in their midst, counting on one of them hearing any incoming calls. My shift was 0230 to 0400, the ghost hours. Pasquez shook me awake, gave me the radio, and returned to his air mattress. I gave the ambush patrol a call. I whispered, "November Three, this is November. If you are ping pong, break squelch twice, over."

After a considerable pause, squelch was broken twice. Maybe they were using the Ricky Hays-approach to radio watch. I spent the next hour and a half fighting sleep, thinking about the incident with Smith, and wanting to get the hell out of there. The desire to see again the Land of the Big PX was becoming all pervasive. I was ready to go.

I had the ambush patrol break squelch again before I carted the radio to Ricky Hays. And again, the patrol took a long time to respond. Oh well. My time was down to a few days, almost hours.

Outta There

Choppers came to get us the next morning. Once again, we were to go to the Kontum airfield. From there, Chinooks were to take us to a location below Pleiku, which itself was 25 or so miles south of Kontum. November was the first platoon to be picked up. The initial lift consisted of four choppers, just enough to hold the platoon's approximately 30 members. Most of the platoon, including myself, were semi-dozing as the four Hueys pounded through the air, when I felt a tap on my shoulder. It was the door gunner. I was sitting on the floor near his seat. He handed me his head phone set and motioned for me to put it on. Once I had it in place, which took some doing because I wasn't used to such fancy equipment, the pilot informed me of a change in plans. A Huey had gone down due to a mechanical problem, and the platoon was being sent to guard it.

A chopper at a time, we dropped down into a small clearing. The Huey sat resting on the rear of its skids and its tail. The skids were eight or so inches in the ground, indicating the machine had come down with a good thud. The clearing was a field that had recently been cultivated. It was about 50 meters by 50 meters and covered with a calf-high scrubby grass. The underbrush and jungle on all four sides were extremely thick. I sent the headquarters group into the vegetation's edge at one corner, and distributed the two squads to the other three corners. It was not a good defensive arrangement, but I couldn't think of another. The visibility and fields of fire into the underbrush and jungle were practically nil. The four groups were too far apart to give one another much support. I looked around the field and saw that all four had disappeared into the woods.

I made a circuit of the field, checking to make sure I still had a platoon. For the most part, the troopers weren't much aroused over our little change-of-pace mission. Many had promptly done what infantrymen were wont to do at any opportunity—sleep. I received a call from someone identifying himself as Hotrod Six. He asked how we were doing, thanked us for helping—as if we had a choice—and promised that he would have us out shortly. After a bit, Sgt. Parker and Sgt. Hernandez ambled over to the chopper. This was a chance to see how the fly boys lived. We began going through the interior, finding neat little survival packs with interesting food items that quickly disappeared. There were also flare guns, map cases, and similar paraphernalia. Anything small enough to fit into a rucksack was fair game.

The arrival of another chopper put an end to the looting. Two riggers were dropped off. They proceeded to run heavy web straps around the injured beast. Shortly thereafter, a Skycrane, a monster helicopter that looked like a big spider, appeared. It gradually descended, as did its wind and turbulence. The clearing quickly became filled with blowing grass and leaves. One of the goggled riggers stood on top of the downed chopper, holding a ring through which all the web straps ran. The Skycrane hovered closer, the rigger made the hook-up and jumped clear, and the sick machine was soon on its way to the chopper hospital. The riggers got the next ride, and then November resumed its journey to the Kontum airfield.

When we arrived at the airfield, Wolfowitz was beside himself. November's side trip had struck some cord in him. He peppered me with questions, as excited as if he'd just conquered Cambodia. I was at a loss to figure out what turned him on so.

But time for post-mortems on the adventure was limited. Some Chinooks shortly arrived, and the company loaded up for the trip south. The flight took us to a place we hadn't seen in a long time—a semi-populated area. It was on a flat dusty plain. A Special Forces camp was nearby, and an airstrip made of PCP, the linked, perforated metal plates. The 1st Battalion's trains were located a little distance from the camp and the airfield. "Trains" is a military term describing not choo-choos but forward support elements. Alpha Company's executive officer, Lt. Kline, was there, as was his assistant and Lima's old platoon sergeant, Sgt. Brown, who was just a few weeks away from DEROSing. Sgt. Brown was no longer the lean guy I had seen departing the field several months before. Life in the rear—the food, the booze—agreed with him. He was filled out, particularly his face. His eyes, however, still had that I'm-tired-of-this-crap look—the thousand yard stare—of the infantryman who had seen enough.

Alpha was to be the palace guard for the next few days. The battalion fire support base was being set up right next to the forward trains. Indeed, one side of the fire support base perimeter was a portion of the forward trains perimeter. The fire support base was an extension, a thumb, of the trains perimeter. As we walked from where the Chinooks dropped us off, a Special Forces jeep drove by. A human skull was mounted on the front bumper. The two guys in the jeep had on a collage of camouflage uniforms and looked damned impressed with themselves. Their cleanliness and well-fed looks, however, told the real tale to the line doggies of Alpha Company—at best these clowns spent a few days a month following a

Montegnard patrol around. The rest of the time they lounged in comfort in their compound, enjoying clean sheets, Armed Forces radio and maybe even TV, air-conditioning, and a steady flow of beer and steaks.

The ground in the vicinity was rock hard. Digging with picks, shovels, and entrenching tools was extremely difficult. Someone had apparently actually realized this and had a bulldozer scrape large holes prior to our arrival. The company spread out over the area outlined by the work of the bulldozers. We tried to construct fighting bunkers from the dozer holes or from scratch, but in either case the results weren't very impressive. By this time, it was getting toward dusk and work ceased for the evening.

It resumed the next day. The word came down that the sleeping areas were to have overhead cover. That was what the bulldozer holes were for. The specter of air bursts from VC and NVA artillery was obviously haunting some senior commander. Sandbags and long metal fence posts were provided. The fill for the sandbags came from the dirt bulldozed from the holes. The theory was to lay the fence posts over the holes and place the sandbags on top. The problem with the theory was the width of the holes. The fence posts bridged the chasm, but not by much. And they were extremely springy. With the sandbags in place, walking across the roofs was like walking across a rope monkey-bridge, with considerable bouncing and swaying. A mortar round hitting one of those roofs would likely send the whole thing crashing down on those inside, crushing them under a mass of 10-pound sandbags. So we built the roofs as ordered but decided to sleep under the stars.

Sometime during that first full day I went over to the battalion trains in search of Lt. Kline. I came right to the point: "Hey, I wanna take my 30-day leave. I'm gonna be a captain in four or five days, and they ain't gonna be making me no company commander. It's time to get back to the World."

"Well, let me get the paperwork prepared. I'll hunt you up when its ready."

"How long will it take? I'd just as soon leave now. There's no point in me leavin' for the field again when the company goes. I'd be a captain platoon leader."

"I don't know. Might be a few weeks."

"A few weeks! Don't gimme that shit. That's numbah ten, G.I. I want outta here. I've been here 18 months. It's time to go home to Mom."

"Well, I'll see what I can do."

"Alright. I've got to get back to helpin' Ricky Hays and the boys build a sandbag roof. See ya later."

I had been mentioning to Wolfowitz my imminent promotion and desire for leave, but following the conversation with Kline, I went for a serious discussion. He said that battalion was already aware of the promotion and that a replacement would be arriving within the next day or so. As far as he was concerned, whenever the guy got there, I was free to go. So I really began thinking of myself as a short-timer.

The next couple of days were quiet. There were squad-size daytime patrols. There was sitting around in the sun. There were hot meals every evening. And there was itchiness. I was anxious as hell to be on my way. Alpha Company was part of my history. I wanted to get on with what life had in store. But before that could happen, one final little bit of unpleasantness intruded. Actually, it was not unpleasantness for me. I kind of enjoyed it. But it convinced me that Wolfowitz's days were numbered.

Evening stand-to was what precipitated the incident. As I've noted, every day at sunrise and sunset all personnel were supposed to go to battle stations, so to speak. For approximately 10 minutes, everyone was to be at their fighting positions, weapons in hand, steel pots on, web gear in place, quietly watching for Charlies. Also, by the evening stand-to, shirt sleeves were required to be rolled down. This was to help prevent malaria.

In short, stand-tos were part of the day's routine. In the field, there was usually little problem. The officers and NCOs had to get everyone's butt moving, but this was accepted. Occasionally, Jerome had gotten cranky at the inevitable delays before all were in position, but it was no big thing. When a company was palace guard at a fire support base, however, lackadaisicalness about standing to reflected badly. And the battalion commander, LTC Shafter, was a guy who noted such things.

Shafter's tent, a five-sided affair large enough for a cot and other amenities, was not far behind November's position. The squad closest to Shafter was Sgt. Parker's, the same Sgt. Parker who had brought a premature end to Shafter's effort at bringing cheer to the troops at Christmas. Toward dusk on our third evening, the call came from the company to begin the stand-to. It was relayed to the squad leaders, and the platoon members began their reluctant amble into position. I was sitting on the headquarters' bunker, noting that Parker's squad was as usual just a bit behind Rickett's squad in ambling.

I wasn't the only one who noticed. LTC Shafter must have been lying in wait. Suddenly he was charging across the 50 meters that separated his tent from Sgt. Parker's squad. He screamed as he charged: "Sergeant, why aren't your men standing to? Goddamnit, you get those men in position! Where the hell's your company commander?"

As did everyone else on this side of the perimeter, Wolfowitz heard Shafter's roaring. Within a wink, the Alpha Company commander was on his way to face the music. And the music was a dilly. Even as Wolfowitz closed the gap, Shafter directed his tirade toward him. It was classic Shafter: loud, long, irrational, and embarrassing to everyone within earshot. No one had called for my presence, but being the platoon leader of the miscreants, I felt it necessary to do more than hide in the bunker. So I took up a position just in front of our hole in the ground, about 20 meters from the screaming Shafter and the cowering Wolfowitz. Sgt. Hernandez appeared beside me. Sgt. Parker was standing at attention about 10 meters beyond Shafter and Wolfowitz.

The tableaux had only one animated element. In the rapidly growing dusk, Shafter's head could be seen bobbing, his mouth could be seen opening and closing, and most definitely his arms could be seen flapping. And there was no escaping the noise. Cursing and threatening, Shafter's voice rolled over the fire support base.

Having seen Shafter in action before, I had developed a degree of immunity. Plus, I was shorter than a frog's hair. An ass-chewing meant little to someone who in a few days would be on the Big Bird to the World. So I entertained Sgt. Hernandez with a running commentary out of the side of my mouth. "Hey, this is good. Look at Wolfowitz. He don't know what to think. Shafter musta been hittin' the bottle in his hooch. Ya realize I'm shorter 'an nine dogs? This baby will all be yours."

Eventually, Shafter wore down. He turned and stomped back to his tent. Wolfowitz made his uncertain way toward me and Sgt. Hernandez. Some commanders might have passed the ass-chewing on, but Wolfowitz was much too shaken. Apparently not having had the opportunity to change glasses, he still had on a pair of dark prescriptions, making him in the evening dusk look even more out of place than he actually was. Before he had a chance to say anything, I jumped in: "Nothin' to worry 'bout, Sir. Shafter treats all his company commanders like 'at. Besides, he's really got it in for Sergeant Parker. They had a run-in at Christmas, and Shafter obviously still remembers."

"Yeah, but Parker wasn't ready for stand-to," Wolfowitz ventured.

"Aw, he was ready, Sir. Shafter just wanted his butt. Ya can't let it bother ya. We'll make sure Parker's okay next time."

He walked off without saying much more. When he had gone, Parker came up. He had enjoyed the show. To him, ass-chewings were just part of the trade.

His chronic state of border-line insubordination ensured that he got more than his share. No big deal. "He was really pissed, wasn't he, Lieutenant?" Parker was laughing as he asked the rhetorical question.

"Yeah, well, you guys make sure you're standing to properly as long as we're here. We don't need no more of this."

"Gotcha, Lieutenant. We'll be right tomorrow."

After he left, I said to Sgt. Hernandez in a high-pitched voice, "short."

My replacement arrived the next day, not a moment too soon. He didn't impress as your typical airborne, elite unit lieutenant. A product of Officer Candidate School, he was a short wizened-looking guy who was in his early thirties—ancient for a lieutenant—but appeared closer to 50. Looks can be deceiving, however. Unlike Wolfowitz, he was confident and not at all intimidated by the fact that he wasn't yet a combat veteran. He asked a few questions and I gave a few answers and volunteered a few additional comments, but he wasn't interested in a detailed picking of my brain. He obviously had his own ideas and was raring to put them into practice.

I found out a couple of months later what one of those ideas was, and the discovery was an eye-opener concerning my own denseness. The platoon was about half black, yet the platoon headquarters group was lily white, assuming you counted the Hispanics Pasquez and Sgt. Hernandez as white. I had inherited the situation and never gave the racial composition of the squads and the headquarters group the first thought. But anyone sensitive to race would have seen right off that, appearance-wise, November had a problem. My replacement was a product of the Army's new attention to racial sensitivity training, attention that was in part due to the growing racial problems in the military of the late 1960s. The problems had not yet registered on my scope. No evident racial difficulties had existed in Saigon in 1966-mid 1967, and racial tensions in the 1st Battalion of the 173rd in the late 1967, very early 1968 time frame were not something I was much conscious of. When I had gone through Military Police Officers Basic in 1965, racial sensitivity was not on the curriculum.

At the first opportunity, my replacement moved a black trooper from Rickett's squad to an RTO position. I happened to run across the company in the middle of March, about six weeks later, and was struck by the sight of a black trooper humping one of November's radios. Immediately, the whole gamut of issues embracing race, appearance, and unintended discrimination crystallized in my brain. "Holy shit," I said to myself, "That's something I should have done." And this in spite of the fact that both Lima and Oscar had black RTOs when I was their platoon leader. In each instance, the headquarters' membership had been set when I took over, and I thought little of the composition.

But that insight on this matter was some time ahead. On this first day with my replacement, I just became aware fairly quickly that he had his own ideas of how he wanted to operate. Realizing your replacement is not necessarily enamored of how you have been doing things is a bit deflating, but I was too anxious to be on my way to care much. Later in the afternoon, I got the word. Lt. Kline came over and said that my leave was approved. I could catch a ride to An Khe, the 173rd's new base camp, the next day. From there, I would go to Cam Ranh Bay for the Big Bird to the World.

On my last night, I made sure Sgt. Parker's squad was in place well before the stand-to time. The following morning, I said a few goodbyes. One visit was over to Lima's area. I came across Lopez, the M-60 machine gunner who had done such deadly effective work at the ambushes back in Tuy Hoa. He was now a sergeant and a squad leader. When I approached, he was having words with an FNG, a PFC with an attitude who I hadn't seen before. At a pause in the conversation, I shook Lopez's hand and said I was on my way. I then turned to the FNG and said: "You'd better listen to this guy, trooper. He knows what he's doing. There's a lotta notches on his gun." But Lopez seemed to have the situation well in hand.

Later in the morning, I took my leave of Alpha Company. Lt. Kline directed me to a chopper pick-up point. A Chinook took a group of troopers to an airstrip, where we caught a C-130 to An Khe. A deuce and a half met the plane and transported us to the 173rd's area.

This was my first visit to An Khe, the massive base camp that had been constructed for the 1st Cav Division when it arrived in Vietnam in 1965. The place had an air of permanence. Solid wooden barracks and buildings sat on concrete foundations. Paved roads carried the traffic. A PX the size of half a football field provided about any good that could be found in a mall back in the World. An elaborate defensive perimeter kept out the Charlies. The perimeter consisted of a berm punctuated by bunkers and watch towers, spot lights, a wide plowed open area, and several barbed wire barriers. Within the defensive perimeter were not only the buildings and roads but also a whole damn mountain. On its top was a state-of-the-art communications facility.

But I didn't want to spend much time enjoying the pleasures of this piece of America in the middle of nowhere. I wanted to get to the real thing. I reported to the battalion personnel section and made arrangements to leave for Cam Ranh

Bay the next day. Then I went in search of my belongings, which I had last seen months before in Bien Hoa. Wonder of wonders, the stuff still existed, resting in a large warehouse. Housed in rooms within the warehouse were several NCOs, one of them being Sgt. Thurmond, Oscar's old platoon sergeant. He had wangled his way out of the field a month or so before and was thoroughly enjoying the good life. Beer and steaks had already added pounds, puffing out his cheeks and expanding his neck. He had a beer cooler in his room, and I quickly downed my first post-boonies brews. With clothing for the journey home, I returned to the main brigade area, had a meal, and repaired to a barracks for transient officers for a little sleep before a dawn trip to the airfield.

One more adventure was in store, however. It was the last of January 1968. Charlie was about to spring what came to be called the Tet Offensive. U.S. and South Vietnamese installations throughout the country were attacked that night and over the next days and weeks. The news was soon to be filled with images of the American Embassy in Saigon under attack, of the city of Hue being ravaged, of death and destruction in populated areas from the Mekong Delta to the DMZ.

Shortly after falling asleep, I was brought to consciousness by the distant thud of explosions and rattle of automatic weapons. The noise was not close enough to cause me much concern, and I lay half-awake wondering if this was a nightly occurrence at An Khe. The question was soon answered by someone who stuck his head in the door and yelled, "Hey Lieutenant! They want ya over at the headquarters building! Charlie's coming through the wire!"

Shit. I didn't need this crap. Eighteen months in the 'Nam, and they were harassing me down to the final hours. I groggily dressed and went over the headquarters building. A group of about 25 disgruntled looking troopers were milling around outside. The area was lit by various street and spot lights. In addition, numerous flares were floating down from the sky. The result of all these light sources was that the whole area was bright as day.

I went inside. A small group was gathered around a desk. As I came up, a captain, a rear echelon type, as they all seemed to be, said to me: "Lieutenant, An Khe is under heavy attack. You're infantry. We want you to take those transients outside and make a reaction platoon out of 'em. Most of them are infantry from the line battalions, either going to or coming back from R&R or some such."

"Well okay, Sir. We don't have any weapons, though." I just wanted to be sure the captain saw the obvious. You never knew about these rear echelon types.

"We'll take ya over to the weapons storage place and get ya some. A deuce and a half will be here shortly."

"Okay Sir." In truth, there was a little feeling of pride and superiority in having the rear echelon boys make like they needed us. On the other hand, this was a hassle. Come daybreak, I was supposed to be on a plane. I didn't want to be assuming responsibility for a combat unit. And I didn't really think there was anything to this. I had been through too many false alarms in 18 months. The chance that this transient outfit would actually see action seemed remote. Surely there were bona fide reaction platoons all around An Khe that would be preceding us into the line of fire.

I went outside to the group. An E-6 appeared to be the highest ranking guy there. I said, "Sergeant, why don't ya fall 'em in, and I'll tell 'em what's goin' on."

"Right, Sir. Alright you guys. Fall in four squads. C'mon, move it." The group shuffled into the semblance of a fallen-in platoon. The sergeant turned to me and saluted. I saluted back and gave the platoon "at ease" although in fact most of them had never come to attention. "Alright, here's the deal. There's some VCs supposedly comin' through the wire, and they're makin' us a reaction platoon. We're gonna be issued weapons, and then we'll see what happens. Is anybody here due to DEROS in the next day or so?"

The question came to me on the spur of the moment. It didn't seem fair to put a guy in harm's way who was about to return to the World. And maybe I had my own case in mind also. Several guys raised a hand. I said, "Why don't you guys step aside. I'll see if we can get ya dismissed. The rest of ya just wait for the truck to get here to take us to the weapons." There wasn't much reaction. Most of the group appeared to be combat veterans, troopers who didn't get worked up unless the action was in the immediate vicinity. My appearance probably served a little to mitigate concern. I was obviously just from the boonies myself: unshined well-worn boots, rumpled dirty jungle fatigues with the only insignia being a lieutenant's bar I had drawn on that morning with a ball-point pen, and a battered steel pot with a faded ripped camouflage cover. A new-appearing camouflage cover was a dead giveaway of an FNG or a rear echelon warrior.

I went inside and said, "We're ready, Sir. I let a couple'a guys go who are DEROSing tomorrow. Don't seem right to send 'em out at this stage." I took the lack of comment as approval for the action and went outside to tell the short-timers to get lost. The truck arrived a few minutes later, and we loaded up. It took us on a five-minute journey to a building near the luggage warehouse. A small portion of the trip was along the perimeter, on the inner side of the berm. The area was brilliantly lit by the spotlights and the flares. No Charlies were visible.

After drawing weapons, we returned to the main brigade area. The captain said to stand by, that we didn't have any instructions yet. I told the troopers to relax in the area. Most promptly found a patch of ground to call their own, laid down, and began cutting Zs. I went inside. The captain and several other officers were gathered around a telephone, a radio, and a map, apparently waiting for orders. The waiting stretched into an hour. Distant artillery and automatic weapons fire continued sporadically. Finally, I suggested that we send the troopers back to their barracks. They could be retrieved quickly. That request was approved, so I broached the important matter. "Sir, I'm due to get outta here to Cam Ranh Bay and the states tomorrow. I'd like to turn over responsibility for this outfit and get some sleep, particularly since it looks like nobody's gonna want 'em tonight."

After a pause, he agreed. I stuck him with my weapon, asking him to be sure to turn it in because I was signed for it. I then headed to my cot.

Bright and early the next morning, I was on the way to the An Khe airfield. Flights, mostly C-130s, were supposed to arrive and leave throughout the day. Several were scheduled for Cam Ranh Bay, and I anticipated no difficulty getting out. The night's activities, however, had made shambles of the flight schedules. Not only was An Khe still considered unsafe, airfields all over the country were under attack or in imminent danger of being so. So we waited. Probably 50 people were gathered in the wooden terminal building.

About midway through the morning, we were spectators to a little action on the other side of the field. The airstrip was on the edge of the An Khe compound. Between the runway and the perimeter berm was about 100 meters of high grass. The terrain had a few folds to it, providing cover and concealment to anyone who managed to get through the wire, across the plowed ground, and over or through the berm. And several Charlies had managed to accomplish those tasks.

To route them out, a platoon-size outfit—maybe the 173rd transient reaction platoon that I had abandoned—formed a line at one end of the airstrip. The line stretched from the airstrip to the berm. The platoon then advanced slowly up the open area. At a point directly across from the terminal, a brief period of firing ensued. Calling it a firefight would have been a misnomer because the Charlies didn't seem to be putting up any resistance. No rounds were whistling in our direction, so no one sought cover. We observed as if it were a sporting event. The firing stopped in short order, and several of the troopers went and stood over a particular spot. We couldn't see what they were contemplating, but presumably it was a dead Charlie or so.

Shortly after the platoon's sweep of the length of the airfield, flights started arriving and departing. Midday came and went, and the afternoon dragged on. I was anxious as hell to be on my way. I paced, walked around and through the terminal, and tried to read. Finally, a flight for Cam Ranh Bay began loading. Our group entered through the rear ramp of the C-130, the plane began taxing, the ramp came up, and soon we were airborne. The flight was an hour or so. In late afternoon, we landed in probably the safest area in Vietnam. The facilities—airfields, roads, buildings, docks—were stateside quality or better. Charlies were not prevalent in this corner of the Republic, and the base itself was huge, keeping the few Charlies around at a considerable distance.

My stay at Cam Ranh Bay lasted only overnight. By noon the next day, I was on a 707 for the land of the Big PX. The destination was McCord Air Force Base, Washington. Most of those on board were DEROSing, some even ETSing. They were a boisterous, happy bunch. I felt a little removed from the general festive mood. I was certainly glad to be going home. But Vietnam was not something I had disliked. I had asked to go there, had asked to stay well beyond the required time, and had asked for the field as an airborne infantry officer. Unlike with many, I had not had a change of attitude after experiencing the realities of combat. And finally, in 30 days I was coming back.

The cross-Pacific flight was close to 18 hours, time enough for the initial euphoria to dissipate considerably and for individuals to go through several mood swings. Most flights transporting U.S. troops to and from Vietnam were civilian charters. They had stewardesses, who were the first round eyes seen by some of the troopers in a long time. The troops generally remained under control, however. The absence of alcohol on board served to keep the rowdiness to a manageable level. The plane stopped briefly in Japan and Alaska, and finally descended into McCord. Once on the ground, the group was subdivided. ETSers had a day or so of out processing to go through. DEROSers and the few oddities like myself faced less red tape and were shortly on our way. I headed for Seattle-Tacoma International Airport—SeaTac—and a flight to the East Coast.

In my few letters over the previous month, I had hinted that I would be coming home shortly but had been vague about dates. I was likewise vague about future plans, not letting on that I would be returning to Vietnam. After I had booked a flight at SeaTac, I found a phone booth. "Yes, operator, I'd like to make a collect station-to-station call to Williamsburg, Virginia, area code 804. The number is CA9-4523." The number came readily to mind, not lost to 18 months of non-use.

"Hello." It was my mother's voice.

"I have a collect call from David Holland. Will you accept?"

There was a short pause, then a "Yes" that had a catch to it.

"Hi Mom. It's me. I'm at Seattle-Tacoma and will be arrivin' at Patrick Henry at 7:15 tomorrow mornin'."

Another short pause, then: "That's wonderful! We're so happy to have you home, that it's over!" The voice was shaky, but she was holding it together. I figured that I should get the bad news out quickly, to keep anyone from being under any illusions.

"It's only for a month, Mom. Then I'm goin' back." I felt like the jerk I was, but the bad news was done. Her pause was a little longer. When she finally spoke, her voice was subdued.

"Well, we're glad you're home anyway. I'll be there in the morning."

"Okay. See you then."

978-0-595-37414-4
0-595-37414-X

Printed in the United Kingdom
by Lightning Source UK Ltd.
123951UK00001B/342/A